A TRENCHARD BRAT AT WAR

THOMAS LANCASHIRE
AND
STUART BURBRIDGE

ISIS
LARGE PRINT
Oxford

First published in Great Britain 2009
by
Pen & Sword Aviation
an imprint of Pen & Sword Books Ltd.

Published in Large Print 2010 by ISIS Publishing Ltd.,
7 Centremead, Osney Mead, Oxford OX2 0ES
by arrangement with
Pen & Sword Books Ltd.

The moral right of the author has been asserted

British Library Cataloguing in Publication Data
Lancashire, Thomas.
    A Trenchard Brat at war. - - (Reminiscence)
    1. Lancashire, Thomas.
    2. Flight engineers - - Great Britain - - Biography.
    3. World War, 1939–1945 - - Aerial operations,
    British.
    4. World War, 1939–1945 - - Personal narratives,
    British.
    5. World War, 1939–1945 - - Prisoners and prisons,
    German.
    6. Large type books.
    I. Title II. Series III. Burbridge, Stuart.
    940.5'44'941'092–dc22

ISBN 978–0–7531–9568–0 (hb)
ISBN 978–0–7531–9569–7 (pb)

Printed and bound in Great Britain by
T. J. International Ltd., Padstow, Cornwall

Contents

Introduction

The fact that I am sitting here, on this wonderful March day, writing the introduction to this extraordinary biography is, in itself, largely down to a huge amount of chance and coincidence.

One day in late 2004, I was surfing the Internet and looking at one of the many Bomber Command related websites that have sprung up in the last few years when a familiar looking name caught my eye. The website was dedicated to the construction of a composite Stirling bomber (of which no complete examples now survive), and one of the entries in the guestbook had been signed by a man named Tom Lancashire. I should add at this point that I am the grandson of one of the 55,000 men of Bomber Command who did not return home, and I had recently spent hours at the National Archives trawling through the Operations Record Book of his squadron in an attempt to try and find out more about my grandfather's wartime experiences. I recognized Tom's name as being identical to that of a man who had flown as a flight engineer with another 97 Squadron crew at the same time as my grandfather had done. With that in mind, I sent off a speculative email to the address that Tom had posted, asking him whether he was a 97 Squadron veteran and, if so, what he could tell me about life at Bourn in that grim and bloody year of 1943. The reply duly arrived, confirming what I had guessed, and I learned that Tom was now in his mid-eighties, living in Ohio in the United States, and to my huge relief and pleasure, that he was very happy to talk about the war years and his personal experiences during those fascinating times.

What followed was a truly absorbing series of email letters which told of his modest Mancunian childhood, his entry into the Royal Air Force in 1936 as a boy apprentice, his early career as a fitter, and his decision to switch to aircrew duties. Before too long, I realized that this was no ordinary tale, and suggested to Tom that he should write it down in autobiographical form so that others could enjoy reading it as much as I was doing. He told me that his family members had suggested the same thing some time ago, but he had never got around to it, and I said that I would be more than happy to write the manuscript for him. Tom agreed and over the next year he sent me a series of long emails covering all aspects of his life, which I then rewrote and organized into chapters. Sadly, Tom's aircrew logbook had been mislaid after he had been demobbed, and as a result I had to revisit the National Archives in Kew and trace his operational career from the official documents that were held there. This meant that the structure of the third chapter had to be somewhat altered from the original submission but, from a personal point of view, this made it the most enjoyable part of the story to write.

When I cast an eye over Tom's life story, the first thing that struck me was how many times he had been, what I would describe as, "touching history". He had been a member of that most famous of all Halton intakes — the 33rd Entry; he was part of the first batch of heavy bomber flight engineers; he had taken part in the first two "thousand bomber raids" as well as the Hamburg "firestorm" and he had been picked up by the famous "Comete" escape line while evading capture in Belgium. After the war he had been involved with the controversial Avro Arrow project (a sore subject in Canada to this day), and was at the forefront of a number of major American aviation projects.

Yet one of the things that stands out for me is the claim that he credits almost everything that he has achieved in his life to the fact that he started out in 1936 as a "Trenchard Brat", a soubriquet that he wears proudly to this day. His affection for RAF Halton, for his courageous and gallant contempories, and for those who taught him there, is a fitting tribute to the highly successful and far-sighted scheme that was set up by Lord Trenchard in the early 1920s and is still going strong. I know that others who began their careers there feel exactly the same way, and that there is a tremendous and special camaraderie between Brats past and present. Long may this continue!

In an age when one can be labelled a hero for scoring an important goal in a football match, for speaking out on a point of principle, or even for fulfilling what one would normally regard as a civic duty, reading Tom's story should remind us of the real and unconstituted meaning of the word. In common with the majority of his fellow fliers, he received no gallantry decorations and nor did he seek them. He completed almost forty operations, the majority of them against German targets, displaying the sort of courage which is difficult to imagine in this cosseted age. Yet Tom's modesty shines out again and again throughout his story. He repeatedly reminds us that he is a "coward" although he is plainly nothing of the sort, and there is none of what is termed (in RAF parlance) "line shooting". He is honest in his appraisals of those with whom he flew, fought, worked and lived and I am quite sure that his views on the mismanagement of the Royal Air Force in those critical days will strike a chord with many.

The year which I spent researching and writing this book was nothing short of being both utterly compelling and thoroughly enjoyable. I know that there are plenty more stories out there that have remained untold and unpublished. The special generations who fought to preserve our freedom are now approaching the ends of their lives and we will all be the poorer for that fact. It is vital that their stories live on and I hope that by helping to tell Tom's, I have "done my bit". I hope you enjoy it.

Stuart Burbridge
Hythe, Kent,
March 2007

CHAPTER
ONE

The Early Years

My story begins just after the end of the Great War, in Denton, on what was then the eastern edge of Manchester. Both of my parents' families came from the north-west. My grandfather Lancashire was quite a senior and successful salesman in the Lyons Tea company, living in Preston, and he and my grandmother had five children between them; three boys (including my father Albert who was born in 1886) and two girls. However, this is only part of the story. My grandfather loved the ladies — any ladies in fact — and his favourite pastime apparently was getting them pregnant! Of course this made him into something of a "wanted man" in the locality, and he managed to avoid being lynched by running away to London with his latest girlfriend and taking her name. Although that branch of the Lancashire family evolved into the Seddons, those he had left behind in the north kept the Lancashire name; the only exception being my Auntie Annie, who also became a Seddon.

Growing up I never saw any of my London relatives, but I did know that that side of the family was fairly well off. As my father grew up he became an apprentice carpenter, but did not remain in this trade for long. He soon got a job managing a music hall in West Gorton in Manchester, which had been invested in by my grandfather. My uncle Tom was the "black sheep" of the family and he was quickly dispatched to the Indian army to prevent him getting into further trouble and to make something of himself. This, I believe, was common practice in those days. As it happened this was indeed the making of him, as he rose through the ranks and retired in 1934 with the rank of captain. He then returned to England with his family and settled in Reading. Sadly, his three sons were all swallowed up by the Second World War, going over to France in 1939 with the British Expeditionary Force and not being heard from again after the Germans attacked. My other uncle, Charles, had also gone to work for the Lyons Tea company.

It is at this stage, just prior to the outbreak of the Great War, that my mother and her family enter the picture. Her name was Frances Skinner, and she lived in Chorlton-cum-Medlock in Manchester where she was born on 30 September 1895. She was one of at least eight children and her father, Grandad Skinner, was a railwayman with the LMS company, working in the local marshalling yards. The family moved to West Gorton some time later and lived at 14 Cromwell Street — a typical two up, two down house of the period, with no bathroom and only one cold water tap in the kitchen. It's difficult to imagine these days just how a large family such as my mother's was able to survive in such a small house without a toilet and hot water, but that is how it was for many working families back at the turn of the twentieth century. I can only remember Grandad Skinner as a drunkard who wore a huge handlebar moustache. On payday, Grandma Skinner would have to meet him from work and claim his pay packet from him so that he wouldn't be able to call in at the pub on the way home and spend it all on drink. He died in 1932 when his liver finally packed up on him.

My father had met my mother in an "oyster bar" — whatever one of those was. As happened even in those days, she fell pregnant in the autumn of 1914 and they married the following March and set up home at 66 Holland Street, Denton. My eldest brother, Albert, was born there on 8 June 1915, followed by my elder sister, Elsie, on 17 September 1916. On 1 February 1917 my father, who had registered for military service in June 1916 under the new Derby Scheme, was finally called up by the army and went off to do his bit for King and Country. He served in France as a Pioneer in the Royal Engineers; he always said that he had joined the Engineers because he had no desire to end up in the trenches, and his wish was fulfilled. He once told me that he never even saw, let alone met, a German in the whole time he was out in France. He had a further stroke of luck in that because he had been a pigeon fancier and breeder before joining up, he became a member of the signal corps, looking after the carrier pigeons that were used to send messages from headquarters to the front line. In January 1919, when he was demobbed, having attained the rank of corporal, he and my mother settled down as a proper married couple. They had moved from their old house into a more spacious three up, three down round the corner at 53 Seymour Street, and it was here where I came into the world on 23 September 1919. Dad again found work with the Seddon branch of the family, who had decided to transform the old local beer hall into a cinema and he was given the responsibility of being the manager. This was a position which gave us a fairly constant income throughout the 1920s, which was just as well as the family continued to expand, with my younger sister, Joyce, being born on 15 September 1923 and younger brother, Douglas, on 28 October 1926. After this point Dad said that he was going to "keep it in his trousers" from then on.

Seymour Street became my whole world during my formative years. The neighbours were all very pleasant and there were always plenty of children around to play with. Although there wasn't much money in the Lancashire household, we still managed to be better off than 90 per cent of our neighbours, some of whom didn't know where their next meal was coming from. When a local child fell ill, which was a very regular occurance, everybody seemed to catch whatever was going around. If you survived, you were therefore automatically vaccinated against the next outbreak. However many of our neighbours didn't survive; such were the times we were living in. Our doctor was a man named Dr Stewart, and my father paid him a penny a week for the privilege of being able to call on him in case of need. House calls were included in the fee, and this "insurance" payment was to prove extremely useful in the years to come, at least in my case.

Living near the breadline also meant that we had great difficulty in trying to keep warm during the winter. One solution to this was the habit of "picking", which saw the local slag heaps in Denton and Hyde invaded by youngsters all looking for the few pieces of coal which invariably got mixed up with the slag, and filling a bag with them to take home for the fire. I soon developed a little trick to supplement this, which was to stand alongside the railway line and wave at the trains as they passed, which more often than not caused the sympathetic drivers and firemen to drop a few lumps of coal alongside the railway tracks for us to retrieve.

A great family who lived two doors down from us were the Holts. Mr and Mrs Holt had four boys and two girls, but they were all older than us. One of the girls, Edith, married a man named Mr Mackie who owned a motorcycle that he permanently seemed to be cleaning and repairing. He used to let me help him clean it and my reward would be a trip as a pillion passenger. One of the boys was named Fred, and he was much closer to me in age. His hobby was making crystal sets, strange primitive radios which consisted of old mantle boxes, copper wire coils and sliders which governed how many turns were required to tune the sets. The electrical circuits would pass through cats' whiskers and black crystals which could be fiddled with in order to try and obtain radio signals. I never did get the hang of making these things but Fred was very good — I think I lacked his patience. Sadly Fred contracted tuberculosis, as did so many in those days, and on his eventual death our friendship was terminated, as was my involvement with crystal sets. We did have a proper wireless set at home which was mainly used to tune in to the latest news. It had a high tension battery, a grid bias battery and a lead acid battery which would periodically need to be taken down to the local wireless shop to be recharged at a cost of 2d. I remember that there was a hole in one of the carpets at home where somebody (not me) had dropped the battery and the acid had leaked out and burnt a hole right through it.

Mondays were always washing days. Our house had a big coal fired tub in the kitchen and all our clothes and bedding was washed weekly. Of course the big problem was in drying such a lot of laundry. On rainless days, which as everyone knows are something of a rarity in Manchester, they were hung out "in t' back". This referred to the open square of land formed when terraced houses met back-to-back and it was a common area where the washing produced by these houses would be hung out. We would also play cricket and football there, with stumps and goalposts painted onto the walls, and on 5 November it would be the venue for a big bonfire. Of course Manchester was an industrial city, and when the local factories were churning out plenty of smoke and pollution, the washing often came back into the house dirtier than it had been before it had been washed. As children we were repeatedly being told to breathe through our noses, but this had the unfortunate effect of clogging them up with pieces of black grit and tar-like residue which we used to call crows. On wet days the washing would have to be dried indoors and Dad constructed some racks which hung from the ceiling of the living room where the washing would be put to dry. This created a kind of labyrinth through which we had to move and I can remember that it made the whole house feel damp.

Thursdays, on the other hand, were baking days, when my mother would make a whole week's supply of bread and muffins. This was quite a feat since the only oven in the house was a cast iron monstrosity in the living room. The oven was an integral part of the fireplace and with the correct manipulation of the dampers, the fire could be forced to heat the oven. It did need an experienced hand in order to ensure that the appropriate oven temperature was achieved. Mother must have had the correct knack because I can't ever remember anything being ruined. The smell of freshly baked bread has never been forgotten and I still remember the taste of freshly baked raisin muffins, hot from the oven and eaten with cheese. I felt at the time that it was food fit for a king.

Dad's main hobby, as I've already said, was breeding and racing pigeons, and he was extremely good at it with trophies everywhere at home to prove it. My elder brother, Albert, was also very interested in the sport and Dad encouraged him, allowing him to help and teaching him the ropes. I always felt that this might have had something to do with the fact I always considered Albert to have been the favourite son. They would organize the clocking in procedure the night before a race, as when the birds returned home a rubber identification band was removed from the leg and clocked in. The clock would then automatically endorse the time sheet within to calculate the winners and losers. The breeding season was the most important time in the calendar, as the birds had to be paired off in order to try and produce the best combinations in a racing pigeon, and this was where real expertise came in. Newly hatched chicks were monitored until it became clear whether or not they possessed the necessary qualities to become winners. Those who were no good had their necks wrung and were brought home to provide the family with a feast. Mother did not like the idea of plucking and gutting them so this job was carried out by a less squeamish neighbour named Bill Meyers, who kept the wings and giblets as payment. I always felt very sorry for the dead birds with their floppy necks when Dad brought them home, but my feelings of pity only lasted until they were served up at the dinner table, usually stewed with liver. Dad sometimes used to cut off a leg and showed us how to make the claws wiggle and move by pulling at the exposed tendons.

I would help out at the end of the breeding season when I would take the new birds for their training flights by transporting them in a basket on my bicycle. First of all I would cycle five miles away and release them, then I would increase the distance to ten, and after that they would be taken to the railway station and sent off to fly back from more remote locations. The railway porters at designated stations would release them on their arrival and return the empty baskets. Dad was quite strict with his birds and, when they returned from these training flights, if they did not fly straight back to the loft, disappearing instead to the nearby fields to hunt for food, he considered them to be not worth keeping. These birds were his pride and joy and after he died Albert stepped into his shoes, but he never quite had the magic touch that Dad possessed. Mother used to say that Dad thought more of the pigeons than he did of her, and there may well have been a grain of truth in that accusation.

For a very long time one of the staple industries in Denton had been the manufacture of housebricks, with the clay being dug locally. The resulting pit had grown over the years into a miniature replica of the Grand Canyon, 100 feet deep, with hills, dales and stagnant water pools, one of which I believe was 30 feet deep. These were controlled by water pumps which were switched on whenever the pools threatened to overflow. The clay was transported from the pit to the brickworks in steel tubs which ran on rails in an endless chain, thereby returning the emptied tubs to the pit to be filled up again. However, the tubs were relatively easy to disengage using a rock and a hammer, and the local children used to release the empty tubs, clamber into them and enjoy a rollercoaster ride down the incline to the pit. Of course the older and more daring would release the tubs higher and higher up the incline and one day the inevitable happened. There was a derailment and the subsequent crash resulted in arrests and prosecutions. I wasn't involved in this, but some of the older boys ended up in borstals. From that time onwards the pit was guarded and there were no more escapades involving the clay tubs.

However the brickyard was still a wonderful place in which to play and to explore. Although it had been fenced off with very visible warning signs, conspicuously displayed, there were still a number of pathways through it which were open to the public. Nobody was supposed to venture off them but of course we didn't pay too much attention to this instruction, and gangs of children from all over would gather and play "Battle", using the lumps of clay as the ammunition. However, if you returned home with clay all over your boots it was difficult to deny that you had been in the brickyard, so we used to get into the habit of taking our boots off and tying them around our necks, so when we returned home there were no giveaway traces of clay. Unfortunately, one day my boots became a casualty of war and, having lost them, I had to return home barefooted with the result that I was suitably punished by my father.

On the subject of getting into trouble, a couple more instances spring to mind. One involved what looked like an old Ordnance Survey map of Denton and the surrounding area which I found one day along with a stack of old magazines, I had never seen such a detailed map before and was staggered to see that it even had Dad's pigeon loft marked. Of course, at this stage I hadn't worked out the relevance of that fact, and I took it into school to show to my teacher. A couple of days later, Dad asked us all if we had seen the map, which it turned out was the most sacred piece of paper in the Lancashire household, and was required in order to verify the winner in a very close pigeon race. I admitted immediately that I was the culprit and that I had taken the map to school, I was told that I was to retrieve it immediately. Mother went with me to the school where we spoke with the headmaster, Mr Pitt, and she explained the situation. The map was returned and we went home. Unfortunately, Dad was still livid at what I had done, and when I gave him back the map, he told me that I had taken something of his which was very precious and without asking, and that he considered what I had done to be theft. For this I would receive the appropriate punishment, in this case ten strokes of the black leather strap which he used to keep beside the fireplace. I had never before had ten strokes, let alone ten strokes on my bare backside, and it hurt a great deal. Whilst I thought this was harsh, I remember thinking as I took my punishment that there had been plenty of times when I had deserved a beating but had never been found out, such as keeping the change when I was sent to pick up the weekly order of meat from the butchers, and grabbing handfuls of broken biscuits from the hinged tin in Mr Lennie's grocery store when his back was turned. I considered that the Good Lord had now caught up with me and was giving me my due. Mother also considered this punishment to be excessive and I remember overhearing them arguing about it later that evening. As well as the strapping, I was also awarded the chore of cutting up the newspapers to make toilet paper. These had to be six inches square and threaded onto a piece of string, as there was a danger that larger pieces would block up the pan. I remember that the ration was three pieces per visit, or as we were told, one up, one down and one for polishing.

Another vivid memory from this period was my regular Sunday morning chore which involved looking after my younger brother and sister, Douglas and Joyce, and taking them out of the house to give my parents some peace. I had very strict instructions not to be back before one o'clock, and to stay in the same clean and tidy state that we had been sent out in, something that was not at all as easy as it sounds. My favourite destination was the nearby Guide Bridge railway complex, where up to thirty tracks would all converge into this one big junction. There were open steel lattice type bridges over the tracks, so that you could stand right above any of the tracks that you wished. I soon got to know which tracks the express trains ran on and so used to stand above these with Douglas and Joyce, awaiting the arrival of the expresses. When they came, they would pass underneath us at high speed with the whistles screaming and this would scare my charges half to death, especially when we would all become lost in the smoke and steam that the engine had produced. This route would also take us through a large graveyard where I would tell them ghost stories about all the spirits and goblins who lived in the graves. Then we would pass through a farmyard where large gaggles of geese roamed free and would sometimes chase us, but we didn't mind because we often encountered the farmer's wife who would always give us a glass of milk each. These were very happy memories indeed.

One day, when I was about eight years old, as I walked home from school I came across an open manhole with a steel bar across it. I thought it would be a good opportunity to try out some high-wire skills and started out balancing myself along the bar. I had just got halfway when the bar rolled over and I fell down through the manhole, breaking my left arm in two places just above and below the elbow. I was taken to see the nearest doctor who strapped my arm to my chest and I somehow found myself at the Manchester Childrens' Hospital, where it was encased in steel and plaster and again strapped to my chest. My mother appeared and took me home. Of course, this meant that I would be away from school until my arm healed and although it healed without any problems, just as I was getting ready to return to school I was struck down by a mysterious illness that Dr Stewart couldn't diagnose. What was happening was that the blood vessels in my feet were bursting for no apparent reason and that this phenomenon was gradually spreading up my legs, and my legs were becoming paralyzed. I overheard Dad discussing my prognosis with the doctor. I remember him telling Dad that he was at a loss to explain what was happening, but that if it progressed to my torso then it was highly likely that I would die. He referred me to a Dr Fisher at the Manchester Childrens' Hospital, and set up transportation for me the next day as I was unable to walk. Thankfully Dr Fisher was able to put his finger on the problem straight away, because after a physical check-up I was immediately put on a course of ultraviolet sunray treatment and prescribed a particularly foul tasting medicine. I had to go to the hospital twice a week for my sunray treatment; this was an experience in itself as plenty of other boys and girls had to undergo the same treatment as I did. Except for a small "fig leaf" covering our privates, we were all naked, thus giving me an early lesson in female anatomy, and prompting questions which my mother would answer very comprehensively. After three months, I was back to normal and able to move my bed back upstairs from the parlour where I had been sleeping each night since becoming immobile. My Dad was also able to move back upstairs, as he had spent each night sleeping on a sofa next to my bed, keeping watch over me. However, someone obviously didn't want me to be at school as two weeks after returning I came down with scarlet fever and had to go straight into isolation.

Being in isolation in those days meant that the local council decontamination squad would come round to your house and isolate your room by taping up the window, door and fireplace and then fumigating it. They would then hang a blanket over the doorway which was soaked in what we called "sheep dip"; a mixture of creosote and water. This was the principal disinfectant during the 1920s, and you could take an empty bottle at any time to the Board Yard and get it filled up free of charge either to give the blanket a good soaking or to put it down the exposed drains that everyone seemed to have in their back yards. It made the house reek, but you soon got used to it as there wasn't really any choice in the matter. In any case, it seemed to work as I was the only one in the Lancashire house to be affected.

By now the decade had come to an end and I had missed two years of school. Dad's solution to this problem was to try and get me into a local grammar school to at least give me the chance to catch up. Although this would be an expensive undertaking for the family, with money for the fees, uniforms and books having to be found, he told me that if I would try my very best he would be satisfied. As luck would have it a new school was due to open in the locality and a desperate search was underway to find pupils to fill it. The new school was called Audenshaw Grammar School. With the help and support of my headmaster and our minister, the Revd. Keely, I was accepted for the start of the new school year in 1932.

I didn't find it easy to settle there at first. The main reason was that my classmates had enjoyed two more years of school than I had, and I soon took up my regular position at the bottom of the class. I also became very conscious of my background, as most of the pupils came from much wealthier homes than mine and my dress and manners reflected my upbringing. My family could not afford to pay for school dinners, so every lunchtime I would have to run home as fast as I could, eat my meal and run back in time for afternoon lessons. When I had to get changed for sports and PE lessons my lack of underwear caused embarrassment, as did the state of my socks, which were always darned and full of holes. However some of the teachers were very friendly and sympathetic, especially my housemaster, Mr Midgely, my French and German teacher, Mr Winder, and my woodwork and metalwork teacher, Mr Lamb, whom I always regard as my "lifesaver". My English teacher, Mr Hutchins, and the Headmaster, Mr Lord, had no time for me and I always got the feeling that Mr Lord thought a boy like me should never have earned a place at his school. I wasn't really very happy at all, so he was probably right.

Around this time I had a brief brush with the law; something that was never repeated but that I look upon as a learning experience. What happened was that a friend of mine came into possession of an air rifle, and near our home was a long interconnecting road about a mile in length which had gas lamps spaced about fifty yards apart. We thought it would be great fun to test our marksmanship by walking along the road shooting out the gas lamps as we went. It was quite a quiet road and after a while we managed to shoot out all the lamps. However when we reached the end of the road we found our way being blocked by a policeman who said to us: "You managed to get them all then, boys? Let's have the gun and we will go and see what the sergeant has to say about it all."

We had to go with him to the local police station where we were booked in, and were then taken to our homes where our parents were told that they would have to bring us to the Magistrate's Court the following morning. The next day we were told that restitution would have to be made to the council and we were both remanded into our parents' care for punishment, which meant being flogged, something which would be unheard of today. Dad used the black leather strap to give me eight strokes across my backside. Half-way through he said to me: "This is hurting me more than it is hurting you", something that at the time I did not believe one bit. However, I did not blame or resent my father for the strapping. I was fully aware what would happen to me if I had been caught during my night of fun. We were all brought up with the understanding that if we broke the law we would be deservedly punished and, in this case, I certainly was.

The Boys' Brigade had a troupe attached to the local United Methodist Church and I joined, becoming a bugler boy. We would meet once a week for band practice and drill, and the noise would considerably annoy the near neighbours. The highlight of the year consisted of us all packing up and heading off to one of the seaside resorts for our Annual Camp. This would take place in August, when all the factories closed for what was known locally as "Wakes Week" and everybody had seven days' holiday at the same time. Our troupe would also take part in the annual Whitsuntide procession, when each church would parade with banners and all and sundry would get dressed up in their new clothes. The parade would end up in the market square where there would be a big religious service. Although our band always did its best we were unfortunately continually overshadowed by the Denton Prize Brass Band, which was the pride and joy of the town. In the afternoon everybody would congregate on one of the nearby fields that a local farmer had opened up and we would have picnics, play games and enter competitions, all while trying to avoid the numerous "purdies" (the local name for cow-pats) which were liberally dotted around. Whitsuntide was always a most enjoyable time whenever the weather was cooperative.

During "Wakes Week", the market place was transformed into a funfair and amusement park, full of music and the sound of people trying their luck at the various stalls and enjoying the rides and roundabouts. My favourite thing was the massive traction engine which was parked in the square and served as a generator to provide the electricity required to run the fair. The rear wheels were six feet in diameter and while it was being used as a generator it was jacked up off the ground, with a flywheel driving a belt to turn the generator which was mounted on top of the boiler. A speed control had rotating weights that whirled round and an extension added to the chimney puffed out steam matching the steady in/out in/out beat of the double acting piston. The hiss of steam and smell of oil, together with the background noise of the fair made for a magical experience, and I was utterly spellbound — perhaps unsurprisingly given the direction that my life would later take. On my mantelpiece at home I still have a small model of a similar machine which serves as a constant reminder of those happy days.

Steam traction engines were fairly commonplace around Denton in those days. A good deal of raw cotton arrived at Manchester docks from America and, once unloaded, the bales of raw cotton would be transported to the mills of Denton and Hyde on four wheeled carts which were pulled by traction engines. These engines would have to slow down on the Manchester Road when they reached the incline, and we would ambush them and raid the carts, pulling the loose bits of cotton away from the bales, We called these strands of cotton that we managed to acquire "ginnybant", and we had quite an ingenious use for them. We used to punch holes in the opposite ends of old Bournville cocoa tins, push the lit and smouldering "ginnybant" through, and then thread the tins on to pieces of wire which acted as carrying handles. By whirling these tins around, air was forced through the holes which encouraged the cotton to burn, and what we would end up with were highly effective hand-warmers.

Guy Fawkes Night was always a memorable occasion in the neighbourhood, when there would be a bonfire (which was known as a "bonty fire") built in the "back". There was a great spirit of competition with the kids from the other "backs" which would extend to scavenging and foraging for anything that would burn well and, on occasions, raiding the solid fuel stocks of the opposition. In order to prevent the same thing happening to ours, we would always rely on the older ones in our gang to keep an eye on things. On the night itself, a great time was always had by all — we were allowed to stay up late, and after the fireworks had all been set off and the fire had burned down a little, we ate roasted potatoes and oatmeal cakes with treacle toffee, finishing up with a camp fire sing-a-long. On one occasion, there was an added treat. A neighbour called Mrs White had died earlier that year aged ninety-six. We all thought she had lived forever and would continue to do so, and it was a bit of a shock when she passed away. However, when her will was read it appeared that she had left the sum of £50 to the local children to have a party in her honour. Naturally it was decided that 5 November would be the most appropriate date on which to stage this party and, as can be imagined when that sort of money was available, a fine time was had, with presents and goodies being handed out to us all. We had seen off Mrs White in style and I am sure she would have approved.

Christmas in Denton was always a special time for us, when my siblings and I all had an opportunity to choose the present we wanted — with an upper price limit, of course. Aunt Annie would always send us each a book of our own choosing and we would go to Lewis' department store in Manchester before Christmas to visit Father Christmas in his grotto, who would give us each a shilling parcel. Preparations for the big day always began in November, when my mother would make the Christmas cakes for us as well as an extra one for her parents. Strangely enough, this was the only thing I ever recall her doing for them. There was some reason why my mother never visited my grandparents' house but I never did find out what it was. In any case, this meant that the job of taking the cake round always fell to me. It was always beautifully decorated, with almond marzipan, icing, roses, candles and sugared silver "ball bearings". I would deliver it two days before Christmas, and the journey to West Gorton always seemed like an adventure to me as it entailed a five mile tram ride, carrying my precious cargo which was safely wrapped up for the journey. On my arrival, my grandmother would give me a penny for bringing me their cake, together with a hug and a kiss which brought tears to her eyes.

As well as the cakes, my mother also made and steamed Christmas puddings. She always made sure to put threepenny bits in with the mixture, which were deemed to be lucky if you came across them at the dinner table; providing of course that you didn't break a tooth in the process. On odd occasions, one or two were accidentally swallowed, but of course they never failed to pass through the system a day or so later with no permanent harm done. There would also be mince pies, Bakewell tarts, Eccles cakes, Chorley cakes and Upside-Down cakes, either baked at home or left by visitors to the house over the festive season. With the exception of one year when we won the church raffle, turkeys were always out of our price range, so the centrepiece of the table would usually be a nice cut of pork. I loved pork, mainly because of the wonderful dripping it produced which we would eat for breakfast on hot toast. Our stockings would also contain oranges and nuts, and I remember one year I had a pomegranate which I had never seen before. I ate all the seeds one at a time with a pin, and Dad said that it had been brought all the way from North Africa just for me. On Christmas Day itself, Dad would light the fire in the front room where the Christmas tree stood and we would entertain numerous aunts and uncles, including Aunt Florrie who would usually have a man in tow. She never married and I remember Dad used to refer to her as a "lady of the night". Of course I didn't know at the time what was meant by that but in any case I liked her, mainly because one year she gave me a whole shilling, the most money I had ever had up until then. We would play games such as Crossed or Uncrossed, Pin the Tail on the Donkey and Guess Who? And, as a family, we were never happier than at Christmas time.

Returning to the subject of my education, my school quickly gained a reputation for its rugby teams' prowess and Mr Midgely encouraged me to take up playing the sport seriously in an attempt to bring me out of my shell a little. I found that I fitted in well, made plenty of new friends and enjoyed being part of something for once and I was soon representing the school. One of the boys with whom I played in that team was called Eric Evans who, in the mid 1950s, gave the school the distinction of having produced an England captain. I knew Eric very well and I remember that even at school he was a born leader on the pitch. I followed his international career even though we never met again once war was declared. I carried on playing for Old Aldwinians even after I had joined the Royal Air Force, because I used to get weekend leave in those pre-war days and I would travel home on my motorbike to take the field on Saturdays.

Playing rugby also seemed to help me improve academically. Although I was still hovering near the foot of the class, remarks such as "He has really tried hard this term" began to appear on my school reports, and this would please my parents, especially when they came from the Headmaster. Eventually, I began to show some real promise in certain subjects such as geometry, woodwork, geography, physics and art, and eventually found myself in the top bracket in these subjects. At last, my school life was beginning to get interesting. However, things were not to last. The cinema building which my father managed was eventually condemned by the authorities, and the Seddons decided not to rebuild it. They gave it to my father to do with as he wished. With the financial help of his sister-in-law, my Aunt Bertha (who was my Uncle Charles' widow), he decided that the best thing would be to rebuild and re-open it himself, in order to provide financial security for the family. Unfortunately, this meant that money would now be at a premium and I overheard a conversation which led me to believe that my future schooling at Audenshaw was in grave doubt. It was looking very unlikely indeed that I would be around for my final exams which I was due to take in 1936.

I began to think about my future. Dr Stewart had suggested to me during the course of my various illnesses that I should consider joining the Royal Air Force. He was the person who, more than anyone else, persuaded me that my future lay in joining the service. When he made house calls he would bring me books and cut out models of aircraft to keep me occupied. These cut out bits of paper would have to be pasted together with glue made from wheat flour by my mother. On one occasion he even brought an airman called Bill Sherlock around to see me and tell me about his experiences. He had been taken on as an apprentice himself shortly after the end of the war and I learned from him all about the life I would soon be leading myself at RAF Halton. Dr Stewart really was a wonderful man who was loved and respected by everybody; a real "family doctor". Certainly, as time went by, the subjects that I found myself doing well in at school were those that would suit a career in the RAF, and I certainly developed a real interest in aeroplanes and flying over the years. I bought and read every magazine on the subject I could find, such as *Popular Flying, Flight, Aeroplane* and an American pulp fiction publication called *Flying Aces*. I wrote to every aeroplane company I could think of, asking for information on their products, and I began to build model aircraft, including a flying model which crashed spectacularly on its maiden flight and was wrecked. The crowning moment was a flight in an Avro 504 biplane from Blackpool Sands with the pilot being a veteran of the Great War who was obviously unable to give up the flying bug and wished to pass it on to others. He was not alone in this, as there was also the famous Alan Cobham Flying Circus around at that time. Alan Cobham (later Sir Alan Cobham) was a former Royal

Flying Corps pilot who had decided at the end of the war to carry on in aviation, and had set up a company which would tour the country, flying from school playing fields or indeed any open space that would be suitable as a landing strip. He would charge people to take them on short pleasure flights around their local area, giving them a unique bird's eye view of their homes. He was responsible for giving many young boys the incentive to make flying their dream, and without meaning to be, was a very successful unofficial pre-war recruiter for the RAF. If you were to ask the young men who flew during the Battle of Britain who it was that took them on their first flight, many of them would all say that it was Alan Cobham. Apart from running this "Flying Circus" he was also an endurance pilot, making long trips between London and Australia to great public acclaim.

In any case, my jaunt at Blackpool cost me 3/6d, which was almost my entire savings for two years. My developing obsession with flight and flight theory meant that the decision to leave school and join the RAF was an easy one to make. The announcement of my intention to apply for entry into the Royal Air Force was met by abject horror from my mother and she was quite adamant that no son of hers was going to join the armed forces. This was due entirely to the fact that her circle of friends at church seemed to look down on those who made the forces their career and were under the impression that such people were either criminally inclined or unable to find any other proper work. My father however, as an ex-soldier, took quite the opposite view and encouraged me to find out more about what was involved. Once again Mr Midgely was extremely supportive and despite a few negative comments from Mr Lord, he managed to convince me that I would pass the entrance exam and that he was behind me 100 per cent.

At this point I should say a few things about the organization I was hoping to join. The Royal Air Force was still a very young service, having come into being as the world's first independent Air Force in April 1918, when all ties with the army had been cut. The man whose brainchild this was, Sir Hugh Trenchard, had established the School of Technical Training (Boys) at Halton in Buckinghamshire in October 1919. The idea behind this was to recruit the backbone of the future peacetime Royal Air Force and train these teenage boys and school leavers in the ways of flight theory, aircraft engineering and general airmanship, thus giving them a strong grounding in the theory and basics which would enable them to go on and make fulfilling careers for themselves within the service, whether as air or ground crew. It was a very successful scheme and by 1935, when I applied, it was in full swing.

After I had done the background research, I had a good long chat with Dad. He reviewed all that was involved and we had a heart-to-heart about it. He pointed out that in order to "Join the RAF and See The World", as the popular recruiting poster of the time said, I would have to give away my life to my King and Country until I was thirty years old. Assuming I would pass the very taxing entrance examination, in view of my previous poor health, there was then the issue of the medical examination. He told me that he would go and see Dr Stewart to get his help in filling out the required medical forms and certificates.

He also told me not to worry about my mother's objections as he would override them. So, with all that help behind me, the forms were duly received, completed and submitted. Soon afterwards, I received notification as to when and where I would be sitting the dreaded entrance examination. I was very nervous but pleasantly surprised in that I didn't find it anywhere near as difficult as I had expected. Two weeks later I learned that I had come 144th out of 900 and that I had passed. I remember that they threw a party for me at school and even the Headmaster made a speech in my honour which, considering he had not had any faith in my ability to pass, made for a very special occasion.

Eventually I received my joining instructions. I was to report to a certain platform at Marylebone Station in London at 14:30 hours on 14 January 1936, where I would be met by a warrant officer who would take me and my future apprentices to begin our new lives as so-called "Trenchard Brats". I was to bring with me a towel and toothbrush, and apart from the clothes I stood up in, that would be it. I had been issued with a railway warrant from Manchester to London and then it was my responsibility to cross the city and get myself to Marylebone Station in time to be met.

By the time 14 January arrived, my mother had still not relented one iota in her opposition to my joining up. I was up bright and early in order to catch the local commuter train which would get me to Wilmslow station to connect with the 08:45 Manchester to London express. Dad was the only one to come to the station to see me off, which was a shame as I had hoped for a bit more of a farewell. As the local branch train rumbled into the station, he grasped me by the hand and said:

> Well, son, from now on you are no longer my responsibility. From now on you will have to take your troubles to your sergeant major. Good luck. I am very proud of you. Do your best as you always have done.

As I got into the compartment with these words ringing in my ears, a couple who were sitting there promised Dad that they would see me safely on the London train as they were travelling that way themselves. With that, the door slammed and we were off. Naturally, I had no problems catching the connection and before too long, the train pulled into Euston station where it had been arranged that I would be met by my Aunt Annie and taken to lunch. This she did, and we went to a Lyons Corner House for lunch. I had never been in such a place in my life. All the waitresses were dressed in black with snow white accessories and I was called "Sir" for the first time ever. We chose lamb chops for our meal, and the chef came out to our table with a large platter of uncooked chops so that we could choose the actual one we wanted to eat. After our meal I was taken to

Marylebone, where I said goodbye to my aunt and managed to find the warrant officer on the platform amongst the crowd of boys of all shapes and sizes who had also gathered there. We were to form half of the 33rd Entry to the No. 1 School of Technical Training and all together there were approximately 350 of us, all about to start our new lives as part of the Royal Air Force. After a final call for all relatives to leave the platform, we were hustled aboard the train which, after a long blast on the whistle, pulled out of the station bound for Wendover, where double decker buses awaited to transport us to our future home, Maitland Barracks. So began the greatest adventure of my young life.

CHAPTER
TWO

A Trenchard Brat

So later on that evening, having reached Wendover and boarded the buses that were waiting for us outside the station, we all found ourselves dropped off at RAF Station Halton, in deepest Buckinghamshire, which would be our home for the next couple of years. We were each allotted temporary beds in the vacant barracks and given our first taste of Royal Air Force food. We were warned that the next day would be a busy one and that following the medical which we would all be subjected to, we would be told whether or not we had been properly accepted into the service. One point that was rammed home continuously was the fact that if at any point we decided that this life was not for us, then we would be free to leave and go back to our families — obviously an attempt to weed out those who weren't sure about their futures and avoid spending huge sums of money beginning their training only for it to be wasted. What we didn't realize at the time was that the previous intakes had been small in relation to ours, and that ours was an "expansion entry", designed to build up the core strength of the Royal Air Force in the light of the fact that Nazi

Germany was becoming a pretty formidable military machine. Basically, we were going to be prepared and groomed for a war that many people in the corridors of power could see coming, even if that fact was being hidden from the public. In hindsight, the timing was perfect as we graduated in December 1938, a few months after the Munich Crisis had taken the country to the brink, and the Luftwaffe was showing in Spain exactly what it could do.

Of course, these events were all a long way off in the future as I got up on the morning of 15 January and, after breakfast, made my way to the sick bay for the much feared medical examination. I was poked, prodded, weighed and measured, all the time being asked question after question. I remembered the advice given to me by Dr Stewart and did not volunteer any information about my previous poor health which might have upset the apple cart. All must have gone well since I was given the status of "Fit for Service" and passed on to the Attestation Detail, where I was again told that before I put pen to paper I was free to go home if I wished. It was without any hesitation that I signed on the dotted line, committing myself to the Royal Air Force until I was at least thirty years old. At the time I remember thinking that 1949 was an extremely long way off and little did I know what fate had in store for me in the interim.

Having signed up, the next stop was the Quartermaster's stores where I was issued my kit, which I then marked with my newly issued service number of 568949. I was also given a bag, into which I was to put all my civilian clothes, in order for them to be mailed back home to Denton, surely a sign that I was now owned by the RAF and that I had well and truly left my past life behind. All those of us who had passed the medical and attested, were now allocated a permanent barrack room which would be home to us from then on. In my case this was in No. 4 Wing. The function, care and maintenance of our items of kit was explained to us and we were instructed to place each item into its specific place. For the first time in my life, I had a pair of pyjamas to sleep in, as well as underwear, towels, socks, boots and gym shoes to complement the wonderful new uniforms which had been issued to us and which would, in due course, be individually tailored to fit. We were also subjected to our first RAF haircut, which was very, very short indeed. This didn't make a great deal of difference to me because my hair was quite short to begin with, but others had beautiful curls and distinctive hairstyles which were soon lost forever once the clippers got to work. Some of my fellow apprentices looked as though they were about to cry as we were all shorn and began to look the same. This was in complete contrast to my grammar school days when you could tell a pupil's social standing from his appearance and dress. Now we were all starting out as equals, and as someone who had constantly been aware of my background at school, this was a great feeling.

Once we were back in our barrack room, we were introduced to the "Macdonald" bed on which we were to sleep. This was a magnificent steel contraption which could be broken down and folded up for inspection purposes during the day, to display our folded blankets and sheets. The mattress consisted of three sections, or "biscuits". These would be stacked one of top of the other, with the folded blankets and sheets placed on the stack. They would then be arranged and aligned along the length of the barracks room, a very pretty and efficient looking sight if done correctly.

Other things learned during that memorable first week were traditions such as the morning routine, which involved the picking up from the cookhouse of buckets of tea for the barracks. The tea was known as gunfire — a name originating in the trenches of the Great War — which would come to us with biscuits (edible ones) and the process was designed to be something of a pick-me-up for the day ahead, or at least I assume that those were the motives behind the ritual. In any case it was a good idea and tea was just what was required at that unholy hour of the morning. Of course, if the weather was bad when my turn came to pick it up from the cookhouse then I didn't feel that way at all and much grumbling was the order of the day. After our tea it was "on parade" for outdoor gymnastics (something the RAF of the day was extremely keen on) and then "on parade" for breakfast. Following breakfast was the daily barrack room inspection and once that was out of the way it was on to our schools or workshops or whatever we were scheduled to do that day. All in all, the week could be broken down into twenty hours of technical training in the workshops, nine hours of physical training, drill and games, and eight hours of general education, as well as homework and other general barrack duties.

The first Friday at Halton was the day that we were introduced to the parade ground, in order to learn the noble art of drill. Here, the drill sergeants showed us how to fall in, fall out, line up, about turn, right turn and left turn, quick march, slow march, stand to attention and stand at ease. This was quite difficult to get the hang of at first and it was strange how tricky it was to follow the commands, as many of us did not seem to know our left from our right. Our instructors, however, had a language all of their own which they used to persuade us to get it right. The first few Fridays on the parade ground were humourlessly funny, but eventually we began to get the hang of it all and we even managed to graduate to the advanced skill of rifle drill. Once we had mastered the art, it became a pleasure to march to work, even more so when we had the added bonus of a piper to keep us all in step.

The workshops at Halton had been built during the Great War by German prisoners of war, and it must be said that they had done an excellent job in constructing them. The first things we learnt were how to familiarize ourselves with the tools of our trade, what they looked like, felt like and what we could make them do for us. We had each been given the rank/title of "Fitter 2". This was because somebody in Air Force Planning had had the bright idea that by combining the trades of Fitter Rigger (airframe) with Fitter Engine (mechanic) it would be possible to cut the manpower requirements down by 50 per cent. Of course this was just not practical, especially with the rapid advances being made in aircraft technology and design at the time, but that was the situation we were stuck with. We were each issued with our own set of tools, complete with a box and a key, as all lost tools would have to be replaced by the individual concerned, naturally at his expense. I should add at this point that we were paid the princely sum of one shilling a day as apprentices, of which we were given four shillings a week to buy such necessary items as soap, toothpaste, boot and metal polish, stamps and writing material. Some weeks there was enough left in the kitty to enable us to go to the flicks, buy a bar of Gleesdale toffee, a Scottish oatmeal cake known as a Banark Bun, or perhaps a "sinker", which was made from the previous day's unused confectionary topped off with icing. The three shillings balance was always kept for us so that when we went on leave we would have plenty of money to burn. When you consider that food, board and lodging was all paid for we didn't do that badly at all, financially speaking.

Being, as we were now, in the possession of tools, we were each allocated a section of workbench with a vice attached. Our first task was to place a steel bar in the jaws of the vice. We were then told that the instructor wished us to chisel a groove down the centre of the entire length of the bar. This groove had to be an eighth of an inch deep and half an inch wide. Our instructor gave us a quick demonstration of how to perform this task, making it look easy, as it obviously was to him. Well, naturally, few, if any of us, had actually used tools in our lives and most had soft lily-white hands without any calluses. This was soon to change. The first hammer blows failed to make any impression on the chisel's attempt to cut a groove into the bar. The advice given by the instruction was simple and concise — "Hit it harder!" These renewed efforts inevitably resulted in the hammer head slipping off the end of the chisel and hitting the thumb, with inevitably bloody results. We all ended our first day in the workshop with bruised, bloodied and bandaged thumbs, and our steel bars were all as yet ungrooved. Added to the discomfort caused by the battered thumbs were painful sores, which resulted in blistering and some of us still carry the scars to this day. These were our first service injuries which I suppose would have won us Purple Hearts had we been in the American Air Force instead of the RAF. Nevertheless, as with most things, practice makes perfect and in time we all managed to master the hammer and chisel exercise.

I was somewhat fortunate as I did actually have a degree of experience in using a hammer. My father, who was a carpenter by trade in his younger days, used to acquire the lumber he used for his DIY projects from local factories who sold their broken wooden boxes and crates to the public at a discounted rate. My job was to break all these boxes down into usable pieces of wood without damaging them further. This task included straightening all the bent nails so that they too could be reused. Although this did not make me an expert, it at least had made me familiar with tools such as hammers, pincers, pliers, files and, most importantly, had put the vital calluses on my hands which toughened them up.

The basic workshop course consisted of ten lessons which covered all of the new tools of our trade and how to use them. This course had to be completed in thirteen weeks. The items which we produced during this time included sets of bend bars for future use in the manufacture of sheet metal parts and a landing/flying wire which would be for use in the art of rigging. Of course, in 1936 we were still in the age when open cockpit biplanes such as the Hawker Hart and Fairey Demon were the mainstay of the service, so the majority of what we learned was relevant to these fairly primitive aircraft. In the next three years we were to see a drastic change in the style and technology of the new aircraft being designed, built and commissioned, but in the meantime we were still a fair way behind the times.

During our early days at Halton, we were initially shown the ropes by a Leading Apprentice from an earlier entry who would help us to become accustomed to camp life. Such individuals were always known as "Snags", and after a while they were to be replaced by those promoted from within our own ranks. You did not apply for promotion, you were watched and scrutinized and if you were considered up to the job of leadership then your name was put forward. So it was that one Friday we were on the parade ground as usual being drilled by Flight Sergeant (Tug) Wilson when out of the blue, he said: "Will Apprentice Lancashire please step forward and face the troops?"

As I did so he said to me: "They are all yours for the rest of the afternoon — Carry on!"

I think that at that moment my heart stopped beating, my face turned crimson and my knees wobbled as I stepped forward in a daze. I tried desperately to activate my vocal chords but nothing happened. I heard a loud: "Get to it, lad!" from Warrant Officer Carswell, our wing Warrant Officer who seemed to have appeared behind me from nowhere. That did the trick and I started to come to life, bringing my charges to attention, turning them to the right and marching them off around the parade ground, all the time trying to conquer my nerves, quieten the adrenaline and decide what my next command would be.

After a series of blunders I managed to get to the end of the afternoon and delivered my charges back to be dismissed. Flight Sergeant Wilson told me I had put up a good show as a first attempt and that I would soon get used to it. He also told me that I had to report to the CO's office at ten o'clock sharp the next morning to answer a charge brought against me by Corporal (Chesty) Reid, and that this needed to be sorted out before I could even contemplate promotion. Thus, at the stated time the next morning I was standing to attention in front of the CO of "C" Squadron, Flying Officer Knight, who informed me that I had been charged with damaging the grass in front of the Mess hall by throwing my knife at worms while awaiting entry to it. I admitted that I had been doing just that but that I was not aware that I had damaged the grass, and in fact the knife was aerating it! A witness, Sergeant

Diddle, stated that he found no damage to the grass and that he was aware that this was common practice amongst the apprentices, although he didn't agree with it. Since there had been no intent to cause damage, the charge was dismissed with the result that Flying Officer Knight instructed Warrant Officer Carswell to put up a notice banning the practice forthwith. With that, Flying Officer Knight congratulated me on my promotion to Leading Apprentice, but strangely enough Corporal Reid didn't.

Now I was officially a "Snag" and found myself in charge of a barrack room, with the additional privilege that I got a room to myself. This was the first time in my life that I had been placed in charge of others, and I was responsible for their "good order and discipline". Thankfully my charges accepted the situation with good grace and I never had any serious or insurmountable problems. I never put anyone on a charge or pulled rank on them during the whole time I held that position. I must have done well enough as a "Snag" because six months later I was again promoted to the rank of Corporal Apprentice, the rank I was to hold during the rest of my time at Halton. It gave me more responsibility and the privilege of being one of the speakers at the passing out dinner

I would now like to return to the subject of the workshops and all that we would learn within them. After the basic course that we had all taken, the next was concerned with aircraft repair. Up until this point, we had not actually seen any modern stressed skin aeroplanes and, in our training at Halton, we were not to do so. We were still solely concerned with fabric and wire braced structured airframes, and looking at seaplane hulls and floats was the nearest that we ever got to the new form of construction that was beginning to revolutionize the repair and maintenance procedures that had been in place since the Great War. In this field, we were to learn why heat treating of duralumin was done in salt baths to noralize it so that it could be worked without causing cracks, and what bend radii and edge distance you had to use in relation to material thickness. All fascinating stuff which we were never once to use after graduating into the real RAF world.

The design and riveting of repairs was also covered, and running parallel to this course were classes covering the theory behind all those mysterious phrases such as anodic treatment, heat treatment, rivet spacing, edge margins, salt water corrosion, stainless steel, and splicing of flexible control cable — all new concepts from a different world that our brains were required to assimilate. The process of repairing fabric covered structures such as damaged wings was also covered. First of all, the wings would be stripped of their fabric to expose the extent of the damage, then the opposite, undamaged side was also stripped so as to give the repairer something to copy. New parts were then made from scratch to complete the structural repair, and then the wing had to be re-covered with fabric. The air loads were transferred to the metal structure by "stringing" which entailed the sewing together of the top and bottom surfaces, with the use of a 12 inch long steel needle. This needle was virtually a lethal weapon and great care was needed while it was being used. Pushing it alongside a rib through the top skin was easy but passing it through the wing and out through the bottom was an operation that had to be completed blind and you had to feel for the point of the needle being in the correct position with your finger. When the right spot was located force was applied to the needle and once it had overcome the resistance offered by the fabric, the tip of the needle would slice through in a great rush. If you weren't quick enough and hadn't moved your hand away in time, the needle would just carry straight on through your hand. I still have tiny scars on my left hand today to demonstrate that I failed on one occasion sixty-seven years ago to keep my hand out of the path of the needle. It went right through and out of the back of my hand piercing and damaging a large vein. Once the fabric had been re-applied then it was "doped" to make it shrink and become taut. Other repair procedures involved damaged tubular structures, such as that of the Warren Truss fuselage which was later used in the construction of the Hawker Hurricane.

This takes me forward a few years in my story when I was stationed at Upper Heyford in Oxfordshire during the Battle of Britain. Our airfield was not a frontline station and our only responsibility as ground crew was to re-arm and refuel any fighter aircraft that landed there for whatever reason. One day, a Hurricane, which had been shot up and suffered damage to two segments of its Warren Truss fuselage, appeared. We had no tubing in stock that we could use to carry out repairs as we had been taught to do at Halton, but an enterprising sergeant managed to locate some piping that could be made to fit. With the toilets now deprived of a vital section of their plumbing, the Hurricane was repaired and sent back into the fray. The repair wasn't one of my best since there wasn't any replacement fabric available either and we just used what string we could find to sew the battered surface together again and apply a coat of paint, which wasn't even dry when the aircraft took to the air again. So much for my comprehensive apprentice training.

Other bits and pieces that we were taught at the time included the skills of the blacksmith as we learned to temper steel tools by heating the steel to a cherry red colour, then we would plunge them momentarily into cold water and watch the oxidization travel down the length of the steel until the required colour reached the tips and then plunge them into water baths. We also learned about case hardening of surfaces, casting techniques and metal forging, with the theory behind the practical being taught as ever in the school classrooms.

These school classes were much the same as those at the grammar school that I had attended prior to joining up, except that the subject matter was very different. All the teachers were experienced civilians who seemed to have the knack of making everything seem interesting. I remember in particular the teacher of flight theory, whose name was Mr Farthing, and who, I believe, was one of only a handful of survivors to have escaped from the burning wreck of the R101 airship when it crashed in France in October 1930. He had a very badly burned and disfigured face, which I always assumed he had suffered during the crash (I can clearly remember the paper boys running through the streets on the Sunday morning after the crash shouting the news of the demise of our country's pride and joy). In fact flight theory was one of my better subjects, with the theory backed up with work in the wind tunnel that was owned by the school. I also enjoyed technical drawing, taught by Mr Williams; also a good teacher but not of the same calibre as Mr Farthing. I had no problems with this subject as it also incorporated the study of geometry (which I had found easy at my previous school). However, Mr Williams' problem was that he couldn't control his classes' behaviour and this weakness was exploited by the students. To counter this, any badly behaved students were made to stand outside the room and, if seen in this location by anyone in authority, they were automatically placed on a charge and given three days' "jankers" on a first occasion, seven days' in the guardhouse for a second offence, and flogged or drummed out of the service for a third.

Other subjects included engine theory (ICE), maths, general studies, physics and electrical theory. All of the subjects were timed to coincide with the relevant practical work being carried out in the workshops, and the two strands complemented each other perfectly. All in all, I found my time spent in the school to be delightful. The facilities were perfect — even the wind tunnel was bigger than that used by the Wright brothers in their early years of experimentation. General studies covered a number of more mainstream subjects such as geography, history, English and religious studies, as well as the current makeup of the RAF including the bases that we had across the world and exactly why they were maintained. These subjects were all, as was usual at Halton, presented and taught in a very interesting manner. I remember that our final exams included what was referred to as a set task. This basically entailed us each pulling a random topic out of a hat (such as Hitler, the Labour Party, and Dickensian England) and writing a book about our chosen subject in our spare time, taking no longer than three months. I drew out "agriculture in England" and whilst I had no problem with my final exams, passing out with an LAC (top) rating, I am afraid I did not win a Pulitzer Prize with my literary effort.

The procedure of rigging was at the heart of all that we learned at Halton and, as we were still in the biplane age, the latest aircraft in the workshops at that time were the Hawker Super Fury, and the hands on airframes that we used were those of the Great War vintage Avro 504, the Westland Wapiti and the Hawker Hart. Rigging was a relatively straightforward procedure. Aircraft were built up from pin jointed sub-assemblies such as the fuselage, tailplane and wings — port upper and lower and starboard upper and lower. All were assembled onto a fuselage, which was placed into position, straight and level on the hanger floor. The parts were then fastened together with wires which were adjusted in order to apply the correct incidence angles, dihedral angles, sweepback and rigidity. It all sounds easy enough, but these things had to be done in a specific order. I remember after I had graduated from Halton and I was stationed at RAF Finningley, a Hawker Hart from another unit made a forced landing in a ploughed field a few miles from the airfield, owing to engine trouble. The field was so muddy that it was unable to take off again and we were told to dismantle the aircraft and bring it back for re-assembly. The NCO rigger in charge showed us how to carefully count the number of turns required to undo each landing/flighting wire, identify the wire's location on a piece of paper, together with the number of turns required to reassemble it again. This was no problem, and when we got back to base we carefully laid all the rigging wires out on the hanger floor ready for the next day when we would complete the work. Unfortunately, when we turned up in the morning, the cleaners had been busy during the night and obviously not appreciating the mess we had made on the floor, had cleared the area of the wires and thrown away the pieces of paper with our instructions written on them. Determined not to be beaten by this setback, the NCO rigger squared off the fuselage with the end of the hanger, we attached the wings and replaced all the wires, before he stood back and instructed us to progressively adjust this wire or that wire until, in his opinion, the aircraft "looked" right. He then checked that the wires were all in safely and declared that the aircraft was airworthy. In fact, so confident was he of his guesswork that he even flew on the subsequent test flight without any hesitation. The pilot who flew the aircraft back to its home base actually said later that the aircraft had never flown better. Needless to say, this was NOT the way we were taught to do things at Halton. However, it was later explained to me that the NCO had known that the top wing's dihedral was zero degrees on the Hart, and that the lower wing took its position from the interplane struts which still had their original lengths since we had had no cause to change them.

Later on in our time at Halton, we took a course on aircraft engines where we went into great detail about the mystery of just how these great big contraptions worked. We covered the processes of carburation and ignition, actually dismantling engines and parts in order to become familiar with them. This meant disassembly, inspection, adjustment, reassembly and testing. Running parallel to this in the school was the class in ICE theory, which involved laboratory testing of components like carburettors and magnetos, as well as complete engines. We were shown how to test an engine to find out what power it was actually developing under the different conditions that it was exposed to. Wonderful words such as dynamometers were explained to us and their workings demonstrated there in the lab before our eyes, with us even being allowed to touch and operate the various knobs and wheels. Also included were lessons in chemistry and physics to explain the theories of combustion, as applied to the internal combustion engine; the differences between the four stroke, two stroke and diesel engines, and the ifs, buts, whys? and why nots? of all of them. We also had time for the odd prank or two, such as shorting out the high tension output from the distributor of a magneto to the zinc topped workbench when some unwary soul had his elbows resting on it — a trick which we were actually taught by the instructor himself, doubtless to his lasting regret.

The eagerly awaited aerodrome course was our first chance to get hands-on experience of what it would be like for us when we passed out and were posted to an operational unit. However, the realism was tempered somewhat by the fact that the Air Ministry had only supplied us with outdated and obsolete types such as the Great War vintage Bristol Fighter, known to us all as the Brisfit, with its Rolls-Royce engine. Other aircraft there were Gloster Gladiators, Gloster Gauntletts, Bristol Bulldogs, Avro Cadets, Hawker Harts and Hawker Furies. These were all operational, but were rapidly being overshadowed by the new monoplanes being developed in a rush by the designers. A smattering of the new Bristol Blenheims and Fairey Battles were starting to appear, but far too late to be of any relevance to our course. I found that the most enjoyable part of the aerodrome course was being marched to and from the airfield with the music of a piper keeping us in step. Sergeant Phillips, who was himself a former pilot, used to be in charge of us as we marched. I remember him as a small but very pleasant chap who took to the air once again when war was declared but was later killed. The route from the camp took us along roads with parallel rows of chestnut trees on the verges and through the beautiful village of Halton; it was a real treat to see.

It was about this time that a delegation from the German Luftwaffe was invited to come across to England and see for themselves the state of unreadiness that the RAF found itself in. Halton was on their itinerary and we were privileged to see them. The head of their party was the famous flying ace from the First World War, Ernst Udet. They appeared to be a superbly arrogant bunch in their long leather coats and highly polished jackboots, who made a great impression on us, as did their peaked caps which seemed proudly to stick up straight at the front. For weeks after they had departed, you could see caps being worn about the camp that had been modified by the owners who had placed a strip of duralumin sheet on the inside front of their cap directly behind the badge. I am sure that the Germans must have been trembling with fear when they saw the "modern" equipment we were being trained upon. Flight Sergeant Tug Wilson said to us at the time: "Mark my words, it won't be long before we shall be seeing those bastards again." A very prophetic comment, and realized sooner than many of us thought.

Every year RAF Halton held a Parents' Day so that our families could see for themselves what a wonderful time we were all having. However, in the three years that I was there, my parents were never able to find the time to come. Mother had never forgiven me for joining the armed forces and Dad would always have an important pigeon race scheduled for that day.

Of course, when war was declared Mother's tune changed dramatically, and almost overnight I became a hero in her eyes as she was able to brag to all the other mothers at church that she was the only one of them who had a son already serving his King and Country. Siblings and other family members were also welcomed on Parents' Day; as a result the camp was flooded with hundreds of young ladies. Our hormones were playing havoc with our girl-starved selves and I remember being introduced to the sister of one of my charges. When our hands touched, the feeling covered my body with goosepimples and I blushed crimson, my heart beating at a record speed. In contrast, I recall the time a few years previously when, after Sunday School, parents would assemble their sons and daughters in the church hall to try and teach them the fundamentals of dancing and, in particular, the waltz. I remember feeling at the time how disgusted I was by having to touch a girl "like that" and even put my arms around her waist. Having said that, I did once get strange feelings when I was paired off with a very middle class girl named Audree Jarvis who had beautiful blonde ringlets which must have been done by a professional hairdresser, and wore superb clothes made of silk or satin. She had wonderful manners and I immediately fell in love with her, but she never even seemed aware of me. I have a class photograph in my collection with her in it and I did try to get in touch but sadly many years later I read in the paper that she had died of cancer. The big finale of Parents' Day was the marching of the massed bands of all the accommodation wings on the aerodrome and the singing of the song *Sussex By The Sea* by all the Brats present. Since all the Brats used the Halton version of the song rather than the original, I'm not sure that it was appreciated by everybody.

We were not the only people to receive our training at Halton in the 1930s. Recruits to the RAF Police, known to us as "Snoops", also learned the tricks of their trade there and used us as their guinea pigs. After their initial basic training where they received the rudiments in the craft of "snooping", they were set free in pairs to roam the camp in search of potential criminal elements amongst our ranks. A very diligent pair was assigned to patrol the workshop area during the break period. Smoking was strictly forbidden anywhere in this area and, in fact, you had to have a pass showing entitlement to smoke if you were under 18. This, of course, did not stop those who wished to smoke from doing so. Those "erks" who had cigarettes, migrated to the toilet block during the break to have a quick drag. On one occasion a trap was sprung and the toilets became crowded with erks all puffing away, with smoke billowing out of the vents as though the place was on fire. This naturally attracted the attention of the snoops who closed in on the block in a pincer movement, with the doors at each end being obediently opened from inside — and then closed again shutting off the means of escape. The two unfortunate policemen were deprived first of their caps, then their tunics, boots, trousers, socks and underclothes as the mob pounced. Then the evacuation began and the smokers joined the rest of us on the bank behind the toilets as we awaited the emergence of the wretched snoops, whose humiliation was compounded by us bombarding them with wet, dirty sods ripped from the bank. The bell then sounded for the end of the break and we all returned to class. Somebody called the guardhouse and told them to pick up the two very unhappy, confused and dejected snoops, who although not physically abused, had suffered a serious blow to their self-esteem. The workshop break period was never again patrolled by the Provost Marshal's troops while the 33rd Entry was in residence.

Halton had its own cinema and this place used to also bring us into conflict with the snoops, who would patrol vigorously both outside and inside in order to maintain law and order. On one particular night the flick house was full and, as usual, the snoops were patrolling up and down the aisles on the lookout for anyone smoking without a pass. They spotted a likely suspect some ten seats in who refused to pass out his permit, mainly because he did not have one. One of the snoops then decided that he would have to go and get it himself, so he began to squeeze his way down the line towards the miscreant. Those who were sitting in the row, having "received" him, promptly lifted him off his feet and once he was airborne, he was passed between the rows, up and down the auditorium until on finally tiring of the game, the audience dumped him in the orchestra stalls. This was not the first time this particular trick had been played on the snoops but some people just do not seem to learn, do they?

At the entrance to the cinema there were a number of cigarette vending machines, unsurprisingly chained down to prevent them from "walking away". They sold Players cigarettes in packets of twenty for 11½d, and you had to place a shilling in the slot with the halfpenny change being secreted in the packet itself. An erk of above average intelligence found the plans showing the inner workings of the machine from somewhere and figured that it should be relatively easy to design and make some kind of gadget that would hold down the pawls that secured the slide, with its packet of cigarettes, between purchases. The said gadget was subsequently designed, made and once the machine had been refilled, applied. I assume that when the cinema was closed, a shilling was inserted and the machine "milked" of the twenty-five packets of cigarettes that it held, with the added bonus to the designer that these contained twenty-five halfpennies, covering the initial outlay with a halfpenny to spare — a fine piece of business. The machines were removed some time afterwards, but the culprit was never caught. As can be seen from this tale, we erks were always looking for a challenge. Someone had the bright idea that removing guns from the Wing armoury could prove to be the most impressive challenge, since the windows were heavily barred and the door double-locked. I don't know exactly how the security was breached, but breached it was and the three culprits removed two Smith and Wesson .38 revolvers and ammunition. They didn't intend to keep them — as they said they just wanted to demonstrate that they had the ability to plunder the armoury at will — but before they could replace the weapons the theft was discovered and all hell broke loose. We all believed that somebody blew the whistle on them. The whole of No. 4 Wing was confined to barracks and every available snoop and NCO was tasked with finding the guns and bringing the culprits to justice; a procedure which took three days. The offenders were duly charged, court-martialled and found guilty. The sentence handed down was public flogging, which was still a part of the penal law at that time. Since they were all under eighteen, their parents had to be notified and their permission obtained. If the parents refused then their sons would be drummed out of the RAF in disgrace. One of the boys was called Percy Boulter and he pleaded with his parents at home in Norfolk to allow him to be flogged as he did not want to leave. They gave their permission but the parents of the other boys did not and they were forced to go. This whole case received plenty of publicity at the time and I believe that it was instrumental in the subsequent removal of corporal punishment from the forces' penal code.

The actual flogging itself took place during a drum head parade when the entire Wing formed a square around a table placed at its centre. Percy Boulter, dressed in PT gear, was held down over this table by two snoops while the senior snoop flight sergeant carried out the flogging. Every stroke was felt by every one of us present at that parade, and to this day I still think that the sentence was grossly unjust. The same parade was also used to perform the equally humiliating "drumming out" ceremony of the other two, and nobody was left in any doubt that this kind of stunt would not be tolerated in future. Incidentally Percy Boulter was one of the many ex-Brats from the 33rd intake who did not survive the imminent war. He was lost over Germany on operations in January 1944, aged twenty-three, while flying as a flight engineer with 514 Squadron. He will certainly never be forgotten by those of us who knew him.

The RAF used to hold an air show at Hendon every year, and lucky apprentices would be shipped off to North London to sell the programmes. One year I was fortunate enough to be chosen for this privileged task, but I didn't sell very many programmes as I was far too busy watching the flying displays. I saw Gloster Gladiators, seemingly tied together, doing aerobatics as well as Bristol Blenheim twin engined medium bombers demonstrating their prowess with dummy bombs. Other modern aircraft were on static display, such as the Fairey Battle bomber, and the new Spitfires and Hurricanes. The tents were filled with all sorts of aircraft information and interested people asking all sorts of questions. I felt completely in my element and had a truly wonderful day. On the bus on the way home we had a sing-along involving lots of changed lyrics using words I can't possibly repeat here. It was a day which was well worth the effort.

The night before we all went on leave would traditionally be eventful. Everybody was wound up and excited and the NCOs had learned from past experience that discretion was the better part of valour and they more or less kept out of the way. We would usually kill time by staging battles between rooms, with the ultimate object being the smashing of every mug in the opposition's territory. I recall on one such evening Corporal "Chesty" Reid took it upon himself to put a stop to all this and install some good order and discipline for a change. Needless to say this did not go down too well. As he entered the block, he was greeted with the contents of a fire extinguisher, something that put him in a very bad mood indeed. The floor at this stage was already awash with the discharged contents of many other fire extinguishers. When, in a high state of frenzy, he persisted in interfering, somebody emptied the sand from a fire bucket onto his head from the top floor, followed rapidly by the bucket itself, which just caught him. Since he was alone and bleeding he decided to make a tactical withdrawal, presumably to drum up reinforcements. As he didn't reappear, I am sure that somebody told him that he should just have stayed well clear and that we should have been left to it without any interference. I suppose he just had to learn the hard way.

Sport played a very important part in Halton life, and was all organized under the umbrella of the PT department, with active teams playing football, rugby, cricket, athletics, boxing and gymnastics. Some American military school had even tried to spread the gospel of baseball by donating some equipment to us. There was great initial interest, but the novelty soon wore off and it didn't really catch on. Speaking personally, of course, rugby was my great love and I had no problem whatsoever in getting onto the squadron team. I played football and cricket to keep fit outside of the rugby season, but I never amounted to much in either sport. I also played table tennis and became quite good at it, as well as snooker and billiards which I couldn't get the hang of. So, as you can see, there was never a dull moment except when "boys were being boys", and trouble inevitably followed.

The four Wings at Halton were surrounded by a ten feet high steel lattice fences. Nos. 1 and 2 Wing shared the same turf, No. 3 was in the process of being built during the first part of our time at the camp, and our wing, No. 4, was some distance away on its own. The high fence was naturally put up to keep us in, so getting past it became our number one priority. If we wanted to go out of camp without a pass then we had to either climb over it or squeeze through it. The fence itself was constructed of substantial laths secured to upper and lower rails with half inch diameter rivets. As we had all been trained in the art of metal cutting and all had the tools required to do the job, it was not at all difficult to remove the rivets from the bottom rail of two adjacent laths. This meant that the top rivet could be rotated and the relevant laths be moved to one side to create a gap through which one could easily pass. Having escaped, we moved the laths back to their original positions and put false rivets in place so it appeared as though the fence was once again complete.

Now that we were out and about, what were we to do and where were we to go? The camp backed onto the beautiful wooded Chiltern Hills with their thick beech trees. We used to explore these and discover who lived there and how we could reach the nearest villages and towns. The area was dotted with large country houses used mainly as weekend retreats by rich Londoners, and their gardens were chock-full of wonderful fruit trees of all kinds, with ripe fruit just asking to be picked. As a result numerous forays were planned, but these could only be carried out at weekends as we had no time off during the week. This meant that they would coincide with the houses being in use, which made it even more of an exciting challenge for us. In actual fact, some of the goings-on at these houses certainly opened our eyes. While conducting our raids we would often stumble across wild parties being held out in the gardens and speaking personally, I had no idea that the supposedly reserved British upper classes were quite so lascivious. Mind you, I suppose my education in such matters had been sorely neglected. I remember once at the flick house in the camp when the newsreel of the night showed a meeting between a man and a bishop, and the commentary intoned that this man had "kissed the Bishop's ring". Everybody else burst out laughing at this obvious double entendre, but I had absolutely no idea what was so funny.

The stolen fruit was carried back to camp in our trouser legs; the ends of which were stuffed into our socks and secured with pieces of string. Although we were never actually caught in the act, the large quantities of fruit that we looted meant that our stocks were eventually discovered. The authorities, however, were at a loss to know where it had all come from, at least until complaints reached them concerning rampaging bands of young men dressed in Air Force Blue, raiding local properties. Some of the culprits had been too greedy and still had fruit hidden in their lockers which was soon discovered. One funny incident I remember concerned one of our number who had managed to put all the fruit he had in his locker down his trousers as the room was being searched, but had not had time to secure his trouser legs and all the fruit came cascading out onto the floor at precisely the wrong moment. Those who were found with fruit were sentenced to time served in the guardhouse, which meant that they were kept in solitary confinement and were kept very busy with parades and other duties in their spare time. Everything in the guardhouse had to be executed in double time. They were at least able to attend their schools and workshop classes, but they were not allowed to fraternize with us. Still, at the conclusion of our time at Halton, all of our disciplinary records were erased and we were able to begin our careers at our first postings with a clean slate.

My life at Halton was now approaching its end. One of our last courses covered the stripping down and repair of an engine, as well as reassembly and static testing. Although we had already been introduced to the workings of Rolls-Royce Kestrels and Vultures which were in-line water cooled types, and radial types such as the Bristol Mercury and the Armstrong Cheeta, the actual engine that we ended up working on was an in-line air cooled one made by de Havilland. This engine had been used in their record breaking Comet aircraft, which had won the England to Australia race a couple of years earlier. We dismantled it entirely and then fitted new main big end bearing shells. This was to teach us how to fit them by scraping them to the crank shaft journals, a very slow and painstaking procedure, but one which utilized the tools and the skills that we had earlier acquired at the start of our time as apprentices. After pre-assembly, the engine was mounted upon a test stand where the airscrew was fitted, and tuned to perfection before the whole thing was started with a manual swing of the airscrew itself. This was the method of starting an engine that we had learned on our aerodrome course. Much to everyone's surprise, the engine did actually cough into life, and ran together with accompanying bangs and wheezes, until the expert hands of the corporal instructor coaxed it into behaving itself with a few twists and turns of knobs and levers. Much to our amazement, our handiwork had actually borne fruit.

In fact, when I left Halton I was to learn that on site repairing of engines did not take place. The entire engine was replaced and the offending piece of machinery was sent away to a separate repair facility to be worked upon. The only time I was ever involved with an on site repair was when we were instructed to change a cylinder on a Cheeta engine, which was fitted to a twin engined Avro Anson. This whole episode turned out to be a disaster. The broken cylinder was removed, discarded and everything was prepared for the installation of the replacement part, when the corporal fitter I was assisting, noticed that the glass front was missing from his wristwatch. Now, even to be wearing one in the hangars was an offence in itself as RAF regulations for ground crew stated that rings and wristwatches were not to be worn on duty and cigarette lighters were not to be carried. These regulations had been put in place to prevent situations such as this one from occurring. A search for the missing glass produced no positive results. The corporal, who was well aware of the rules, decided to install the cylinder and say nothing about the missing glass. Initially, all was well and the aircraft flew without incident, but a few weeks later it again developed engine trouble; it was examined and evidence of ground glass was found in the oil filter. Thankfully for the corporal and myself, the glass was never officially linked to him. However, our good old flight chiefy, Flight Sergeant Keogh, realized what had happened but decided to say nothing, thereby preventing a court martial, which would also have convicted me for assisting the corporal to cover up his mistake!

As I have already said at the start of this chapter, when we arrived at Halton back in January 1936, we occupied the reopened No. 4 Wing, with No. 3 Wing being under construction. When it was finished a year later our entry was split into two. One half moved into the newly completed building, and the other half stayed where they were, in order to act as "Snags" for future entries. We still retained our status but those of us who moved wings replaced our orange cap bands with new red and black chequered ones. I was one of those who moved, and I was pleased to see that although the format of the new wing was the same, the new building was a great improvement on the old.

All in all, little happened that was worthy of note during the time that I was in the new wing but a new type of scandal did raise its ugly head. It appeared that the station warrant officer, Warrant Officer Routledge, had a preference for young boys over young girls and the inevitable happened. He was found out, court-martialled, convicted, sent to jail and dismissed in disgrace. In my innocence I was informed that one of his crimes was sodomy; a word I did not then fully understand, even after I had looked it up in the dictionary. It did, however, clarify the meaning of the words in one of the songs the old boys sang, *Maria Monk*, which went: "The old sod, the dirty old sod, The bastard deserves to die." For obvious reasons Routledge's victims' names were not made public.

Autumn 1938 saw the imminent end of our time at Halton, and was characterized by set tasks, shop tasks, oral and written exams. All that was left was to practise hard for the big march past and final parade and, speaking personally, to prepare the speech that I was required to give at the passing out dinner on 20 December. In any event, the parade itself was cancelled due to a then record snowfall, so all of our practice was for nothing. This was a great disappointment to us all, as well as the legions of family members who had descended on Halton. It goes without saying that nobody from the Lancashire household attended to see me pass out. My speech at the dinner did not quite come off as I expected either. It was meant to last for five minutes but I could not make myself heard above the momentous din and excited chatter and, in any case, nobody was really interested in what Corporal Aircraft Apprentice Lancashire had to say. As a result my one chance to make a name for myself as a distinguished after dinner speaker vanished into the general hubbub. I do, however, remember the principal guest and speaker saying, amongst other things: "Gentlemen, within one year we shall be at war with Germany." How true this prediction was to be and quite how drastically all our lives were to be changed by that war, we could not have guessed.

The following day we had to say our goodbyes as the 33rd Entry split up and we all went our separate ways to our first postings. Mine was to RAF Finningley then the home of both 7 Squadron, a Bomber Command unit equipped with twin-engined Armstrong Whitworth Whitley bombers, and 78 Squadron. Our instructors were conspicuous by their absence that last morning, having said their goodbyes the previous evening. My best friend at Halton had been Alan Keogh, who was posted to RAF Abingdon in Oxfordshire. Sadly, our farewells were very final since he was killed less than a year later on 18 October 1939; the first of many of the 33rd to die. He had been flying in a 52 Squadron Fairey Battle light bomber which had crashed near Oxford after a mid air collision with another Battle, and somehow his head had been in the wrong place at impact and he was decapitated. I will never forget him or the others I knew whose lives were cut tragically short by the war.

So it had come to pass. For me my time at Halton was, and remains, the greatest experience of my life. The education that I received there in all aspects of life was well worth the subsequent twelve years that I gave to my King and Country. If I had my time again I would not hesitate to repeat my three years there. Sir Hugh Trenchard, I am very honoured to call myself a "Trenchard Brat". You were a genius.

CHAPTER
THREE

To War

After the excitement of passing out with the rest of the 33rd Entry in December 1938, coupled with the sadness of realizng that I was going to be parted from some very good friends, it was a question of enjoying Christmas at home with our families and then on to the challenge of beginning our RAF careers outside the safe confines of Halton. For many of us, it was a time of contemplation as to what we had got ourselves into. For all of us, shortly to be swallowed up in the most devastating war in history, service life would take a very different direction to that which had been advertised by those classic recruiting posters of the early 1930s, which encouraged us to "Join the Royal Air Force and See the World". Although a few of my fellow Brats had jumped at the chance of taking far-flung postings within the Empire, the vast majority of us remained within the United Kingdom. I was posted to RAF Finningley, near Doncaster in South Yorkshire, and I knew little about the place. The most important thing about it, as far as I was concerned, was the fact that it was the nearest available posting to

Manchester and that I would be able to make regular trips home without too much inconvenience.

So on 5 January 1939, I presented myself to the guard house at RAF Finningley. The Provost Sergeant in charge looked me up and down, and said: "Ah, another boy wonder come to solve all of our problems. Just sit there, son, and somebody will be along to look after you." I did as I was told, and nearly an hour later I was collected and taken to the orderly room where I was booked in. Following this procedure, I was then led over to one of the barracks and handed over to the erk who had been placed in charge of that particular block. He allotted me a bed, gave me an orientation lecture and took me on a tour of the camp. By the time we had finished, the working day was over and my new "family" had returned to the block. They took over the induction procedure and were extremely friendly, answering my numerous questions and taking me to the Mess hall for dinner. The next morning I again reported to the orderly room where the very fatherly station warrant officer took me under his wing and making me feel very welcome — not the type of behaviour I had come to expect from senior NCOs.. He took me to meet a flight lieutenant, who in turn introduced me to a Flight Sergeant Keogh, who had been detailed to come across and collect me. After some small talk, I went back with him to the hangar where I was to meet my future work mates. I was pleased to see that I already knew some of them as they lived in my block, and it wasn't long before I stopped feeling as though it was my first day at school. With the masterful handling of my new "chiefy", Flight Sergeant Keogh, I soon fitted in and began to feel like one of the boys.

I rapidly lost my stage fright when I was assigned to a ground crew which was responsible for a couple of the newish Whitley bombers, as well as two of the old outmoded Handley Page Heyfords which were more or less ready for the scrapheap. I spent the next few days watching and listening in order to acclimatize myself to this new life and to learn what would be expected of me. The impression that I gained was that the whole set-up in the "outside world" was a great deal more gung-ho, lax and unprofessional than the rigid order of Halton, but I learned to adapt my ways, and within two weeks I was considered competent enough to be given my own aircraft to look after. I also learned to my delight that, as a member of the ground crew responsible for the aircraft itself, I was in a fairly respected and privileged position and that for a small fee, we were entitled to be looked after by batmen types who would polish our buttons, clean and buff our boots, and make our beds in the morning — I even began to feel a little bit important.

We would have compulsory PT sessions early each morning after our batmen had brought us our "gunfire". On Wednesday afternoon we would all take part in sporting activities. It was here that I discovered the existence of a motorcycle club — to my surprise this officially constituted a sporting activity. I became extremely interested and as a result I decided to splash out on a second-hand bike. I chose a now defunct make called a Calthorpe, and arranged to have it delivered to the nearest railway station. It cost £20 and I had to buy it "on tick". This meant that I had to persuade my father to co-sign the purchase agreement. In the Lancashire household it was considered a cardinal sin to pay for anything on credit and I had a very difficult time persuading Dad to agree. Fortunately he did, and once I had taken delivery of my bike, my new-found mobility made a huge difference to my life at Finningley. I was now able to take advantage of the fact that once we had packed up our tools at lunchtime on a Saturday, we were free until our first parade of the week on Monday morning. This meant that I would be able to ride home across the Pennines to Manchester and only have to return late on Sunday evening. For a small fee I was able to provide someone with a lift, and I was able to make a little pin money that way. The camp had facilities for housing the bikes and it was easy enough to carry around a small petrol can with you and top it up while refuelling the aircraft. I was constantly tuning up my new pride and joy, whether it needed it or not. I remember that I would dismantle my bike completely at least once a month and thoroughly enjoy putting it back together again. The motorcycle club's Wednesday afternoon rides through the Yorkshire Dales were absolutely wonderful, and we began to develop the sort of camaraderie within the club that reminded me of my Halton days.

During the first half of 1939, the threat from Irish Republican terrorism escalated dramatically, culminating in a vicious summer bombing campaign which claimed several innocent lives. The IRA had reportedly threatened to attack RAF airfields and bases, and this resulted in a directive from on high being issued, which decreed that all available units would be forced to supply armed guards to patrol the perimeters. Since the RAF Regiment had not yet been formed, the onus fell upon us to manage our own security, even those of us who had trades to perform. The problem was that we did not have enough arms and ammunition available to mount all of the patrols that had been demanded. We did apparently have sufficient quantities of ammunition stored somewhere on the base, but the problem was that nobody seemed to know where it was. On many occasions I found myself on duty, facing the unseen and malevolent IRA threat alone except for an unloaded and empty 1914 Lee Enfield .303 rifle. Still this state of affairs did at least cancel out the thorny problem of having to ask the duty officer what to do if a terrorist suspect did actually appear, as shooting him dead was hardly an option. I had been introduced to weapon handling at Halton, but this had not exactly been a comprehensive overview and we had only been taken to the range on two occasions, shown how to load ammunition, and allowed to blast off five rounds each. I hardly think that this qualified us as marksmen, and I'm sure that the only reasons we had rifles given to us at Halton were to lug them around the parade ground and to give us something else to clean and polish. Of course, having to carry out guard duties meant that we could not do our real job of servicing and looking after the aircraft. I was not privy to the high level discussions that took place in order to thrash out the RAF's anti-terrorism policy, but they must have been hilariously chaotic. It was not long before our guard duties were abandoned, and I never did learn whether or not any other strategies were put in place, or whether the IRA ever attempted anything. With the prospect of war looming, our Keystone Kops performance certainly gave me food for thought, and I wasn't exactly surprised that Adolf Hitler didn't really consider us much of a threat to his future plans.

We began to carry out more and more war exercises and these would often overrun into our free time at the weekends, meaning that I would be lucky to get home at all. It was during these exercises that I got my first experience of night flying as in those early days ground crew were used as air gunners and were paid a small amount extra to perform that role. This was a far cry from the days to come, when air gunnery in itself would come to be regarded as a highly vital and skilled trade. There were no power turrets in 1939 and, in my case, I didn't even have any guns to play with; neither did my aircraft have any bomb racks or bombs. Owing to a complete lack of suitable flying clothing, I would almost freeze to death in the unheated tail end of the Whitley. I soon realized just how unprepared for the onset of war we really were. Even the aircraft themselves were wholly unreliable, with the Armstrong Siddeley Tiger engines that they were powered by being next to useless — the concept of designing and manufacturing an efficient 14 cylinder double banked radial engine was something that the Americans were later able to perform, but we hadn't quite managed it by 1939. The engine flaws eventually led to the Whitley being superseded, and then replaced by the end of the year, by the Handley Page Hampden. Some Whitleys were later built using Rolls-Royce Merlin engines, but these too proved to be easy meat for the enemy's Messerschmitt 109 fighters and production soon ceased completely.

Our war manoeuvres took us to a place called RAF Acklington, on the coast a few miles north of Newcastle, where we were supposed to carry out plenty of gunnery practice and night flying training (NFT), although it was difficult to accomplish any of the former as we still had no guns or ammunition, let alone target towing aircraft. We were supplied with obsolete Gloster Gauntlet aircraft to assist us with our fighter affiliation exercises, but once gale force winds set in, these were grounded as it was too dangerous for them to fly. Everything that could go wrong had gone wrong and, fed up, we returned to Finningley and it was arranged for the night flying training to be finished off there.

By the time summer arrived, 7 Squadron had been re-equipped with the Hampden, but we still had no bomb racks to play with; so as far as bombing was concerned, there was no discernable difference from the Whitley. The Hampden was, however, fitted with defensive armament in the shape of four Lewis guns — two on the top of the pencil thin fuselage and two in the belly, both firing aft. We were to find out the hard way, during subsequent gunnery practices, that there were no interceptor stops to prevent the gunners from shooting their own tail units off, and once this flaw became known, all subsequent gunnery practice was suspended until someone could come up with a way of designing and fitting movement restrictors. I am proud to say that this challenge was eventually taken up and met by a fellow Brat, but typically I don't believe he actually managed to get any credit for his sterling efforts. Another initial problem with the Hampden was that nobody had been told how to maintain the new Bristol Pegasus 18 engine, and no training courses existed for us. This meant that in the early stages the process of starting the engine became for us a matter of trial and error, or should I say "chain-swinging", until starter battery packs arrived. This was all very well, but we had no recharging facilities, so once they went flat, that was it. Gradually, we got a little more organized and groups of us were sent to Radlett, Bristol and de Havilland's factories, in order to learn about the airframe, engines, and the new hydromatic variable pitch propeller, respectively.

As the summer progressed, we also began to receive a number of Avro Anson twin-engined aircraft, and rumours began to circulate that 7 Squadron was going to convert from being a front line bomber squadron to forming an Operational Training Unit (OTU). Of course, we had to endure the same problems with the Anson as we had with the Hampden a few months previously — namely that nobody knew the first thing about them, and the concept of "trial and error" was again the order of the day. By now, it was the end of

August and war seemed imminent, Germany was making aggressive territorial demands to Poland, whose independence Mr Chamberlain had guaranteed, and Hitler and Stalin had signed a non-aggression pact. It looked as though we'd be at war within days and nobody really knew what to expect. The powers that be decided that we'd all be far safer and much less of a target if we moved to our dispersal aerodrome, which was at nearby Doncaster Airport. This came as an almighty shock to the officials there, who were not in any fit state to receive us at such short notice. Chaos reigned and my role in all of this was to act as a switchboard operator, since the civilian operator had been sent home. I didn't really have the first idea what to do, and I certainly found myself in at the deep end. On the day that war was declared, it seemed as though every member of the Officers' Mess had the sudden impulse to telephone as many people as they could, and "my" switchboard was swamped with calls to wives, girlfriends, parents, brothers, sisters and so on. I was getting more and more frustrated until, in a fit of desperation, I lost my temper and pulled all of the plugs out, with the inevitable result that I was promptly put under arrest by the orderly officer for dereliction of duty. So started the Second World War for this unhappy airman.

Before too long, the rumours about our becoming an OTU had become reality, and we moved to RAF Upper Heyford in Oxfordshire, together with our collection of Hampdens and Ansons, in order to form No. 16

Operational Training Unit. An OTU was responsible for preparing raw young aircrew for operations, and moulding them into crews. They would have already completed their trade training at specialized establishments, and an OTU was where it would all come together. Later on in the war, with the advent of four-engined aircraft, Heavy Conversion Units (HCUs) were set up to bridge the gap in skills between crewing medium bombers such as Wellingtons and heavy bombers such as Lancasters. For now, this was all a long way off and OTUs were directly responsible for churning out the men who would lead the way in taking the fight to the enemy in those early days.

Training the new crews was a hazardous and risky undertaking for all involved, and casualty rates amongst aircrew were extremely high. Our Ansons gave us no trouble and were easy to fly and maintain. The Hampden was a different matter, and it transpired that the engines had a nasty habit of cutting out on take-off, with often fatal results. This was caused by the mixture control sticking, and there was really not a lot that could be done about it. However, just in time we took delivery of a number of what we all believed would be the solution — the new and upgraded version of the Hampden, called the Hereford. This was basically a Hampden airframe powered by two New Napier Halford "H" engines. Unfortunately, these engines were prone to overheating and failing on take-off, so casualty rates remained high. It appeared to us as though we were killing more crews than we were actually managing to train. These new Herefords were swiftly taken out of service and, I believe, shipped to the Isle of Man where they were disposed of. So much for our long awaited solution.

As 1939 became 1940, we were subjected to one of the harshest winters on record, which severely curtailed our flying activities. Nevertheless, in between the frequent heavy falls of snow we did at least attempt to continue with the training programme, despite the conditions making things very uncomfortable for all. At least the Germans were prevented from paying us the occasional visit, but this worked both ways as I don't remember any "nickels" or propaganda leafleting raids being made by our unit either. These sorties, which dominated the early months of the war, were often the domain of OTU crews nearing the end of their training, giving them practical experience of working together as a crew over enemy territory. They were often ridiculed, both within the RAF and in the national press, and would come to symbolize Neville Chamberlain's conciliatory and cautious approach to waging war. With the spring came warmer weather and with the warmer weather came the Germans, first into Norway, and then later into France, Holland and Belgium. The war was coming closer, and a change in government would mean a change in approach.

I was still at Upper Heyford when the Luftwaffe began what would become known as the Battle of Britain, and we soon found ourselves in the thick of it. Our new remit was to refuel and rearm the fighters which used the airfield as an emergency landing ground, and although we didn't receive the daily attentions of the Germans, as did the front-line bases such as Manston and Biggin Hill, we soon found ourselves a target for roaming Messerschmitt 110 pilots who would strafe us for fun in their attempts to demonstrate who was the boss. I soon developed the very useful skill of being able to dive post-haste into the nearest ditch. Our Lewis gun posts were initially unmanned, but even when steps were taken to keep them permanently crewed, the gunners had to obtain permission from the duty officer before engaging the enemy; such were the strange protocols that governed life in the Royal Air Force in those days. Of course these defensive emplacements soon attracted the attention of the Germans, and our unit started to suffer its first casualties of the war. Our primary role remained the training of bomber crews, and the Luftwaffe would also have their fun here as well. Night fighters would regularly infiltrate our landing circuits during NFT exercises, line us up in their sights, and give us everything they had. This tactic soon led to the suspension of all night flying as our satellite aerodrome, Brackley, had no Lewis guns to defend it.

These acts of war made me feel extremely angry and began to spark thoughts of retaliation, but there was little that I could do beyond my ground crew maintenance duties at Upper Heyford. However, the RAF had been developing the idea of using four engined heavy bombers, and towards the end of 1940, the first of these was to enter service. The Shorts Aircraft Company of Belfast had designed and produced the Short Stirling, a behemoth of an aircraft and, as it turned out, the largest bomber used by the Allied air forces until the arrival of the American B29 Superfortress in 1944. The difference between this aircraft and those already in service, was the fact that looking after the engines and the fuel supply while in flight, amounted to a fulltime role, and it was unrealistic to expect the pilot to fulfil this as well as all of his other responsibilities. As such, a new aircrew trade was created, that of the flight engineer. There had been no efforts made, up until this point, to actually train volunteers from outside the service, and with our specialist knowledge of the aero engine, fitters such as me could well prove vital. In fact, as it turned out, the Air Ministry was thinking along those same lines and had actually told the service to give recruitment priority to ex-Brats who were Fitter 2s and Fitter 1s — Airframe/Engine. This was my opportunity, and I immediately put myself forward for flying duties.

My application was successful at the first stage, and I was informed that I would have to undergo a medical examination in order to check that I was fit to fly. This examination more or less consisted of me being asked "How do you feel?" by the doctor. Unsurprisingly, I passed with flying colours, having supplied the right answers, and I was subsequently told to report to a receiving unit at RAF Newmarket in Suffolk. This was little more than a basic gunnery school, and when I say basic, I mean basic. As trainee flight engineers, we learned that we would also be required to man the Stirling's power operated machine-gun turrets, should the need arise. Consequently, all we did at Newmarket was to learn the noble art of trap shooting, using shotguns, in an effort to drill into us the principles of "lead and lag". The problem was that we had plenty of shotguns and plenty of clay pigeons, but as usual no cartridges and shells to fire. This resulted in a ludicrous situation where we had to follow the clay with the weapon and shout "BANG." at the appropriate moment, so that the instructor would know that we had fired. I never did find out if I "hit" anything, funnily enough. From here we moved on to the slightly more functional surroundings of RAF Pembrey in south Wales. This was an actual bona fide air gunnery school, so we were able to ditch our shotguns, take to the air in old Wellingtons and Blenheims, and shoot at targets being towed along behind even older Fairey Battles. It was here that I learned how to be continually airsick, but that wore off and thankfully didn't hinder my progress. Now that we had graduated from Pembrey, it was time to learn about this new monster and we were dispatched to the Morris MG factory near Oxford, which had been converted into a shadow factory building the Stirling. Here we were instructed in the finer points of the aircraft, its engines and fuel supply, and we learned how to perform the type of emergency repairs and maintenance that would keep the bomber in the air over the dangerous night skies of the Third Reich. The course itself was extremely interesting, but before too long it had ended and we had become fully fledged flight engineers, with the substantive minimum aircrew rank of sergeant. I still have a photograph, taken at Pembrey, which shows me among my class of thirty-seven fellow ex-Brats — many of whom I had been with at Halton. As I look at it now, I can only account for three other individuals who made it through the war, and only one other that I am aware was still alive in 2002. All that technical expertise thrown away because of a lack of planning and foresight — it still upsets me to think about it.

So, Sergeant Thomas Lancashire was ready to take to the air, but all he needed now was a crew. In late September 1941, I reported to RAF Wyton, near St Ives in Cambridgeshire, which was the home of 15 Squadron. There, I was lucky enough to meet up with the crew of twenty-two year old Pilot Officer Dennis Parkins, who had arrived the day before from a Heavy Conversion Unit, and who were short of a flight engineer. They were the veterans of six operations in Wellingtons, but the Stirling was a totally different kettle of fish and we were all in it together. Dennis Parkins, from Buckinghamshire, was an absolute gentleman, and a very capable, efficient and brave captain. I always feel that I owe the fact that I survived my first tour of duty to him and his superb leadership skills. The only other commissioned officer in the crew was the navigator, Pilot Officer Dick Strachan. As his name suggests, he was a Scot and before the war he had been a chartered public accountant. Dick didn't care for rank and formality, and we got on very well. He survived the war — we stayed in contact and a year before he died I visited him and his wife, Celeste, at their home in Ayrshire. In the nose of the aircraft was the bomb aimer (and part time front gunner), Sergeant

Ron Quartly. Ron was an east Londoner who had joined up almost straight from school. He often talked about his girlfriend at home, and how much he looked forward to getting married to her once the war ended. He was another one who survived the war and did actually stay in touch with Dick Strachan until his death a few years ago. I never did find out if he eventually married his sweetheart.

The crew member I was closest to, both in a geographical and emotional sense, was the wireless operator, Sergeant Robert (Bob) Milne. Geographically, because our stations were in close proximity to each other, and emotionally, because he was the only person I could see during the long hours of terror that followed, and we would often find ourselves staring wordlessly into each others' eyes, just waiting for what we thought would be our inevitable fate. Bob was twenty-eight and had been a teacher before joining up, with ambitions to become a headmaster. Sadly he was never to realize that aim. Like me, he undertook a second tour as a Pathfinder and, almost inevitably, met his end on 22 March 1944. He had been granted a commission and had reached the rank of flying officer before the final op to Frankfurt that claimed his life. A sad loss to the world of education and a very brave man.

Of the permanent crew, that left the mid-upper gunner, Sergeant Alec Picken, and the rear gunner, Sergeant Birch. Alec Picken was a twenty-eight year old Glaswegian, a butcher by trade, and very much a man of the world. We younger men would sit spellbound as

Alec related his nocturnal adventures on the streets of his home city, talking freely about sex and the women he had known. He considered it hugely funny that I had never been intimate with a girl, and urged me to take advantage of as many WAAFs as I possibly could. He had a point, in that we aircrew were seen as the glamour boys and there was no shortage of local girls who were keen to be seen out with us. Our camp padre was regularly called upon to counsel young girls who had got themselves "into trouble". They often showed up at the guardhouse with their furious parents in tow, demanding to see the guilty airman responsible for this unfortunate state of affairs — high casualty rates meant that this was not always possible, for obvious reasons.

Sergeant Donald Birch was the youngest member of the crew and had joined up straight from school. He did not complete his tour with us, for reasons that I shall come to later, but he did at least survive the war. We were quite a sociable lot and I do remember a number of enjoyable parties and excursions to nearby Huntingdon, where there was a fine hotel called The Criterion. We endeavoured to get traditionally drunk and I don't remember there being room for many deep and meaningful conversations on such occasions.

That accounts for the six permanent crew members with whom I began my operational flying career. The Stirling was designed to carry a crew of eight, including a pilot and a copilot, but the co-pilot's seat was usually filled either by a rookie pilot who was learning his trade, or a spare bod who had been detailed to fly. On many occasions, the seat was just left empty. Since joining the squadron in late September 1941, our own skipper had completed a number of trips with a more experienced crew, in the role of second pilot. Now that he was judged to be competent enough to captain his own crew, we were going to be out on our own. On the morning of 27 November we were told that we would be making our first operational sortie that evening, and that our target would be the Belgian North Sea port of Ostend. We were to carry a number of 500lb bombs, a reconnaissance camera and a number of propaganda leaflets to drop over the town. This first operation, as part of a small force of Stirlings and Wellingtons, was traditionally known as a freshman trip, and was usually pretty simple. Being on the coast, Ostend wasn't too difficult to find, despite the heavy cloud that blighted our arrival, and even that began to clear after a while. Unfortunately something was wrong with the aircraft's bomb release mechanism and we weren't able to drop our load on the target. As it turned out, we weren't the only crew with problems that night: out of eighteen aircraft, for a variety of reasons only seven were able to hit Ostend. We did eventually manage to jettison the bombs just off the French coast, much to everybody's relief. Returning to base with a full load of ordnance was not a good idea and put many lives at risk on the ground, as well as the obvious risk to the poor aircrew. The port defences had been reasonably strong, with plenty of heavy flak, and finding oneself being shot at was something of an eye-opener for us all. We would all get used to it very quickly in the months to come.

The Breton port of Brest, on the Atlantic coast, had begun to receive substantial attention from Bomber Command. This was owing to the fact that a number of German battlecruisers had docked there and were believed to be preparing themselves for a dash through the English Channel to their home port of Kiel. Chief amongst these were the *Gniesenau* and the *Scharnhorst*, who had been wreaking havoc amongst Allied shipping in the Atlantic. No available British ships were capable of catching and outgunning them, so the job of damaging or destroying them was awarded to us. On the morning of 18 December we awoke to be told that we had been listed to take part in a daylight raid against the cruisers which were still in port. Daylight bombing was not something that we had trained for and we all felt extremely uneasy about the prospect. Nine Stirlings, including ours, were to form up in flights of three and make our way across the Channel. The weather was perfect and visibility was excellent. We had been given an escort of Spitfires, but Brest was at the extreme limit of their range and this meant that they could only take us there and had to turn round and return as soon as we had reached the target. We were left to the mercy of the ever eager Luftwaffe day fighters, and there was intense opposition over the port. As instructed, Dennis Parkins dived from 17,000 feet to 14,000 feet on the bomb run, and we released our load at 12:38 hours exactly. Our photograph showed that along with one other crew, we had scored a hit on one of the ships. Not that we were that concerned at that point with our achievements as we were too busy trying to see off the multitude of Messerschmitts and Focke-Wulfs who were intent on seeing us off. One of the disadvantages of bombing in daylight is that nothing is hidden from you, and when you see other aircraft all around you blowing up, going down in flames and spinning out of control, it does affect the nerves somewhat. The Americans would come to learn this in the months and years to come, but for my part, I was more than happy to work the night shift.

Christmas 1941 was spent on the base, being kept on standby in case the German ships decided to risk what ultimately became known as the "Channel Dash". We did go out and have a look for them on 27 December, but bad weather combined with failing navigational signals put an early stop to proceedings, and once again our bombs were jettisoned over the Channel. Our next trip, two days into the New Year, was once again to Brest. Ron Quartly was absent on this trip and his place in the nose was taken by a Sergeant Morgan. It was here that we had our first real brush with death. Over the target, we were subjected to more intense flak than we had been before, and this state of affairs resulted in a shell hitting the tailplane, but miraculously passing straight through without exploding. Had it exploded, the aircraft would, at best, have become unmanageable and, at worst, the tail would have blown right off. Either way, we'd have been in big trouble. Thankfully, we managed to evade the flak by diving to 10,000 feet before setting course for home.

Our next trip, on 14 January, took us to Germany for the first time, with the target being Hamburg. We were briefed to attack the shipyards on the Elbe and an airframe factory. Unfortunately, once over the German coast I began to notice that the starboard inner engine was playing up and reported this to the skipper. The decision was taken to try and find a suitable target in the vicinity and then turn back and head for home before anything more serious developed. We managed to find a cluster of searchlights on the coast between Wilhelmshaven and Emden and dropped our bombs on them from 17,000 feet. The journey home was reasonably uneventful, but I was kept busy nursing the troublesome engine.

February passed relatively uneventfully for me, with one "nickel" raid to France as a guest in Squadron Leader Sellick's crew and, on 12 February, a fruitless search over the Channel for the three ships which had, as expected, left Brest for Kiel and managed to evade all attempts to track them down. However changes were taking place behind the scenes at Bomber Command headquarters, which would soon come to affect all of us.

1942 was to be a watershed year for Bomber Command. The famous Butt Report, completed in August 1941, held some uncomfortable truths for the top brass. It had emerged that for every 100 bombs dropped on inland targets by British aircraft, only three landed within *five* miles of the aiming point. We were wasting our lives throwing high explosives at cows and sheep and this situation had to change. The government was also of this opinion, and the resident

C.-in-C, Sir Richard Peirse, was replaced in February by the famous Sir Arthur "Bomber" Harris.

Harris was an advocate of technological advancement coupled with the aggressive policy of "area bombing". This was the indiscriminate flattening of residential areas in an attempt to crush civilian morale, thereby affecting industrial output. The Germans had pioneered this tactic at the start of the war and it had worked well in certain places. Harris wanted to take it to the next level. On being appointed to the post, he said:

> The Germans entered this war under the rather childish illusion that they were going to bomb everybody else, and that nobody was going to bomb them . . . they have sowed the wind, and now they are going to reap the whirlwind.

We were the ones who would be doing his bidding in the months and years to come, and the change in tactics wasn't long in coming.

On 3 March, we were briefed for a raid on the Billancourt Renault factory, just to the west of Paris. Apparently the Air Ministry had asked Bomber Command to attempt a raid on one of numerous French factories known to be producing war materials for the Germans, and this establishment fitted the bill — it was producing some 18,000 lorries per year for the Wehrmacht. We took off at 18:42 in our newly allocated Stirling, R-Robert, and headed out to the target as part of a force of 235 aircraft which would be bombing in three waves. The factory itself was relatively easy to find as we managed to pick up the ribbon-like Seine river which guided us through Paris, and then on into the western suburbs. We were to bomb at low level in order to maximize accuracy and made four runs over the target. Our crew's entry in the Squadron's Operational Record Book notes that we finally released our load at 2,500 feet and that the first four bombs were seen to hit the factory's power plant before the resultant drifting smoke made target identification impossible. There was no flak over the target, and we suffered no interference from fighters either. All in all, the raid had turned out to be one of the most successful of the war to date, but we didn't know that at the time, nor that 367 French civilians had also lost their lives during the attack. Such were the inevitable results of the new, more ruthless, approach that we were now taking.

There now followed a series of three uneventful trips to Essen as we familiarized ourselves with the Ruhr, or "Happy Valley" as the area was ironically christened by bomber aircrew. These may have been somewhat quieter than we expected, but our later visits to Essen would not prove to be quite so comfortable. In the meantime, on 28 March we were briefed to hit the ancient north German town of Lübeck with everything that we had. This raid was actually the brainchild of Bomber Harris and was his attempt to demonstrate the damage that a medium sized force could do to a German target, if conditions were in his favour. He chose Lübeck as it was on the coast and thus relatively easy to find; the buildings were made of wood and would therefore burn easily and he knew that it was not a priority target and was not heavily defended. We were sent out to do a job and we certainly did that. The fires that we had stoked were still visible eighty-three miles away as we flew home, and the target photographs the next day displayed to everyone the absolute devastation that we had caused. However, the raid hadn't been an absolute cake-walk for us, as I remember that we were caught in searchlights over the Kiel canal, and had to dive down to ground level from 14,000 feet in order to evade them and the subsequent attention from radar-controlled flak batteries. Escape them we did, and as we landed back at Wyton at approximately 04:00 I was able to chalk up my twelfth op in my logbook. We were now becoming a reasonably experienced crew and, despite the odd temporary change in personnel from time to time, we were knitting together well as a unit and were beginning to have great confidence in one another, and especially in our skipper.

Around this time, a photo journalist from the *Illustrated London News* visited Wyton in order to compile a feature entitled *A Bomber Goes To Germany*. The aircraft that was chosen to feature was our trusty R-Robert, and also featured in the photographs was the squadron mascot, Flight Lieutenant Bill Prune. Flight Lieutenant Prune was a very grandiose name for the ugliest bulldog you could imagine, but nobody begrudged him his rank as he was in fact a veteran of several operations over Germany, always flying (unofficially) with the crew of former

London bobby Flight Lieutenant Boggis. Bill's face was a mass of scars and he could always be found in his regular haunt at the top of the steps leading to the Sergeants' Mess, drooling profusely. Newcomers were afraid to go past him but they needn't have worried as Bill had only two real enemies, RAF lorries and empty four-gallon petrol cans. He would attack the latter whenever he could find them, biting them in the middle so as to be able to carry them around in his mouth. On one instance, I found him on the top floor of one of the barrack blocks trying to make his way down the stairs and, of course, he was holding a battered petrol can in his mouth. He refused to put the can down and, because he could not see where he was going, he had to feel very gingerly for the next step. Inevitably, he missed his footing and overbalanced, crashing to the floor at the foot of the stairs — but still proudly clenching the flattened can between his jaws. He became something of a celebrity but his dangerous habit of chasing lorries inevitably resulted in his sad demise, and he had the honour of having his obituary published in the *Daily Express*.

RAF Wyton was an established pre-war RAF station, which had been built during the expansion programme of the 1930s. The accommodation was permanent — brick and mortar barracks as opposed to the draughty Nissen huts I was to encounter later in the war. If you were lucky, you would have your own room in the Sergeants' Mess but if you were unlucky you would find yourself in a room with fourteen beds, together with your fellow tradesmen but not your own crew. This was not ideal, because it gave us the opportunity to make friends with members of other crews, many of whom would invariably disappear and it became a case of "here today, gone tomorrow". You were never supposed to talk about those who had not returned — grief was a personal thing in those days. You would sit silently in the large ante-room in the Mess, together with their ghosts looking over your shoulders, and try and take your mind off what you had to face. I used to be a devotee of the *Daily Express* crossword (when I could find one lying around that hadn't been completed) so I would occupy my time that way. If you were fortunate enough to have a wife, girlfriend or sibling to write to, in order to take your mind off reality, so much the better, but as I did not I would shed silent tears for my friends and try to make some sense of it all.

Back to the war, and again to Essen. Our trip on 6 April marked our first sortie in a brand new R-Robert — with a serial number of W7513. It wasn't a successful raid as weather conditions over the target were atrocious with severe storms, icing and 10/10 (total) cloud cover. We believed that we hit the target but could not be certain and, as the authorities in Essen reported slight damage and no civilian casualties, it doesn't seem very likely that we did. We went there again six days later but didn't really do much better although we did have some success using our IFF (Identification Friend or Foe) beacons against the German searchlight batteries who seemed to leave us pretty much alone. That certainly wasn't the case on our next op, which was against Dortmund on 14 April. Once again the weather was not in our favour, and when we arrived over the target at about 02:00 we were almost immediately picked up by a radar-guided searchlight, then another, then another, until we were completely "coned".

It is difficult to describe fully this overwhelmingly terrifying state of affairs. The principle of "coning" is that all the available searchlights would be drawn to the aircraft caught in their beams, and that by using the angles of the lights and by accurately estimating the height of the trapped aircraft, the flak gunners would be able to concentrate on one target. By being able to observe the results of their efforts in the brilliantly illuminated sky, success would invariably follow with the destruction of the bomber. That is how the situation would appear to those on the ground. For the unfortunate crew, the reality was nerve-shattering, with up to twenty high-intensity lights turning night into day, and the deafening noise of concentrated bursts of high explosive just the other side of the thin metal skin of the fuselage. This is where the flying skill of the skipper is often the difference between the life and death of the crew, and thankfully we had Dennis Parkins in the pilot's seat. His first response was to attempt violent evasive action, or "corkscrewing" as it was termed. This manoeuvre failed to evade the lights, and at the exact moment that the skipper began to put R-Robert into a steep dive, a shell burst just underneath the tailplane and the blast pushed the aircraft into a vertical descent. Down, down, down we went, seemingly heading straight for Germany and with all the searchlights and guns still fixed rigidly onto us. We were all thrown around inside the aircraft. Suddenly, having plunged to 4,000 feet, the nose of the Stirling pulled up and we went into a steep and rapid ascent. So steep and fast was this climb that the constant speed units that controlled the airscrews were overridden and the airscrews went to maximum course position. In this condition, the RPM of the engines dropped rapidly and the aeroplane stalled. This resulted in silence from the engines and it was at this point that I was aware of the tremendous noise of the shells exploding outside. The port wing dropped and we again found ourselves diving towards the ground. The reverse now happened, with the constant speed units now putting the airscrews into maximum fine position and causing the engine RPM to increase rapidly with a deafening roar. Suddenly, after the aircraft gave a mighty shake, we levelled out and to my relief I could see that the lights had vanished — we were free of the searchlights at last. After a brief period during which we all picked ourselves up, dusted ourselves down and returned to our stations, the skipper's voice came over the RT. I still remember exactly what he told us:

Well chaps, from the time that we were picked up in the lights to the time that we were straight and level again, nobody was flying the aeroplane. The high G forces prevented me from doing so.

I was glad that I hadn't known that at the time. We quickly ditched our bombs and set course for home. Poor old R-Robert had taken a pounding and was quite badly damaged, but the important thing was that we made it back and I for one was extremely grateful for the ability that our Stirling seemed to have to return to its original trimmed configuration after being thrown all over the sky.

There was no respite, for R-Robert or for us, and three days later we carried out an incendiary raid on Hamburg as part of a force of 173 aircraft, four of which were from 15 Squadron. Thankfully there was no repeat of the drama of the previous trip and we made it back without any problems. My eighteenth op, on 22 April, was a new experience for me as it involved the art of "gardening", or the dropping of sea mines in shipping lanes used by the Germans. These were often long haul flights, mostly made over the sea, and relied upon superb navigation and pinpoint accuracy. We were spared the hazards of the Ruhr searchlight batteries, but low flying RAF bombers were tempting targets for the many bored gunners on small German surface vessels, and more than one crew got a hot reception from an unexpected source. These mines were top secret, and the Navy was adamant that if they could not be dropped in the right place, they should not be dropped at all. The unpleasant scenario of having to land back at base with a large amount of high explosive on board was not one that we all looked forward to, so every effort was made to ensure that we got it right. A further quirk of these mines, or "vegetables" as they were officially termed, was that they had to be dropped into the water from below 1,000 feet or there was a danger that they could explode on impact. Since you would have no idea what the barometric pressure was at the drop zone, you would never know what the height was when the mines were dropped. In these circumstances, the only way to deal with the situation was to cross your fingers and hope for the best. When no explosions could be heard there was an audible sigh of relief over the intercom.

The first of these gardening trips took us to the Baltic on 22 April where we placed four mines in the correct area despite having been spotted and fired upon by an unidentified ship of some 5,000 tonnes in weight. The next night we reverted to carrying bombs, with the Baltic port of Rostock being the target. This was the first of four successful Bomber Command raids on the town, carried out in the manner of the Lübeck operation of the previous month. Incendiaries were dropped and the narrow mediaeval streets burned well. We went again three days later with similar results, although on this occasion our gunners did identify and fire at a night fighter which strayed a little too close to us. I remember that on one of these Rostock trips, the aiming point that had been chosen was a large church in a residential area. We brought back a great photograph of this church which confirmed that we had dropped our bombs right across the aiming point. This showed that we could bomb accurately in good conditions and with light opposition. Having said that, we did pick up a little flak damage on the homeward leg as we crossed the Danish coast. Baltic targets were generally considered to be easier than others, because at that stage of the war the route across the middle of Denmark was reasonably free of defences. This would change later on as Berlin was repeatedly attacked, but at the time we were more than happy with the situation. It was also nice to know that the sanctuary of the Swedish coast was nearby should you get into trouble. Rostock was of no real military value and these raids were little more than destructive shows of strength, of the type that would become the speciality of Bomber Command as 1942 progressed.

On 2 May we went to Kiel Bay, to mine the approaches to the canal, with a Pilot Officer Haines in the co-pilot's seat. This was followed by an abortive trip to Hamburg the next night, when turret problems forced us to turn back in excellent weather conditions. There then followed a stand-down period of about two weeks before we again set out across Denmark to mine the Baltic sea lanes. On this occasion, Sergeant Birch was temporarily replaced in the rear turret by a Sergeant Rainbow, and a Sergeant McLaren took over the co-pilot's seat. Because this was a maximum range operation, our additional fuel tanks were used. These additional tanks formed the inboard leading edge structure skins and they were not self-sealing. When the wing structure flexed under load, there should have been clearance left between the tank skins and the structure itself. However, in these days of mass production, this wasn't always the case and chafing occurred. It was a problem on this trip, and the subsequent leakage resulted in fuel flooding into the compartment that I shared with Bob Milne. This built up until I found myself standing in a lake of petrol which was gradually increasing in depth and not draining away. I informed the crew of the situation and told them that under no circumstances was anyone to smoke or to carry out any tasks involving electricity. Since our compartment was directly over the bomb bay, I decided to use my screwdriver to try and punch holes in the floor to allow the petrol to trickle through into it. My thinking was that if the doors were then opened using the manual override system, the resultant suction and air pressure change would quickly suck the petrol out through the holes in the floor. This worked to perfection and the danger passed. This incident did highlight a fault with the Stirling and perhaps goes some way to explaining why so many aircraft simply blew up or disappeared without trace over the North Sea, far from the enemy's guns and fighters.

Our next op, on 21 May, was no less dramatic. We had been briefed to mine the Gironde estuary in the Bay of Biscay, which was an area of intense U-Boat activity. It was a long haul, and we set off at 22:01 and headed south-west. The weather conditions deteriorated the further we flew and visibility was reduced to almost nothing. By the time we reached the drop area all that we could see were the small white caps of the waves and it was impossible to get a land fix. Gingerly, we descended lower and lower — until CRASH! It seemed that R-Robert had flown straight into a number of fishing nets that had been hung out to dry on a small island at the entrance to the estuary. The skipper instinctively pulled back on the stick and we climbed away from danger and turned back out over the Atlantic. It was hopeless trying to find a fix in these conditions, so we were forced to turn back, since fuel levels were low and this had been a maximum range trip with very little to spare. Our troubles were far from over, as the bad weather had followed us to the English coast and the entire southern half of the country was boxed in by fog. We found ourselves flying over Devon and Cornwall at 5,000 feet with no real plan as to what to do next. We were advised to turn south and head out a short way into the Channel before descending to low level and returning towards land whereupon searchlight crews would try and pick us up and point us in the direction of the nearest airfield. By the grace of God this plan worked and we were able to put down safely at Exeter. This was a fighter base and the runway was never intended to host lumbering four engined bombers. As a result we managed to overshoot the runway and carry on into a neighbouring farmer's field. We were still carrying the mines but thankfully we came to a halt on our wheels and with no damage to the aircraft. As we got out we could see that there were fragments of fishing net hanging from various parts of the underside of the aircraft. The next morning, the ground crew informed us that they could not find any trace of petrol in the fuel tanks, and were amazed that such a large aircraft had attempted to land on such a small airfield in such dense fog. We refuelled R-Robert from numerous four-gallon cans and landed back at

Wyton with our mines intact, much to everybody's relief.

Eight days later we were briefed for an operation against the Gnome & Rhone factory at Gennevilliers near Paris. This was not a particularly successful trip on any level and subsequent photo reconnaissance showed that the factory had been left almost completely untouched by our efforts. Our part in this raid was described in detail in the Operations Record Book of 15 Squadron:

> Flight Lieutenant Parkins was late in reaching the target owing to following the wrong river and finding another similarly defended factory. The Y-shaped docks were also identified 20 minutes late. One run was made at 5,000 feet, but searchlight glare made bombing hopeless. The height was now 8,000 feet and he was 30 minutes overdue, so the mission was abandoned. All the bombs except one (4000lb "cookie") which was jettisoned in the sea were brought back.

That more or less says it all, and what should have been my twenty-fourth credited op was nothing more than a write-off in my log-book.

Operation Millennium was the name given to Bomber Command's largest and most ambitious effort so far — the first raid on an enemy target comprising over 1,000 aircraft. Harris wanted to build on the limited successes of the raids on Lübeck and Rostock by dishing out the same treatment to a major target, as well as supplying the public with a welcome morale boost. Success in this operation would also send out a message to the numerous critics of area bombing, and undoubtedly demonstrate the growing destructive capability of the Royal Air Force. The target was to be the city of Cologne, and the date of the attack would be 30 May. Every available aircraft was earmarked to take part, and the numbers were considerably swelled by the inclusion of half trained crews from OTUs up and down the country. As it turned out, 1,047 Wellingtons, Halifaxes, Lancasters, Stirlings, Whitleys, Hampdens and Manchesters were eventually made ready — with R-Robert taking its place as one of twelve Stirlings from 15 Squadron.

Take-off was at 22:46 with the usual crew on board and a vacant co-pilot's seat in the cockpit. As before, this was to be an incendiary raid in an attempt to try and get the city burning fiercely. We found the target without any problem, and the aiming point was identified with the help of the reflection from the great River Rhine, which flowed through the centre of Cologne. Our huge numbers that night seemed to simply overwhelm the defences and, as a result after we had bombed, it was possible to circle the target and get a great view of the largest fires seen since the London Blitz. With over 1,000 aircraft seemingly intent on doing precisely the same thing, it was an absolute miracle that only two of them actually collided over the target. Although the desired "sea of fire" never actually materialized, we did a good job and the local fire brigade reported fighting over 1,700 separate conflagrations that night. On our way home, I remember that we were tasked to drop thousands of teabags at 1,000 feet over Holland — hopefully benefiting the obviously thirsty Dutch civilians rather than the German occupiers. We arrived back at Wyton just after 04:00 and went to bed following a debriefing, knowing that we had taken part in an historic raid which would certainly make the front pages later on that day.

Harris' intention was obviously to try and keep the pressure on the German defences following the success of the Cologne op, and two days later the second raid involving a huge force was planned, this time against Essen in our beloved "Happy Valley". Only 956 aircraft could be mustered for this trip, and once again R-Robert was bombed up and prepared for action, with Pilot Officer Haines rejoining us in the co-pilot's seat. Little did we know that the night of 1 and 2 June was going to be rather different for us — we had suffered near misses before but had never come as close to disaster as we did on this occasion. Take-off was at 23:15 hours and the raid started ordinarily enough as the target was again easily located and we dropped our incendiaries right on track. Although the effect wasn't quite as spectacular as it had been two nights earlier, we still felt safe enough to circle the target area, taking in the sights. After a while the skipper turned for home, but we had drifted to the north of the city and found ourselves on a different heading to the rest of the force. Initially this wasn't a problem, but we soon found ourselves flying towards a defended area, as indicated by the banks of searchlights and flak batteries directly in front of us. Unable to get a ground fix to confirm our position, and with no cloud cover to assist us, the skipper took the decision to drop down to ground level. Before too long, it became apparent that the defended area ahead of us was in fact Antwerp docks, and that we were heading straight into the middle of it. At the time, the searchlights and 88mm guns mounted on top of the flak towers were busily occupied with illuminating and firing at elements of the main force which were flying overhead, and nobody had spotted R-Robert sneaking through beneath them. It looked as though we might even make it past them undetected, but unfortunately an eagle eyed gunner spotted the huge Stirling skimming the water and suddenly the lights descended upon us, the guns followed and all hell broke loose. We were nothing less than a sitting target and we took numerous hits on our fuselage and tail section as the skipper pulled back on the stick and took us clear of the water. The firing continued initially, but then ceased as the Germans realized they were actually in danger of shooting at each other across the docks. We knew where we were now and Dick Strachan quickly worked out a course to get us home. We returned to low level and flew along the Scheldt estuary and out into the North Sea. The engines were seemingly undamaged and were behaving themselves, but a quick crew check resulted in silence from the rear gunner, Donald Birch. I was sent back to check out the situation and as I passed through the aft fuselage I could see that it closely resembled a colander as a shell had passed through and actually exploded inside the aircraft, spraying shrapnel everywhere. The mid-upper gunner, who had been with us for a few trips now and whose name was Sergeant Donald Drake, was miraculously uninjured. He had been protected by his armour plating, and by the fact that his turret had been facing towards the explosion. The controls and the electrics were all still functioning, but the aft intercom had been knocked out, which explained the earlier silence from the back of the aircraft. The rear turret had been penetrated from inside the fuselage and I could see Donald Birch struggling to free himself from its confines. His face was covered in blood and he was hysterical. I couldn't handle him on my own so I went back to my compartment and got Bob Milne to come and give me a hand. Between us, we managed to get him up to the bunk which was located amidships between the wing spars, and strapped him down securely. I couldn't locate any penetration of the skull and it became clear that he had merely suffered flesh wounds, which appeared at first sight to have been a lot worse than they actually were. We did the best that we could under the circumstances and just made sure that he couldn't get up off his bunk and do himself harm.

We had an uneventful trip back to Wyton where we requested a priority landing slot and the presence of an ambulance and a crash wagon. On the landing circuit, the port landing gear failed to descend properly and I was told to get back and lower it manually, before being reminded that we'd only get one shot at landing. I vividly remember going aft and saying to myself "Port gear, left — port gear, left", in a desperate attempt to try and remember which side of the fuselage the correct crank handle was on. Unfortunately, I forgot that I was facing the wrong way and, I started to wind down the wrong side. In time — or so I hoped — I realized my mistake and frantically changed sides until I heard the magic words from the skipper that told me the green light had appeared signifying that the wheel was fully locked down. I braced myself for touchdown which was remarkably light and smooth, considering all that R-Robert had been through. However, unbeknown to us one of the tyres had been punctured by shrapnel and as the Stirling continued to settle on the tarmac and the weight transferred itself to the wheels, the rim bit into the runway and spun the aircraft around so that it veered onto the grass verge where the wheels dug into the soft ground and tipped the bomber up onto its nose, with the propellers just scraping the surface. Thankfully my training paid off as my first reaction was to turn all the petrol tanks off, followed by the engines, which reduced the risk of fire. It was 03:45, pouring with rain, and we had made it home at last.

Getting a wounded man out of a bomber which was standing on its nose was not easy, but we managed it and Donald Birch was taken away to hospital to receive treatment. Three weeks later, on 23 June, the *London Gazette* carried the announcement that Flight Lieutenant (as he was now) Dennis Arthur Parkins (102961) of the Royal Air Force Volunteer Reserve, serving with 15 Squadron, had been awarded the Distinguished Flying

Cross for his actions that night in getting us all home. The official citation read:

> One night in June 1942, this officer was the captain of an aircraft which participated in a bombing attack on Essen. Despite unfavourable weather, industrial haze and smoke, and in the face of heavy anti-aircraft fire, Flight Lieutenant Parkins made repeated runs over the target to ensure accurate bombing. His aircraft was extensively damaged but, displaying fine airmanship, he flew it safely back to base. This officer showed great determination and devotion to duty throughout. He has completed numerous sorties and, on all occasions, he has shown courage and reliability.

Perhaps not quite how I remember it over the target, but never was a gong as richly deserved as that one.

One thing that I remember most clearly during my first tour was the appearance, on three separate occasions, of what were (and still are) termed Unidentified Flying Objects. We had no idea what these could be, but on each occasion they appeared over the Ruhr valley. They took the form of bright orange spheres which flew on our beam at the same speed and altitude as us. One minute they were there and the next minute they were gone. We reported their appearance at debriefings and nothing more was said so we assumed they were just something that the Germans were developing. At the end of the war it transpired from Luftwaffe records that their night fighter crews had seen exactly the same thing and assumed that they were an RAF invention. The pot was stirred further still with numerous daylight sightings from American crews. I wonder what any aliens on board would have made of it all?

Our time as a complete unit was coming to an end as we were nearing the end of our tour. Donald Birch never came back to us after his ordeal over Antwerp, and our original mid-upper gunner, Alec Picken, returned to the crew and took his place in the rear turret. Because the skipper had flown a number of trips as co-pilot before our first op to Ostend, he was closer to finishing than the rest of us. I still had seven to do, and the first of these was a return to Essen as part of a small force on 5 June in a new aircraft, N3759 Q-Queenie. This was because R-Robert had been so extensively damaged that it would never fly again and so we now had to get used to a new kite, with all its quirks and idiosyncracies. Pilot Officer Haines, who had been with us over Antwerp, once again deputized, and although we found ourselves coned for five minutes over Essen after delivery, the shelling was not as intense and we eventually evaded the lights using more conventional methods than before. The next night, we paid a first visit to the Frisian port of Emden on the Dutch border, and did a cracking job. We were guided in by the clearly identifiable outline of the estuary, and bombed from 13,000 feet in good visibility. The defences were not that concentrated, and we made it home without any problems.

The next trip was a gardening expedition on 11 June back to the area of the Frisian Islands. This was another smooth trip with minimal losses amongst the force of ninety-one aircraft sent out. For us this was to be a poignant occasion, as it marked the end of the skipper's first tour of thirty ops. As was the routine, he would receive an extended period of leave and then be sent to an OTU to instruct. I was aware that when crews split up at the end of a tour, the pilot and flight engineer usually stayed together as an instructing team. The other crew members usually went their separate ways. Naturally I was keen to stay with Dennis Parkins, so I approached the Commanding Officer, Wing Commander Ley, and asked if I would be able to accompany him to his next posting, which was to 1651 Heavy Conversion Unit at nearby Waterbeach. I was then a few trips short of the end of my tour but I didn't realize fully quite how rigidly the RAF hierarchy stuck to these protocols. I was told that I had to complete my tour and that was that. Little did I know it then, but this refusal on the part of the CO was ultimately to save my life.

Along with Alec Picken and Donald Drake, I was now a spare bod — without a regular crew but available to fill in for anyone who needed a spare engineer. I didn't have long to wait. Together with Alec and Donald I found myself making up the numbers in the crew of Flying Officer King, a newly arrived skipper from 15 OTU. On 22 June we returned to Emden with a cargo of incendiaries and caused some damage, and then on the 25th we bombed Bremen as part of another raid by Harris' famous "Thousand Force". We made a follow-up visit to Bremen on the 29th, and then all of a sudden, after a good three weeks on the sidelines, I was being briefed for my final op against the submarine yard at Vegesack on the River Weser, once again with Flying Officer King.

The orders here were to ignore residential areas and concentrate on blowing newly completed U-boats off their slipways before the Germans had a chance to launch them. The importance of this raid was stressed to us at briefing, and once again we were to bomb at low level if weather conditions were appropriate. Unfortunately, the entire area was completely cloud covered and we were forced to bomb using the Gee electronic navigational aids in order to estimate our position over the target. Naturally, this wasn't the most reliable method of delivery and subsequent reconnaissance photographs showed that not one aircraft managed to hit the submarine yard. Still, at 05:40 hours, when we arrived back at Wyton, I had the ultimate satisfaction of knowing that my tour was over and that I had come through unscathed.

In the light of this, I was somewhat perturbed to discover that my name remained on the available crew listing for the next night's operations, and so I went and found my flight commander to see if there had been some mistake. He passed me up the chain to the CO and, when I reported to his officer to discuss the matter, I was asked whether or not I had lost my nerve. He gave me a long lecture about duty and responsibility, and then finished by requesting that I stayed on a while longer. With great conviction, I said "No thank you, Sir", before being dismissed with some none too complimentary words ringing in my ears. I was expecting to have been thanked for the thirty completed (thirty-four in total) operations that I had carried out as part of 15 Squadron, but instead I got the distinct impression that Wing Commander Ley considered me to be only one step up from a "Lack of Moral Fibre" case. So I ended up leaving Wyton under something of a cloud, which was a shame as I had enjoyed my time there.

The last time I had spoken to Flight Lieutenant Parkins had been the evening before he had gone on leave prior to his reporting to Waterbeach on 12 July. He was in excellent spirits as he was about to get married — having delayed "taking the plunge" while on operations. He said that he was looking forward to teaming up with me at Waterbeach and he hoped that by keeping our noses clean and being in the right place at the right time, we could spend the rest of the war as instructors. He had reminded me that I was actually in line for a medal as a result of my conduct on the Essen raid but, strangely enough following my subsequent interview with the CO, no such award was forthcoming. I didn't really mind too much as the only person who was likely to be impressed was my mother, and she would be able to brag to her friends at the Methodist church that her son was a hero, which was completely untrue of course. In fact, I used to try and keep my family as much in the dark as possible about my flying duties so as not to worry them. I even used to remove the flight engineer chevron from my uniform when I was home on leave so as to fend off any awkward questions.

It was now late August 1942, and with my extended leave over, I reported to 1651 Heavy Conversion Unit at Waterbeach in order to meet up with my former skipper and begin my career as an instructor. Or so I thought. On my arrival I asked for him by name but nobody seemed to have heard of him. After making further enquiries, I discovered that he had failed to return from an operation against Hamburg on 28 July when he had captained a brand new crew. A maximum effort had been called for, and once again training units were used to make up the numbers. The weather in the North Sea had been particularly poor, although the target area had been reasonably clear. The big problem for the crews that night had apparently been icing, something to which the Stirling Mk I was especially susceptible.

I recalled that on one occasion during my tour we had been returning across the North Sea at about 9,000 feet after dropping our cargo. We were flying in 10/10ths cloud of unknown depth and, as we were starting to run low on petrol, we rigged the aircraft into a very shallow descent, with the engines in auto-weak mode and the RPM as low as possible, but still able to keep the engines warm and to stave off the danger of ice forming as we dropped through the cloud. The conditions were such that the air temperature and humidity were ideal for icing, but we had no alternative other than to come down through the cloud. All of this was pretty standard and we knew that we would eventually break through the cloud base with plenty of altitude to spare. I was monitoring the cylinder head and oil temperature in order to know when to open up the engines to keep their temperatures high enough for safe running, and I noticed a rapid increase in oil temperature and a drop off in oil pressure. This was a dangerous and illogical situation and I couldn't see what could have gone wrong. The engines were already at their lowest possible RPM setting and to decrease them further would have spelt disaster. What had actually happened was that the oil coolers, of a honeycomb type construction, had become blocked with snow and ice which had stopped the cooling air flow. There was nothing that we could do except keep our fingers crossed and hope that the outside air temperature started to increase the lower we flew. We broke cloud at 1,000 feet and the skipper increased the engine power and RPM, and I watched with great relief as the oil temperature fell and the pressure increased. Only the skipper and myself knew the danger that we had been in, and when we got back home the experts managed to figure out what had gone wrong. The cooler design in the Stirling Mk I was never changed and the official line was that in future all such hazardous flying conditions were hopefully to be avoided. I couldn't help but wonder if this neglectful attitude had caused Flight Lieutenant Parkins' disappearance.

The Stirlings that we had been using had been replaced at Wyton towards the end of my tour by the improved Mk III, and the obsolete Mk Is were sent off to the training units. The oil coolers on the new model were relocated from the wing to a circular housing underneath the engine cowling just behind the gills. These oil coolers incorporated ice guards and air cleaners in the forward section of the housing while the cooling section was equipped with thermostatically controlled shutters. I couldn't understand why the HCU's obsolete Mk Is were allowed to proceed through hazardous weather conditions over the North Sea when it was known to all and sundry how dangerous this could be, and I began to feel a huge sense of anger at the way that my skipper's life, and those of his crew, had been endangered in such a reckless manner.

I brooded on this, and ended up by confronting the engineering officer, Squadron Leader Ely. He was extremely indignant at my attitude and informed me that he would be reporting me to my flight commander. It so happened that I had previously decided to apply for a commission as an engineering officer and this application had required me to sit a written technical examination, under the direct supervision of Squadron Leader Ely. This examination consisted of ten questions, which gave me no problem at all. My flight commander was aware of my application and he was a great deal more understanding of my anger than the engineering officer had been. For the sake of my career and my promotion prospects, he stated that he would pass over the complaint and not institute any formal disciplinary action. I was extremely grateful for this, and undertook not to rock the boat any further as I now knew that I wouldn't get anything in the way of answers or explanations in any case.

Two days later, I was loaned to the flight engineers' ground school at St Athan in south Wales in order to give future aircrew pep talks about the joys of operational flying, and to tell them how interesting life would be for them in the months to come. I had been specially briefed beforehand not to discuss such matters as aircraft losses and survival rates. This sort of thing did not go down too well with me — telling these keen new recruits that everything in the garden was rosy whilst knowing that their chance of surviving their tour was less than 50 per cent. Before too long, I requested to see the CO at St Athan and explained to him that I had put in for a commission and would ideally like to return to my unit to chase up my application. Luckily, he remembered me from the previous week when I had been the orderly sergeant on guard duty and I had challenged him as he returned to the camp late at night. I wouldn't let him pass without seeing his identification. He obviously approved wholeheartedly of this approach to security because he smiled, said "Good show, Sergeant," and promptly authorized my return to Waterbeach before wishing me luck.

When I arrived back at Waterbeach, I managed to team up with a pilot, Flight Sergeant Mac Mackie. We had both been at Wyton with 15 Squadron so knew each other quite well. Now Mac was a man whose fuse was certainly shorter than most and he was currently in a spot of bother with the hierarchy of the Sergeants' Mess.

I need to pause here to explain the set up of the Mess. Senior NCOs comprised two very distinct groups — those who flew, and those who did not. The non fliers were mainly members of the old guard who had taken years to attain their present ranks and who deeply resented the influx of fliers, whom they regarded as little more than spoilt, undisciplined brats. From time to time, tensions between the two groups would bubble to the surface and result in violent confrontations, usually involving those with a quick temper such as Mac Mackie. I hadn't been there at the time, but it was easy to believe the oft repeated story that blows had been exchanged between Mac and the station warrant officer. Coupled with this was the fact that Mac had also fallen out with our flight commander. The reason for this was that as a response to mounting operational losses, the decision had been taken to issue a large batch of decorations to aircrew personnel in an effort to try and improve morale. Mac was one of those who was selected to receive a medal, but he disagreed profoundly with this method of doing things and, after he had been given his gong, he stormed into the flight commander's office and threw it at him, simultaneously informing him as to where he should put it. He undoubtedly had an abrupt way of expressing himself, but he was, in my opinion a wonderful instructor and the very best Stirling pilot in the unit. Since I had previously known him at Wyton and since we got on very well, I decided to stick with him. This was not a decision which was to do me any favours in the long run as far as the engineering officer was concerned, as I was thereafter labelled guilty by association.

I remember another incident when Mac once again clashed with authority, and I was actually present this time to witness it. We had been forced to put down on one of the many American airfields which were springing up all over the place in that part of the world and, as soon as we touched down, an angry American voice shouted "Get the hell off this airfield". Without saying a word Mac taxied to the control tower, parked in front and then cut all the engines. Only then did he reply, stating that they had better go and get their CO, as he was about to come up there, give them a lesson in manners, and then lodge an official complaint against whoever was in charge. We subsequently deplaned, "invaded" the control tower, and refused to move until a senior officer arrived. Eventually one turned up, listened to our side of the story, and promptly placed the culprit under arrest. A fortnight later an official American apology arrived at group headquarters, but Mac's reputation had obviously preceded him as he was reprimanded for taking matters into his own hands.

In addition to our instructing duties, we also had the task of flight testing aircraft that had been in for repair. These were usually Mk I Stirlings, and Mac had been more than happy to offer to perform these tests, as it meant that he would get the opportunity to fly the aircraft to their limits, something he would not be able to do in the course of our instructing duties. These flights were among the most wonderful that I was ever to experience. We would begin by climbing to altitude on days when about 6/10ths cloud cover existed at about 10,000 feet and "fair weather clouds" filled the sky. We would fly in between the canyons, valleys and towering peaks formed by the clouds which rose up to 20,000 feet, and it was easy to imagine that we were in a different world — one which was at peace. Mac showed me how to fly the Stirling, and we even simulated landing on top of clouds. As well as this we would drop down to the deck and skim over the flat fenland landscape of East Anglia, resulting in numerous complaints from irate farmers accusing us of upsetting their cattle and chickens. They had no problem in identifying us as the guilty parties, as we had been low enough for them to read the aircraft's identity code. On one occasion we had flown so low that we had clipped leaves from the tops of a number of trees, but it wasn't long before we were told that we had to put a stop to these antics.

On one such test flight, during a steep diving turn and subsequent pull up, it was noted that the port wing tip rose more than usual above the outboard engine nacelle. This rise was a normal side effect of the wing bending under load, but on this occasion it seemed to be due to greater pressure on the wing as we completed the manoeuvre. This was indicative of a structural weakness, and the aircraft itself had completed a great number of circuits and landings — many of them heavy — and so we promptly entered the defect onto Form 700 in order for it to be properly examined and thought nothing more of it. The next morning the aircraft was again scheduled for flight testing and we were informed that it had been examined and subsequently declared airworthy. We again flew the aircraft and found it to have the same problem. Once again, the defect was entered onto Form 700, but this time in red ink for extra emphasis. It was not put up for test flying again and I assumed that the fault had been addressed and rectified, and promptly forgot the incident.

Some weeks later, a trainee crew were taking part in circuit and landing exercises when, following a heavy landing, the wing fractured near the inboard engine. Thankfully nobody was hurt, but as we were not flying on that particular night, we didn't hear about the incident until the next day. We immediately went to check the Form 700 to see whether this was the same aircraft that we had had concerns about, but the paperwork had been removed and could not be found. We approached my old friend, Squadron Leader Ely and asked him about the aircraft but he was extremely angry and again told me that I was poking my nose into matters that did not concern me and that he would once again be making an official complaint.

The next day, I was informed that my application for a commission had been rejected. The reason for this was that I had only answered half of the twenty questions that comprised the written examination. Further enquiries revealed that only one sheet of two had been submitted. Once again I confronted Squadron Leader Ely, who could not keep the smirk off his face as he told me that he could not be held responsible if I had failed to complete the examination, which of course I had. I discussed my position with my flight commander who told me that there was unfortunately nothing that he could do about it. He advised me to change my application to a general duty commission rather than a specialist technical one, as the number of operations I had completed virtually guaranteed that I would receive one. Once I became a pilot officer it would then be relatively easy to apply to re-muster as an engineer officer. I agreed and submitted the appropriate forms.

A week later, Mac and I found ourselves posted away from Waterbeach and back to operational flying duties, but to different locations. I didn't actually find out where Mac ended up, but I did hear that he survived the war. For my part, I was posted back to my first unit, 7 Squadron, at Oakington in Cambridgeshire, but I was almost immediately re-assigned to 97 (Straits Settlements) Squadron, a Pathfinder unit based at nearby RAF Bourn. I had made it my maxim never to volunteer for anything and, being a born coward, I had no great desire to be a Pathfinder. The Pathfinder Force had been developed in 1942 by an Australian, Group Captain Donald Bennett, with the aim of training an elite force to arrive at the target first and illuminate it using brightly coloured flares, target indicators and skymarkers. The Pathfinders would also be responsible for dropping the first bombs and the main force would follow on behind and bomb the markers, thus ensuring accuracy and concentration. It was a dangerous role, and the tour of operations was somewhat longer. However the benefits of being a Pathfinder were more rapid promotion prospects, a better chance of being decorated and the sense of prestige that one felt at being part of an elite unit. Not that I cared about any of that. 97 Squadron flew Lancaster Mk IIIs and I had never even seen one before but I was handed a copy of Air Ministry publication AP 2062 — training notes for the Lancaster. I was told to read, learn and inwardly digest the contents, and that when I had done this, together with my experience on Stirlings, I would be able to consider myself fully qualified to act as a Lancaster flight engineer. Needless to say I wasn't too enamoured at the prospect.

Having been promoted to flight sergeant during my time at Waterbeach, I arrived at Bourn at the beginning of July 1943 and was not impressed by what I saw. Unlike Wyton, which had been comfortable, permanent and well organized, Bourn was a collection of draughty Nissen huts and prefabricated buildings which had been scattered over the bleak and exposed landscape with reckless abandon. It seemed that no thought had been given to the comfort and welfare of those who were to be stationed there. I also felt a little apprehensive that I was now considered to be a "trained" Lancaster flight engineer without ever having set eyes upon one, let alone having flown in one. On the bus from Cambridge to Bourn, I had met up with Flight Sergeant Steve Powell who was wearing an observer's wing on his tunic. My first thought was that he must have been left over from the First World War, but he didn't seem old enough. In response to my curiosity, he told me that the post of observer had not yet been made obsolete and that he was a bomb aimer and had also been trained in navigation. He had no operational experience thus far, and had been posted from Pathfinder HQ in Huntingdon. Like me, he had never seen a Lancaster. This didn't exactly fill me with confidence.

We duly arrived at Bourn and I checked in at the orderly room, where I was shown to my sleeping quarters and given directions to the Sergeants' Mess. I was left to my own devices and told that I would be picked up the next morning, given a guided tour of the airfield and introduced to the routine. Since the camp consisted of clusters of huts dispersed around the runways, with no signs to show where everywhere was in relation to everywhere else, a lorry was sent to collect me and my fellow new arrival, and take us to the station headquarters. On the way, all of the places of interest were pointed out to us, and we were informed that this journey by lorry was a one off, and that in future we would have to make our own way around the camp on foot or by bicycle.

On arrival at headquarters, we were introduced to everyone and the process of "crewing up" began. I was assigned to the crew of Flight Lieutenant Covington, who had already completed a tour on Lancasters with 97 Squadron. I think it is fair to say that I didn't really take to him at all. He had been born with a silver spoon in his mouth and came across as a completely spoiled individual who seemed to think that he was invulnerable. I remember that he drove a Triumph Twin motorcycle which we all admired, although we could never quite work out where he managed to get the petrol from in order to run it. Covington was acutely aware of his status as a commissioned officer, and wasn't at all interested in getting to know the NCOs in his crew, preferring to spend his time with the navigator, Flying Officer Canham. He was the only other officer in the crew, although he had previously been awarded the Distinguished Flying Medal so he had obviously begun his flying career as a sergeant, and he also had a tour of operations under his belt.

Our bomb aimer was Steve Powell, the friendly Liverpudlian "observer" I had met the previous day on the bus. He was the only member of the crew I was really able to get to know — indeed our stories were to be very closely intertwined over the next three years. Unfortunately, I don't remember all that much about the remaining crew members.

The wireless operator was a Canadian from Vancouver, Sergeant Sammy Ramsden, who had joined up from high school and had no operational experience, and the two gunners were Sergeants Jackson and MacKnight, in the mid-upper and rear turrets respectively. Sadly, I don't remember a single occasion when we went out and socialized as a crew, as we had done at Wyton on a number of occasions. The whole atmosphere at Bourn was not what I was used to at all. I recall one instance when Steve Powell and I were walking up to the station headquarters when an aircrew squadron leader approached. We did not salute him but said "Good morning, sir" as we passed. He took us to task in no uncertain terms and we were both made to feel like new recruits. On 15 Squadron, aircrew were not expected to salute each other but apparently on 97 Squadron that was not the case.

My new skipper didn't seem to be that concerned that I had no flying experience on Lancasters and when I was shown our assigned aircraft, which was JA716 OF-V, I was all eyes and ears. I was given a guided tour inside and out and explained my position to the ground crew chief, arranging further meetings with him in order to gain familiarity. The aircraft was certainly different from the Stirling. It had a higher ceiling, a heavier bomb load and a far greater top speed, although the wingspan was considerably smaller. It was powered by four Rolls-Royce Merlin engines, and my crew station was now in the cockpit with the pilot rather than aft of the cockpit with the wireless operator, as it had been in the Stirling. All in all, it was certainly a different kettle of fish, but trying to master the Lancaster was an interesting challenge that I was quite keen to accept. However, unlike on 15 Squadron, we did not have discussion sessions in order to compare the operational experience of others and pool our knowledge, nor do I remember taking part in the emergency drills which had been mandatory at Wyton. Perhaps the powers that be thought that as we were all volunteers, we were experienced enough in such matters and that they did not need to be constantly practised.

My application for a commission had not been forgotten and I was called to group headquarters in Huntingdon where I found myself being interviewed by none other than Group Captain Bennett. He asked me a number of questions about my previous tour and my experiences as a flight engineer on Stirlings. He concluded the interview by saying that he would have to hold back his approval until I'd completed some time as a Pathfinder, but that he wouldn't delay matters by any more than two months. It looked as though I would soon be a commissioned officer, as long as I was able to stay in one piece and didn't make too many mistakes — a far cry from that day in January 1936 when I arrived at Halton for the first time.

So, I was back to operational life for the first time in just over a year. In my absence matters had been stepped up a few notches. The long and bloody Battle of the Ruhr was coming to a conclusion, with huge damage to the vital German industrial region on the one hand, and thousands of dead RAF fliers on the other. This concentrated assault on German war production had begun in March 1943 and had benefited from more advanced navigational aids and vastly superior tactics, which demonstrated how far the Pathfinder Force had evolved. The abrupt change in approach and tactics were to be demonstrated to me on my very first operation.

On the morning of 24 July, I learned that we would be one of seventeen aircraft from 97 Squadron to carry out an attack on Hamburg, and that we would be deploying a brand new defensive tactic that would hopefully bamboozle the defences and greatly improve our chances of survival. The idea was ridiculously simple. It had been discovered that the radar systems that the Germans used would be vulnerable to jamming by the jettisoning of thousands upon thousands of thin aluminium strips above the target area. This had apparently been known for some time, but the authorities had decided that they should wait for the right moment to use it. The opening raid of what would come to be known as the Battle of Hamburg was deemed to be that moment, and supplies of these metal strips, codenamed Window, were loaded aboard our aircraft along with the high explosive and target indicators that we would be dropping on Hamburg.

We took off at 22:04 and joined the stream which was heading out across the North Sea. On arrival in the target area, we dropped our Window and did our job, which involved backing up the target markers for the benefit of the main force. It was a huge relief to see the searchlights waving ineffectually across the sky and the flak being fired blindly and at wildly varying altitudes, the radar screens of their controllers having being completely blanked. As it turned out, only twelve aircraft out of a total of nearly 800 were lost that night, an enormous improvement and a great testament to the effectiveness of our new weapon. Of course it would be a case of making hay while the sun shone, as we knew that it wouldn't be long before the Germans worked out a way to counter the problem.

We, however, had a few problems of our own on the way home. The weather over the target and on the approaches was mainly clear but with a degree of cumulonimbus cloud towering up to 30,000 feet. These clouds did not pose a serious threat, since the static electricity that they generated would light up the sky from time to time and make them clearly visible, and hence easy to avoid. You just had to be careful never to fly through them. It was a great surprise then, when I realized that we were about to do just that. Once inside these clouds, the terrific energy that they generated resulted in the aircraft being lifted vertically, as if it were a leaf caught in a draught. This manoeuvre placed everything in the aircraft under negative G-forces which resulted in me being thrown to the floor, where I grabbed what I could and held on. I knew that when the aircraft burst out of the top of the cloud, the effects of the G-force would be reversed and I would be thrown against the canopy — I was not strapped in, unlike the skipper. True enough, this happened and the Lancaster's nose dropped into a vertical dive.

While all this was happening Flight Lieutenant Covington had said and done absolutely nothing. The speed of the dive dramatically increased and when he finally came to his senses and pulled back on the controls nothing happened. The excessive speed of the aircraft was placing too much load on the elevators and they could not respond. The skipper panicked, pulling back on the controls like a madman. Since I was already on the floor I was near to the elevator trim wheel and I reeled it back to provide assistance to the elevators. Thankfully, this seemed to do the trick and gradually the nose of the aircraft rose up and we regained straight and level flight. After the skipper had recovered his senses, he composed himself and said "Right, let's go home, chaps". Nothing more was ever said about the incident to anyone, including the debriefing officer.

The next night we were off to my old stamping ground of Essen once more, as part of a force of 705 aircraft. We again used Window, and once again the German defences were in total disarray. It was my responsibility, as the flight engineer, to dispense the aluminium strips. I had to go to the back of the fuselage, carrying my parachute, and drop bundles of these strips out of the flare chute, using a stopwatch to ensure that the best coverage was gained. This was a deeply unpleasant task to have to perform at 25,000 feet over the target area and so I devised a plan to make this process a little less arduous. I wanted a hole cut in the metal skin of the aircraft's nose to allow the Window to be dropped without any need for me to go aft to the flare chute. I figured that by placing the hole in a particular spot, the air flowing around the curvature of the nose would create a negative pressure and so suck the strips out. I got the ground crew to carry out the modification and tried it out on subsequent operations with great success. Naturally, this tactic came to the notice of the authorities and I was taken to task for damaging one of His Majesty's aircraft and for interfering in matters that were none of my business. Not that it particularly bothered me as the benefits of this vandalism far outweighed any possible punishment.

After a night off, on 27 July we returned for a second time to Hamburg. The Battle of Hamburg was to become one of the most devastating and talked about

124

conventional operations of the Second World War, only superceded in terms of loss of life by the attack on Dresden and the American raid on Tokyo in February and March 1945 respectively. The dry summer conditions, coupled with a concentrated incendiary attack, created a firestorm in which separate fires joined together at speed and sucked all the oxygen out of the area. This had the effect of creating the force of a storm, but fire took the place of wind and the conflagration spread rapidly throughout a large section of the city. We were one of the first aircraft over the target and did not see the effects of the subsequent destruction. One interesting point about this trip was that we had Flying Officer Peter de Wesselow aboard as a second pilot. At this stage, he was just gaining operational experience, but in February 1945 he had risen to the rank of squadron leader and was appointed to be the master bomber on the Dresden raid, directing operations while circling the target. Perhaps he had applied some of the lessons that he had learnt while sharing a cockpit with Flight Sergeant Lancashire over Hamburg one night.

Forty thousand people are estimated to have died in Hamburg that night and two-thirds of the city's population fled out of fear of further raids. Bomber Harris was determined not to relent and two nights later the bombers came again, though without me this time as my crew had been given a break from operations. We were back in action on 30 July, however, with the hitherto untouched Ruhr city of Remschied being attacked by 273 aircraft, including thirteen from

97 Squadron. This raid was a great success and it was later estimated that 83 per cent of the city was devastated. We were having a good run of successful raids, but this was to come to an end on 2 August when we were sent back to Hamburg, with weather conditions not in our favour. Electrical storms, icing and turbulence over Germany meant that we were unable to locate the city and had to bomb on dead reckoning, never the most accurate method. We were only carrying high explosives that night and there was absolutely no guarantee that we even got anywhere near Hamburg. We touched down at Bourn just before 05:00, having spent an extremely uncomfortable return journey over the North Sea, and I went gratefully to bed.

There then followed a short period away from operational flying, which ended with an uneventful but cloud covered trip to Mannheim on 9 August. The next night the target was Nuremburg, a long way inside Germany, and this was to be a night I will never forget. This was my sixth operation as a Pathfinder, and it was to be my last. We took off at 21:37 and headed out across the North Sea. We were due to arrive at the target area before the Mosquitos dropped their initial target indicators. This was always an extremely stressful period as the Germans would not operate their searchlights or deploy their 88mm anti-aircraft guns, but they would be plotting and tracking, waiting for the right moment. Our role was to act as a kind of decoy, while the Mossies sneaked in at low level and under radar cover. The hope was that we would attract the attention of the defences as we circled at altitude, presenting ourselves as a very attractive target. As the first flares lit up the target area, all hell would break loose and the defences would let go with everything that they had — you just had to hope that their aim was poor. Thankfully, on this occasion it was and we were able to carry out a normal bombing run, backing up the initial markers and dropping our 4,000lb cookie. We turned for home, but after a while a routine navigational check indicated that we were flying much further north of track than we should have been, and out of the relative safety of the bomber stream. The navigator advised the skipper to head south to where the stream should have been. Flight Lieutenant Covington didn't change course but merely asked the crew to try and get a ground fix so as to confirm the navigator's findings. This took valuable time, but I managed to recognize the city of Mannheim with the help of the reflection of a distinctive bend of the Rhine. It was now obvious to all that we were a good deal further north than we should have been and we were a sitting target for prowling German night fighters. For some reason the skipper did not do anything, but continued on the same course, flying straight and level.

The reason why it was important to remain within the main stream of aircraft was that the greater the density of aircraft, the more difficult it was for the enemy to get a fix on a potential victim. The night fighter would be guided within visual range of a target, and then would position itself underneath the bomber, in the blind spot where he couldn't be seen. The pilot would then raise the nose of his aircraft into a position where he would be able to fire into the belly of the aircraft, with the wing root fuel tank being the favoured place to strike. A week later, a more fearsome night fighting weapon made its debut — twin upwards-firing 20mm cannon mounted at a 45 degree angle on the top of the fighter's fuselage — but this stall method was effective enough. You would not even be aware of the enemy's presence until it was too late. This is the reason why it was suicidal to be alone and why it was essential to be part of the main bomber stream, taking precautionary evasive measures to disrupt the aim of any fighters closing on you from below.

So the stage was set. We were alone, some considerable distance from the stream, and flying straight and level at 14,000 feet over the Belgian province of Namur. Unbeknown to us, a Messerschmitt 110 night fighter from 5/NJG 1 based at St Trond and piloted by Sergeant Otto Fries, was flying just below our Lancaster and he was making his final alignments to fire into our port wing fuel tanks and send us into oblivion. Flight Lieutenant Covington was sitting in his seat 100 feet above him, wondering what to do, when all of a sudden tracer showed itself, rising from behind and under the port wing, vanishing in front of us. Sergeant Fries' first burst had ripped through the port inboard engine and numbers 1 and 2 fuel tanks. Fuel spilled out of the holes, ran along the trailing edge of the wing and ignited. We were doomed and we didn't have long to evacuate the aircraft.

128

I looked at the skipper to get eye contact and confirmation of that fact, but he just stared straight ahead, gripping the control column just as he had done on our first trip to Hamburg. I shook him by the arm and, as I had an overall view of what was happening, I shouted into the intercom "Everybody get the hell out, abandon aircraft, abandon aircraft". I gave the skipper the thumbs down, to indicate that I was bailing out, and I bent down behind the pilot's seat to retrieve my parachute just before a further volley of 20mm cannon shells tore through the fuselage.

In his position in the nose, Steve Powell had opened the escape hatch and was kneeling on the edge, ready to go. Cannon shell splinters were ricocheting through the nose but miraculously he was not hit, even though the front perspex window was taken out from within. I pushed him through the hatch and followed him out into the night sky, as our doomed aircraft began to fall towards its eventual resting place near the small Belgian town of Hazinelle. Little could I guess the tremendous scale of the adventure that I was about to embark upon.

CHAPTER
FOUR

Shot Down and on the Run

As I fell through the clouds, I could feel that it was raining and very windy, and although I don't actually recall pulling the ripcord, I must have done since I felt a huge pull on my harness and looked up to see that my parachute canopy had opened. As I descended, I can remember that the buffeting wind caught my parachute causing air to spill, so that I dropped like a stone before it pulled up. This continued all the way down and caused me to vomit into the blackness, although I would imagine that the sickness was caused more by fear and shock than anything else. With the countryside being blacked out, I had real problems trying to gauge where and how far from the ground I was. Perhaps then, it was no surprise that I actually hit the deck at more or less the same time that I saw it rushing up to meet me.

As luck would have it, I appeared to have landed in a field of recently harvested wheat, complete with straw stubble pointing up towards the sky. This stubble could not have been more painful to me had it been made of steel, as the backs of my hands were badly lacerated in the landing. As I tried to release my parachute canopy, which was dragging me along the ground, the gusty wind made it more difficult. Eventually, I managed to slip the harness off and the parachute collapsed. I was safely down on terra firma, and my first reaction was to pass out where I lay. Whether this was from a combination of fear, relief, shock, panic or pain, I don't know, but I woke up where I lay some ten hours later. The time was about 13:00, the rain had stopped and, as I sat up and took in my surroundings, I found myself in open countryside just adjacent to the uncut half of the wheat field.

My first attempts to stand up failed. I could feel a severe pain in my pelvis at the site of my coccyx, but I gingerly examined myself and came to the conclusion that I hadn't broken anything and discovered that I was able to crawl, so I spent the next few hours retrieving my parachute and crawling into the uncut part of the field so that I could conceal myself amongst the stalks of wheat. Once there I managed to dig a hole where I buried my parachute and any other items I felt it would be wisest to get rid of. I looked around but I couldn't see any buildings nearby and before too long my exertions got the better of me and I fell asleep again, waking again at about 21:00 as it was starting to get dark. By then the pain in my pelvis had subsided somewhat and I found out that I could stand up and walk about, albeit with some discomfort. The rest of me was in reasonable shape, despite the fact that my face was still caked in dried blood — I assumed that this had been the result of the straw stubble dragging across

131

my cheek as I landed. I decided to wait until it was dark before making my move.

At 23:00 I headed off towards a distant row of poplar trees. I was aware that in the Low Countries it was common practice to plant such trees along exposed roadways in order to act as windbreaks and, on reaching the road that I had guessed was there, I sat down for a minute or two to try and weigh up my options and decide which way to go. Suddenly, I heard the sound of someone approaching on a bicycle and moved into the ditch to let them pass. I saw to my relief that it was an elderly man and after he passed me, I moved out into the road and said (in my best schoolboy French) "Bonsoir, monsieur". He took off like a rocket as if he'd received the shock of his life. I decided to move off in the same direction, assuming that he had been heading towards some degree of civilization and before too long I came to a sign which pointed to a place named Furneaux. I followed the sign and soon came to a small village. I passed a small farmhouse and saw a bicycle propped up against a wall so I guessed that the old man I had seen was inside. I took a deep breath, approached the door and knocked. There was no response so I knocked again and eventually heard scuffling on the other side. Slowly the door opened to reveal a little old lady who, quite frankly, looked scared to death, which was hardly surprising under the circumstances. She was faced by a strange foreign man in RAF uniform, with dried blood plastered all over his face, in a tatty and unkempt state, long after the official curfew had begun. She said "Monsieur?" and I replied

"Bonsoir madame, je suis Anglais. RAF. Anglais". With that she closed the door in my face and I heard the sound of frenzied discussion coming from inside. The door soon re-opened and I was told: "Entrez, entrez tres vite."

I stepped inside and was confronted by three generations of a Belgian farming family aged between four and eighty. None of them could speak English, but I managed to explain to them in my best French what had happened and they understood me all right — my grammar school French teacher would have been proud of me. I was given a hot drink, some bread and some cheese. This was the first food I had eaten since leaving England the previous night and it tasted wonderful. I was asked to be patient while someone in the village was spoken to, and my heart sank as I thought that the game was up and that I was to be handed over to the police. However, after what seemed like hours, a man arrived at the house, together with his wife and, to my relief, they were English speakers. I was asked what had happened to my aircraft, what I had done with my parachute and where I had buried it. Armed with my answers, the man left and returned a short while later, obviously having located my parachute and effects. I was told to accompany the couple to another location, where I would be given accommodation for the night. We traipsed across seemingly endless fields until we reached another farmhouse. There I was cleaned up, given clean and dry civilian clothes, had my aches and pains checked out by someone, was given another hot drink, a blanket and

133

bid goodnight. I was led into a barn and told not to smoke any English or American cigarettes — the few I had on me I gave up to them.

The next morning I was given some breakfast and informed that a monk would pick me up and direct me to my next contact. I was quite anxious to know whereabouts in Belgium I was, but any such questions in connection with this resulted in my being told in no uncertain terms that security was the paramount concern, and no mention would be made of anyone that I had come into contact with since my arrival. In fact, I was not to find out the names of anyone who had helped me until long after the war's end.

The monk duly arrived and, oddly, he asked me for my home address in England before explaining what we were going to do next. He then asked me for the English money that I had with me, explaining that he would keep it safe and return it to me eventually. We left the barn and walked some considerable distance through a forest, with him always no less than 100 yards in front of me. As instructed, I stopped dead every time he did, and only moved again once he had given me an agreed hand signal. He had also told me that if he met anyone I was to get out of sight immediately. Eventually we broke clear of the forest and he briefed me on what to expect next. We walked along a wide pathway which led to a group of buildings some 150 yards away. I had been informed that this was a resort area and that my eventual destination was a large outdoor restaurant. The monk had told me that the restaurant would be thronging with German troops but that they would be off duty and on leave and would not be the slightest bit interested in me. He told me to stay calm and walk steadily through the middle of the restaurant, to a set of double doors at the back. I was to go through these doors and stay put. He told me he was leaving me to it, said "Au revoir", and wished me luck. I was on my own.

Taking a deep breath, I did as directed, walked through the restaurant and through the double doors, entering a darkened room. By now I was sweating blood. The swing doors opened behind me and a waiter appeared. Without a word, he took hold of me and led me through another door into a room which was completely empty, except for a table and a chair, upon which sat a man drinking a glass of beer. The waiter turned to me and said: "May I introduce you to your friend, Flight Sergeant Powell?"

It was a great relief to see him and we soon got down to the business of swapping stories and comparing our versions of events. He told me that he remembered something (i.e. me.) pushing him out into the wide black yonder and his parachute opening cleanly. His descent was much the same as mine — unsurprising, given the unhelpful weather conditions — but it appears as though he had enjoyed a much softer arrival, landing on his feet and consequently not being dragged. He had actually been spotted by friendly locals and had been approached by them. They helped him to gather and dispose of his parachute, before hiding him and sending him down the escape line.

Unfortunately I can't remember the details of his story from then until we met up, beer in hand.

We next met up with a member of the Belgian Resistance — L'Armee Blanche — and she briefed us on our next move down the Comete escape line which had been set up by twenty-five year old Andrée de Jongh, the daughter of a schoolteacher from Brussels. Dédée, the name by which Andrée de Jongh was known, had been captured by the Germans and imprisoned some months earlier but, of course, I didn't know that at the time, or that the famous 1970s television series *Secret Army* would be inspired by her exploits.

We were to be sent to a safe house in the Ardennes area, and to get there we would have to travel by train. The procedure would be that we would walk to the local branch station and buy a ticket to the hub station of Dinant, which was two stops down the line. Once there, we would buy tickets to our final destination, a town called Voneche. Our guide, also known as Dédée, supplied us both with the correct fare and explained the etiquette for travelling by train in occupied Belgium, as the area was expected to be crawling with Germans. We were told that we would have to split up and act as individuals and, if one of us was picked up, he should surrender without resistance and say nothing. Once leaving the train at Voneche, we were to go directly to a café at the entrance to the station, order a beer and sit down at a table — our beer money was also provided. Once Dédée had established that no Germans were in the vicinity and that we were not being watched or followed, she would join us at our table. She also passed on an extremely interesting piece of information to us, namely that we were not, under any circumstances, to pick our noses. This was because any Germans nearby would consider this to be a gross insult and the last thing that we were to do was draw attention to ourselves.

This journey may seem straightforward and easy some sixty years on, but I can assure you that the effect on one's nervous system was ten times worse than actually being shot down. This feeling was exacerbated at one point when we were on the train between Dinant and Voneche. We had been split up with Dédée in one coach and Powell and I sitting at opposite ends of another. At the first station out of Dinant three German soldiers boarded and one came and sat in the vacant seat next to me. I didn't react and spent the rest of the journey staring out of the window — my insides in turmoil. He ignored me and when we reached Voneche I said "Pardon, monsieur" and squeezed past him to the exit, having lost about ten pounds in sweat.

After finishing our beers at the café in Voneche, we were joined by a man I knew only as "The Lieutenant" — the leader of the local Resistance group — and he led us out of the town and across a number of fields, before we reached a large farmhouse. We all entered and were met by the other six members of the local Resistance group, as well as the farmer — who I was later to discover was named Monsieur Pochet — his wife, and his daughter, Blanchette. This was the safe house where we were to spend the night and the farmer

137

had certainly laid on a wonderful spread for us. When the eating and drinking was over, we were given a tour of the house, which had obviously been used to shelter evaders on plenty of previous occasions.

The house had four storeys, with the top one having been specially adapted to house the likes of us. This was because the gable ends of the roof had been modified to permit entry from the attic, with the entries being sealed off to simulate the attic ceiling, even down to the fact that if the entry doors were tapped, they would make the same noise as the rest of the attic ceiling made. We were told to familiarize ourselves with the layout of the upper floors, as we would need to know where everything was in case of trouble. This was fortunate advice to receive, as unbeknown to all present, the local Gestapo were planning a sweep of the area, in order to try and pick up those Belgians who were attempting to avoid being deported to Germany to be used as forced labour.

At 05:00 the next morning the daughter of the house woke us up from the deep, cognac-induced sleep we were enjoying. She whispered urgently "Vite, vite, les Boches, les Boches". My first thought was that this was all a big joke, as those lines were surely only ever used in Hollywood films, but I soon realized that this was no laughing matter and Powell and I, together with the Resistance members, hurried up into the attic and into the gable end as we had been shown, with someone sealing the trapdoor behind us. There were eight of us in total, all clad in only our underwear, huddled together in a tiny space together with the local village records. "The Lieutenant" was crouched against the exit with his revolver drawn, ready to shoot his way out if necessary. We were all so quiet I could hear only the sound of breathing and the thump of beating hearts.

Before too long we could hear French and German voices the other side of the gable end, repeated banging on the attic ceiling, and then, after an eternity, the noise of footsteps receding into the distance. Some time later, we heard gentle tapping on the other side of the door, and a female voice telling us that it was okay to come out. The Gestapo had managed to locate a Belgian on the farm who was avoiding deportation, and this was enough for them to arrest Monsieur Pochet for the crime of harbouring fugitives. He was never to be seen by his family again, and after the war I learned that he had died in Flossenburg concentration camp in 1945, shortly before the end of hostilities.

Since this farmhouse was now a marked place, it was never again used as a safe house by the escape line. We were forced to spend the next few days staying with the Resistance, in a hide in the nearby woods that they used as a base for their operations. We did not join them on their escapades and asked no questions about what they got up to, but it became apparent that their main priority was executing local collaborators. Some evenings we would go to a nearby village or farmhouse for a hot meal or to spend some of our plentiful escape kit Belgian francs on beer and food.

We were subsequently passed on down the line, and at our next stop we were picked up by another mysterious man called "The Captain". He accompanied us as we were driven to a small town named Haversan, and we were left at a tiny garage while the driver filled up with petrol. I found this a little unusual as I was aware that strict petrol rationing was in force, but we were then taken to a private home in the town, fed and watered, before being provided with bicycles and an escort to our home for the night some six miles away in the village of Sinsin. We were told that it would be too risky to remain overnight in Haversan, as there were suspicions about the loyalty and reliability of the driver of the car that had taken us there.

The next morning we were again picked up by "The Captain" and driven into the bustling city of Brussels, where we were taken to a large house owned by a young married couple with small children. Here we were introduced to our fellow guests, six American B-17 crewmen and three Dutchmen who were trying to get out of the country. However, my suspicions were aroused by the fact that we were asked to fill out certain forms with our personal details, and I approached the senior officer there, an American captain, and told him of my concerns. He told me that in his opinion there was nothing to worry about and, as far as he was concerned, that was that. I still wasn't convinced and Powell and I only filled out the bare minimum of name, rank and number on our forms. We were then taken out in pairs to a department store in central Brussels called "La Bonne Marche" where we had our pictures taken so that they could be used on our travel and work permits. We joined the queue at a kiosk in the store where a very pretty attendant positioned us, said "smile", and pressed the button. While she was dealing with me she leaned close and said "Vous êtes Anglais, n'est ce pas?" My heart skipped a beat as behind me in the line was a German sergeant, but to my great relief he didn't even lift his eyes from the newspaper that he was reading.

Once we had all been through this procedure we returned to the house to await the arrival of our forged work permits, identity cards and rail tickets. The thought did occur to me that it would be easy for the Germans to use these booths as good places to pick up suspected evaders and fugitives and I discussed this with the Dutchmen as I considered that of all of us, they were the ones who had the most to lose — their lives.

Once our forged papers arrived we were all briefed on our next move. We were told our new identities and that we would have to learn by heart the details that we had been passed. I was given the name of Jacques Regout and my new birthplace was Charleroi, in southern Belgium. We were to be taken to the main railway station in the city to catch a train to Paris. A guide would be on hand to keep an eye on us en route, but he wouldn't contact us and railway porters would show us to our reserved seats on the train. When we reached the Franco-Belgian border we were to stay put and a German customs officer would board the train and examine papers. This was all to be fairly routine stuff. The train would then continue on to a town called Charleville, just inside France, and we were to disembark. Our unseen guide would then make himself known to us and give us further instructions.

Unfortunately, as I boarded the train, I discovered that someone had decided to sit in my reserved seat, and to compound my feeling of unease, a lady walked past me and as she did so, said "Good luck" in English, making me wonder if my nationality was as obvious to everyone else as it had been to her. However, all appeared to be well, and after the first couple of stops I was able to claim my own seat when the interloper left the train. At the Belgian border town of Givet, the platform seemed to be alive with Germans and naturally we all assumed that they would be looking for us. As predicted, the German customs official got on board and travelled the length of the train checking the passengers' documents. When he reached our compartment he executed a typical Prussian heel-click and said: "Bonjour messieurs, vos passeports, s'il vous plaît?" It occurred to me that this was probably the only French that he knew or was ever likely to use. He examined our forgeries, stamped them with a huge swastika and thanked us, before leaving the compartment. As the train pulled away from the platform and crossed the border into France, I was tempted to flick a "V" sign at the Germans at the station, but soon thought better of it.

On arrival at Charleville, our carriage was diverted to a less busy platform and we disembarked, to be met by our guide. He told us that we now had a three hour wait until our connection to Paris and that we would be going into town for lunch. We were ordered to split up into twos and threes and leave the station as inconspicuously as possible, before proceeding through the town, following him at a distance of fifty or so feet. He told us that he would pause before crossing a particular road, and that we were to bunch up, cross all together and follow him into a building on the other side, where we were to go into a room on the first floor and close the door behind us. I had a nagging feeling that this wasn't quite right and that we were being led into a trap, but I couldn't see that I had any alternative other than to do as I had been told. All went as planned, and we crossed the town centre without actually seeing a single German. The place seemed as dead as a doornail as we entered the building, found the correct room on the first floor, and shut the door behind us. Then, all hell broke loose as the door and windows were flung open and the room was filled with gun toting German soldiers, shouting at us in comic book fashion to put our hands up. I found myself standing face to face with the German sergeant in charge, looking directly down the barrel of the American Colt .45 revolver that he was pointing at me. I can remember that I could even see the head of the bullet, so close was the "business end" of the weapon. For some unknown reason, my immediate reaction to this unexpected turn of events was to laugh hysterically and put my hands up. I can only attribute this to the built up adrenaline being released, because our situation did not in any way, shape or form constitute a laughing matter. One thing I could not understand was why the Germans had put so much effort into capturing a few airmen and harmless civilians, and I was not to find out exactly why until I found my way home after the war and was fully debriefed about my time as an evader by MI9 — the special intelligence section formed during the war with the sole responsibility for assisting and organizing the evasion lines in occupied Europe.

It appeared as though the three Dutchmen, far from being the harmless civilians they purported to be, were actually three of the Gestapo's most wanted men in Holland, and that they were being tracked down the evasion line which led through Belgium and France and into neutral Spain, our ultimate destination. The Gestapo had successfully managed to infiltrate the line in Brussels, and from then on, our fate was sealed. The Germans had organized the Dutchmen to be mixed in with our little group of fliers to allay any suspicions that the men may have had and from then on, it was a simple matter of just putting us all in the bag. I was told that the traitor had been "The Captain" who, in actual fact, was a Luxembourger working for the Gestapo, but who didn't live for long afterwards as he was promptly assassinated on orders from London. However, he had been given time enough to have betrayed the six brave members of the Resistance unit that Powell and I had briefly been mixed up with, by telling the Germans of the exact location of the woodland hide. The group was ambushed there a week after we had left them and moved to Brussels, and tragically all six of them lost their lives. The wife and daughter of the farmer — who was taken away by the

Gestapo during that dawn raid — managed to survive and I was to meet up again with them and with many others who helped me some time after the war — a chapter of my life I shall cover in much greater detail later on.

For now though, self preservation was the key and as instructed, I surrendered. We were lined up, searched and everything that we had was taken from us. After this was done, we were all taken outside to a waiting lorry, one at a time, and put on board. The lorry was sealed from the eyes of the outside world with canvas flaps and off we went at marching pace, surrounded by German troops. Eventually we arrived at what looked like a military barracks and, when the gates had been closed behind us, we were taken off the lorry. We were all told in no uncertain terms that after we had been taken to our quarters, if we showed ourselves at the windows or at the doors then we would be shot dead. We were then marched upstairs to a large room on one of the upper floors of the barrack block, and to my great surprise, I noted that there were exactly eleven bunks inside — someone had obviously booked our accommodation in advance.

At 04:00 the next morning we were rudely awakened by the Gestapo and subjected to intensive questioning. The Dutchmen were taken away in shackles but the rest of us were allowed to go back to sleep once our ordeal was over. We were, after all, only the bit-part players in this grand production staged by the Germans. Later on that morning, we awoke to the sound of a marching band passing by in the street outside. I worked out that it was a Sunday and that this performance must be a weekly treat put on by the Germans for the benefit of the locals, who I'm sure must have been immensely grateful. We were allowed the chance to wash, fed a surprisingly good breakfast, given the circumstances, and told that we would be leaving at noon. We were given ragged old captured uniforms that approximated our own status and our civvies were taken away. I was particularly embarrassed by my own issue as it was a very poor fit and barely covered my privates. Now that the Dutchmen had gone, security dropped down a notch or two and our transportation to a beautiful French chateau was carried out in less oppressive circumstances. This chateau was situated in the middle of a beautiful forest of oak trees, and it had obviously been taken over by the local German garrison and transformed into headquarters. We entered the building, passing impressive looking sentries standing at attention, and found ourselves in a huge, magnificent entrance hall with a plush scarlet carpet and walls adorned with enormous oil paintings. The carpet fitted the length of the hallway and disappeared up a grand central staircase, making it appear as though the whole scene had been transplanted straight out of *Gone With The Wind*. There we were addressed by a smiling army captain, who told us that our overnight accommodation had been arranged and that in the morning we would be taken to Germany to visit the Luftwaffe interrogation centre in Frankfurt. The sleeping quarters turned out to be high up in the attic of the chateau, a room with no plumbing except a bucket, and small windows all around which only gave us a view of the tops of the oak trees that surrounded the building. Despite these privations, once again we were well fed by our captors.

The next day we were taken to the local railway station and supplied with our rations for the journey ahead — slices of bread and some ersatz jam to spread on them. With a number of German guards acting as our travelling companions, we set off. On arrival in Frankfurt, we got out and fell in for what turned out to be a rather hairy march through the city centre to our eventual destination. The problem was that the previous night the RAF had successfully bombed a nearby target, and many people had been killed. Frankfurt itself had also taken a pasting from the Allied air forces although I couldn't take personal responsibility for this as I had never taken part in a trip there. As a result, local feeling was raw and tensions were high. Word appeared to get to the locals — possibly from our unsympathetic guards — that these eight ragged strangers passing through their midst were shot down Allied airmen and I began to feel as though I was becoming the target of a lynch mob. We were in deep trouble and people began to bombard us with anything they could lay their hands on. At this point, when it looked as though we had had it, suddenly our saviours appeared in the unlikely guise of two SS officers, who drew their sidearms and forced the crowd back, before ordering our guards to do their duty and guard us. These SS men remained with our party until we had reached a stationary tram and were bundled onto it, taking us out of the city centre and away from the mob. We arrived at Dulag Luft, some eight miles away to the north-west, without further incident and amidst great relief on our part. Once there we were placed in a room, without amenities, with thirty other new arrivals. They had not been fed all day and were generally feeling riled, shouting and yelling over and over again at the sight of a guard at the door. On one occasion, a very discontented prisoner had started chanting and before too long, we were all doing it and creating the most terrific din, such as a football crowd would make. I was sure that the Germans would lose their temper and come into the room, guns blazing, if we didn't stop, but thankfully their reaction was nowhere near as extreme. I believe that this must have been part of the official Luftwaffe softening up process as a precursor to being placed in solitary confinement, as was the subsequent hardship of having to sleep on the floor with hardly enough space for half of our number.

After a long and restless night we were given mugs of ersatz coffee, allowed to go to the toilet and were each taken to individual cells to await our interrogators. The first person who spoke to me was a wonderfully smartly uniformed individual who introduced himself as a Swiss Red Cross official. He stated that his role was to ensure that news of our survival and capture reached the UK, so that our family and friends would know that we were alive. To those ends he presented me with a very official looking Red Cross form and asked me to fill it out with all of the personal information that was requested. While I had been at Wyton with 15 Squadron I had seen a copy of this form during a lecture on escape and evasion, and I played it safe and only filled out my name, rank and serial number. The official wasn't pleased and pointed out to me that I had been caught in civilian clothes and in possession of forged papers and documents, and that it would be a wise move not to annoy my captors, who would be within their rights to shoot me as a spy. I refused and told him that I was filthy, had not shaved for four days and not eaten anything substantial for three. The official left me in my cell and shortly afterwards the heating was turned up. All I had to drink was water, which I could request when required by pressing a call button. I wasn't given anything to eat at all. However, word of Powell's and my capture obviously reached home successfully — the 97 Squadron Diary entry of 3 November 1943 records that:

Flight Sergeant T. Lancashire and Flight Sergeant S. Powell reported Prisoners Of War (missing with Flight Lieutenant Covington's crew on 10th August).

Three days later, by now really annoyed, I was taken from my cell to a marvellously plush office, where I was to meet my next interrogator, who sat there in all his Teutonic glory behind a magnificent desk. He introduced himself to me as Major Junge, the Chief of Interrogation, and asked me to sit down, before offering me a Players cigarette which I gladly accepted. He lit it for me and told me to relax. In all my stinking misery, I managed to control my emotions and smiled, and we now had a man-to-man talk. He told me that he was disappointed that I had refused to fill out the Red Cross form properly, but that it didn't really matter as he was going to disclose to me anyway all the information that the Luftwaffe held on me. All that they had been trying to do was confirm that it was accurate. Major Junge then proceeded to supply me with a complete history of my RAF service. He began by telling me that I had joined the Air Force on 14 January 1936 and served a three year apprenticeship at the No. 1 School of Technical Training, RAF Halton, graduating in December 1938. He embellished this by recounting all sorts of incidents from my time at Halton, together with the names of instructors and teachers, all of which were very impressively accurate. He then told me that I had been flying in a Lancaster when it had been shot down and that I operated out of RAF Coningsby. He then began talking about gliders, which he stated were also based at Coningsby and then told me that, as one engineer to another, he was absolutely intrigued by the new Typhoon fighter. I put on a spellbound expression and told him that: "It's incredible and positively amazing what you know. You know even more than I do." This was absolutely true. 97 Squadron operated out of Bourn, of course, although I do believe that the squadron had previously been based at Coningsby, leaving there in the April of that year, a few months before my time. There may have been gliders at Coningsby for all I knew, but there were certainly none at Bourn. The conversation carried on in this vein for a short while longer until I had had enough. I told Major Junge that the miserable physical and mental condition that I had been reduced to was hardly conducive to further cooperation and that I had nothing more to say. I told him to do his worst. He responded by offering me another cigarette which I politely refused. I was then returned to my cell, where I remained for a short while before the Luftwaffe decided that I was of no further use to them and I was moved into the transit camp next door to await my fate.

CHAPTER
FIVE

Prisoner of War

Emerging from the interrogation centre and finding myself in the transit camp was a little like emerging from hell and finding oneself in heaven. My first stop was the bath house where I had a much needed shave and enjoyed the best hot shower of my life. I was then given a set of clean clothes and made my way over to the cookhouse where I was given a bowl of hot soup and a few slices of black bread — surely the best tasting and most welcome meal I have ever had. To top things off, I was given a pack of Gold Flake cigarettes and even the matches to light them. Things were definitely looking up for me. My next stop was the camp's reception area, which was run by the highest ranking RAF prisoners. However I again had cause to remember the previously mentioned lecture at Wyton when it was suggested that Germans may have been infiltrated into these reception committees in order to eavesdrop, spy and generally make nuisances of themselves. As a result I kept my cards pretty close to my chest but I needn't have worried as there were no cuckoos in this nest. I was sorted out with a bunk and informed that when sufficient numbers of prisoners had been collected together to justify a complete shipment, we would be on our way to a bona fide prisoner of war camp. As to where we'd eventually be going, nobody seemed to have the slightest clue. I did find out that Flight Sergeant Steve Powell, our bomb aimer and my erstwhile travelling companion, had been shipped off somewhere with the last batch. For now, it was time to wait.

In due course, enough men had accumulated and we were loaded onto the usual form of transport — freight wagons. These were hooked up to a train and off we went. Conditions on board weren't too bad, the trucks weren't that crowded and we had the luxury of a black pot-bellied stove in the middle of the floor which churned out plenty of heat. We were now well into the autumn and it was starting to get a bit chilly. There were the usual buckets scattered about "for our convenience", there was plenty of hot soup and Red Cross goodies were available. As far as the rail planners were concerned, we were classified as "non-priority freight", so we seemed to spend lots of time standing idle in sidings, waiting for spare engines to arrive to take us on the next leg of our journey. The nights could be interesting, especially if the rail yard became the subject of RAF air raids, although we used to comfort ourselves with the thought that the bomb aiming would undoubtedly be so lousy that we were bound to remain unscathed. I remember being underneath one such raid on the town of Bitterfeldt during our journey, and I am still here to tell the tale, so we must have been right. We measured our progress by the names of the places we stopped at. We spent the last night of our journey in Dresden, before arriving at our ultimate destination of Neuburgsdorf. Our carriages (we had managed to pick up two more en route) were diverted onto a side track which led off to the town of Mühlberg, and we were ordered out for a roll call. After it had been successfully established that nobody had disappeared during the trip, we were marched off through the flat landscape towards Mühlberg and the prison camp there. The area was characterized by two things, firstly by the six inches of snow on the ground which made everything look clean, peaceful and beautiful, and secondly by the dreadful smell caused by the fertilizer which had been spread all over the fields. After four or five miles we reached the camp that was to become our home for the next two years — M-Stammlager IVB.

Once we had passed through the gates, we were halted and told to form up opposite a large brick building. A German sergeant major looked us all over and ordered us to take off all our clothes, bundle them up and mark them clearly with our names. These bundles were to be industrially deloused and cleaned while we were given a hot shower and a medical check-up of sorts. Bearing in mind the fact that we were standing in six inches of snow and being whipped by a bitterly cold wind, this was not a pleasant experience. Thankfully, it wasn't long before we were ordered into the wonderfully hot showers, given pieces of soap and told not to hang around. Then we were herded into drying rooms, where huge fans blasted air through at room temperature, drying us off in double quick time. From the drying room the next stop was the haircutting salon, where several manually operated sheep shearing machines awaited our pleasure. As each of us progressed down the line, we turned the handle of the machine for the one in front. Our barbers were Russian POWs, and they started at the forehead, and then drew the shearer over the head and, in four strokes, we were as bald as coots. It was quite amusing looking at the anguished expressions of those in front of you. We were then taken through into the next room for a medical examination of sorts. Still stark naked, we were looked over by more Russian POWs masquerading as medical staff, told to put our hands above our heads and swabbed down with a liquid that seemed to be agricultural disinfectant. No nook or cranny was spared from this process, armpits, groin — you name it, it was swabbed. The grand finale of this "examination" was a typhus vaccine injected directly into the chest, and then it was on to another room where we were gratefully reunited with our freshly fumigated clothing. This process was not, as may be imagined, the sadistic and humiliating requirement of the arrogant Nazi captor, but that of the Red Cross under the articles of the Geneva Convention, which dictated how we were to be treated as prisoners of war. After we had been officially documented, fingerprinted and photographed, we were given a piece of aluminium on a string which had been stamped with our prisoner numbers, of which mine was 222829IVB. All that remained was to be officially welcomed to the camp and have the Riot Act of Stalag IVB read to us — this could be effectively condensed into:

Obey the rules and you live — ignore them and you are dead.

We were then shown to our huts and allocated bunks, and turned over to our respective appointed national representatives for the required introductions to camp life. It had certainly been a day to remember.

Yet again I caught up with Steve Powell, whose destination had also been Mühlberg, and I started to learn a little about the history of the camp. It had only just started to house RAF prisoners owing to the Luftwaffe POW camps becoming overcrowded, and the majority of the prisoners were from the Army. M-Stammlager IVB had originally been a base camp for the initial documentation of prisoners of all nationalities, from where officers had been shipped out to their own camps, senior NCOs were retained as residents and all others were detailed to join work commandos. So the camp had been home to all manner of senior NCOs of all Allied nations until the beginning of 1943 when the influx of prisoners increased dramatically and RAF personnel began to arrive.

Traditionally, it was possible to move about the camp at will as long as one stayed inside the "death wire", which was strung some twelve inches above the ground, ten feet from the perimeter fence. This wire was so named because if you failed to get permission from the guard in the watchtower before crossing it, to retrieve a ball for example, you would be promptly shot dead. This was accepted practice on both sides. However this did not stop some people from being foolish. I learned that the previous year a British sergeant major had decided that the rule was nothing more than a bluff and completely ignored it, stepping over the wire in order to retrieve a cricket ball. He had survived the entire North African campaign without a scratch, but was immediately shot dead by the guard in the watchtower, who was fully justified in doing so. Of course a sergeant major, of all people, should have known better, but some individuals never seem to learn, do they?

Before the ever increasing number of RAF prisoners began to swell the ranks at the camp, the senior NCOs who had been resident there for some time had managed to settle into a comfortable pattern of existence. Some had been there since May 1940, when they had been captured at Dunkirk, and they had learned, by being good soldiers and model prisoners, to get along very well with the guards. Their attitude had been one of not rocking the boat, and they had managed to win privileged status as prisoners and had assumed the natural mantle of leadership amongst all the other nationalities present. When the boys in blue arrived these leaders considered it to be their duty to show them the type of discipline and good order that was the norm in the Army. However they didn't seem to realize that we weren't used to this sort of rigid discipline and as a result we were looked upon as a bunch of naughty schoolboys by the Germans and the Army NCOs, mainly because we adopted a policy amongst ourselves of being as awkward as possible when in contact with the German authorities. As a punishment for our unhelpful attitude, we were rapidly segregated from the rest of the prisoners and locked away in a different part of the camp until we decided to grow up and toe the line. However this policy contravened the articles of the good old Geneva Convention and before too long the commandant was forced to back down and give us the freedom of the entire camp. A small victory had been won. Pilot Officer James Branford of 149 Squadron, who arrived at Mühlberg at exactly the same time as me, was quoted in an official report after the war as saying that:

> Had we allowed it, the bullying arrogant guards would have made life a pretty good hell. The RAF did all they could to wear them down. Turning up late for parade, talking, booing the guards whenever they kicked anyone for small offences. Finally their attitude changed and they gave it up as a bad job trying to keep us in order. (*Secret Camp Histories of Stalag IVB* — WO/208/3274)

This restoration of our freedom meant that we were once again able to take part in the well established camp activities which were part of life in Stalag IVB. These included a football league, with teams adopting the names of English clubs, an international football tournament, and cricket and rugby "test matches" and leagues following the same pattern, with equipment provided by the Red Cross. Theatre groups were formed by the various nationalities, and a barrack block was set aside by the Germans for conversion into the camp theatre. There was also a well stocked library, again thanks to the Red Cross, and chess clubs, debating societies and the like flourished amidst the boredom of being prisoners. There was a large German-run hospital situated outside the camp and small sickbays were established within, staffed by captured medical staff and, of course, supplied by the Red Cross. The British sickbay was run by a Major Whyte, of the Royal Army Medical Corps, who had been captured in North Africa some time previously. All religious groups and denominations were catered for by various padres and holy men who had been captured by the grace of God (and the Germans) in order to care for and minister to the prisoners, and I am sure they performed magnificently under the watchful eye of the Almighty although, not being a religious man myself, I can't confirm this. I can state that the religious prisoners I knew did seem to derive a great deal of comfort from their presence and they did help them through the traumatic ordeal of being POWs. Praise the Lord and pass the ammunition was my motto in those days, however.

Another important club was established and organized by the RAF boys: the escape committee. The object of this was to organize and discover the existing talents of the prisoners and harness these in order to use them to assist anyone who wanted to escape. You would be amazed at the huge variety of people we had with us, from all walks of life. There were the lowest and the highest, the ignorant and the genius, the saints and the criminals. What was improvised and accomplished within this camp was truly staggering. One clever trick I enjoyed was seeing a can of Spam opened, the meat extracted and then replaced with exactly the same weight of soil, and then re-sealed so that to all intents and purposes, it was a bona fide can of Spam once more. It was then considered the done thing to exchange the tin for cigarettes (the established camp currency), bread or eggs with a gullible guard.

As in most POW camps, an attempt was made to dig a tunnel out under the wire, and this activity kept many of the prisoners happy — a most important factor in the day-to-day life of a POW camp — until one day, when it collapsed after something heavy inadvertently passed over it. The commandant found this failure very amusing and congratulated its builders on doing a very professional job. He then ordered them to fill it in by emptying the contents of the camp cesspools into it — not quite "The Great Escape". Thankfully, I didn't actually have any part in the digging of the tunnel and, in fact, I didn't even know about its existence until it collapsed. However it did explain why I had been ordered to contribute two of my bed boards to the project, so that they could be used to act as shoring and supports for the tunnel ceiling. The inevitable result was that my bed was then much more uncomfortable to sleep on, with the new and ever-present danger of my mattress and I falling through onto the bed beneath. Yet the discovery of the tunnel did not eradicate the desire of some to escape and plenty of other methods were devised and explored. One of these involved changing places with an army private who was due to leave the camp as part of a work commando. There were always plenty of soldiers willing to swap as the prospect of working for the enemy was never a very attractive one for them and, as far as the Germans were concerned, one was just a number anyway and hardly any close attention was paid to the members of the commandos. It was the luck of the draw as far as these were concerned, as some would find themselves working in a nearby coal mine and others would end up on a farm, helping with the daily tasks. In any case, it was generally agreed that the chances to escape in these circumstances were a good deal less risky than taking one's life in one's hands and crawling down a tunnel.

Amongst our number were plenty of radio experts who were able to build and supply us with working receivers, the component parts of which were easily obtained by exchanging the usual camp currency of Red Cross cigarettes. Our only problem was how to conceal them, as the Gestapo and SS would periodically descend on the camp in order to carry out searches for such items. Our eventual policy was to construct working decoys and hide them so that they would be found, but only after a "cat and mouse" game of sufficiently convincing complexity had been arranged, in order to divert the Germans' attention away from the craftily hidden main sets. The BBC news was never withheld from us, and the guards would regularly rely upon our radio men for more accurate news of the progress of the war in order to keep the commandant appraised. One other source of contact with the outside world was the fact that the commandant allowed small working parties to travel to the local railway station at Mühlberg to assist with the unloading of Red Cross shipments and to help transport them back to the camp. To this end a party of ten men was picked and each was asked to swear on their honour that they would not try to escape, before being placed in the custody of a solitary guard. This apparently lax security situation was the result of the commandant believing in the honour and the integrity of an Englishman's word being his bond. He considered us to be gentlemen, but would not extend this privilege to the Americans, whom he did not trust one bit, and consequently would not let out of his sight. Every railway station in Germany, even the smaller ones, would have its own station master, and these trips were a heaven-sent opportunity to barter with and bribe Mühlberg's station master who also ran the small bar and could not resist the real coffee and Red Cross cigarettes which were proffered by the prisoners.

So as we approached Christmas 1943 things were not all that bad, considering my circumstances. I kept myself occupied and I didn't really have too much to grumble about, in direct contrast to many who felt extremely sorry for themselves and hated their lot as POWs. No amount of effort on our part seemed to cheer these men up, and it was often the case that, after the war, such prisoners returned home as physical and mental wrecks, unable to deal with the fact that they had been their own worst enemies during their time behind the wire. Sadly, this group could count vast numbers of men within their ranks.

However the advent of Christmas made even Stalag IVB seem like a happier, cheerier place. Variety shows were put on by the various different national groups, and even the commandant and his staff were welcomed into the audience. As I recall, the highly appropriate name of the show that the British prisoners put on was *Birds In A Cage*. Our Christmas dinner was supplemented by our being given extra rations by order of the commandant and we had sufficient Red Cross parcels in stock to enable us to issue one between three without drastically depleting our stores for the coming month. Visits were made to the barracks of our Allies, where carols were sung and tales of Christmases past were shared. However the most heart rending visit was to the compound housing the masses of Russian prisoners. Their forces were fighting the Germans in one of the most savage confrontations the world had ever seen, and the articles of the Geneva Convention, which protected us and our rights, had no relevance here. These men were completely at the mercy of the individual kindnesses of their captors and, in order to try and help them through this difficult time, we set up a charitable fund to which the rest of the camp contributed. This was an act that was much appreciated by the Russians, and helped us to feel as though we were at least contributing to the spirit of the festive season. There were other memorable moments. I vividly remember one prisoner starting to sing the well-known carol, *Silent Night*. More and more people joined in as the sound travelled throughout the camp, and eventually 10,000 voices, including those of the German guards, could be heard, transcending national differences and conflicts, and all singing together in their various languages. If there was a more poignant moment in my time as a prisoner, then I can't remember it. This act was repeated a week later, with the singing of *Auld Lang Syne* as the new year of 1944 was welcomed in with gusto. We all hoped that this would be the last year of the war and that we would be spending the next Christmas at home with our families and friends.

Almost straightaway our vital and beloved supply of Red Cross parcels began to dry up owing to the relentless and successful bombing attacks on the German rail and transport infrastructure. Although the Red Cross tried to compensate for these difficulties by sending aid by road, this was a Herculean and ultimately hopeless task as only 10 per cent of goods reached their destinations, and much of what arrived at the camps had been pilfered en route as it passed through Portugal, Spain and France. Although we rationed out what was left, the reserves gradually diminished until all that remained was that which we had earmarked for Christmas 1944, or a victory party — whichever came soonest. I should point out here that the crime of stealing from fellow POWs was considered to be the most serious offence that could be committed

164

behind the wire, even more so than murder. This was not the attitude of the German authorities, but that of all of us. The responsibility for enforcing discipline in these cases fell upon the POW council and, if an offender was caught, he was tried and sentenced to a beating. These beatings would sometimes prove to be fatal as even the medics were disgusted by thieves and would often refuse to treat the injured. It came to be seen as a very harsh and effective deterrent.

German rations now assumed a far greater significance in our lives. They were stored outside the camp and were brought in daily by carts which were either towed or pushed by the prisoners. The Russians, who were in a far worse condition than us, would habitually line the roadway and try to distract the guards as the carts rumbled past, thus giving their more daring comrades the opportunity to steal from them. The Germans would often react to this by issuing a warning, which was invariably ignored, and then shooting to kill. Many starving Russians met their ends in this way. In a direct contrast to this sad state of affairs, the Germans never failed to supply our basic rations, even as the end of the war approached and food became scarce for the civilian population on the other side of the fence. We were allowed to grow our own vegetables to supplement our diet and our bread ration was never cut. It is entirely probable that, as a POW, my diet in 1945 was far better than that of a German civilian, which is more than a little ironic.

The camp was located a few miles south of a Luftwaffe training airfield, and the rookie German pilots, knowing that RAF aircrew were being held at Stalag IVB, would spend plenty of time showing off their newly acquired talents at low level over the camp. Such mock strafing runs were usually carried out adjacent and parallel to the fence, along which prisoners would often walk in order to get some exercise. Tragically, on 30 April 1944, a pilot with obvious limited flying ability and experience misjudged the sink of his Junkers Ju 88 when we pulled up from a dive and actually skimmed the football pitch, killing a Canadian airman named Sergeant Mallory and seriously wounding another. The pilot got away without facing a more serious charge in relation to this, but we were informed some time later that he had been reduced to the rank of private, and transferred to the infantry before being posted to the Russian front. There were no more impromptu flying displays put on for our benefit after this incident.

An important commodity which was steadily being eroded was the camp coal ration, which came to us in the form of compressed soft brown coal briquettes, approximately 8 inches by 2 inches by 3 inches in size. It was not long before the entire ration was allocated to the cookhouses and the bathhouses, being stored in the basement of the cookhouses which were completely off limits for the likes of us. Naturally we RAF prisoners regarded this apparent inaccessibility as a wonderful challenge, especially as our huts were adjacent to the cookhouse. Any stealing would have to be carried out at night and this would entail breaking into the cellar through the loading ramp, transporting the briquettes and hiding them in the barracks. The guards would have to be bribed with cigarettes so as to prevent the orderly sergeant from doing his rounds at an inopportune moment and catching the culprits red-handed. As it happened, the entire operation went off without a hitch. The loot was hidden in the barracks by our removing sufficient floor bricks and digging a hole of the required size beneath, before filling the hole with the briquettes and replacing the bricks on top of them. However once the theft came to the notice of the commandant, he guessed what had happened but informed us that all we had done was gone to the unnecessary effort of stealing our allocated coal ration as the briquettes had been destined for use in our own cookhouse. We had outsmarted ourselves.

As 1944 wore on the number of POWs passing through the camp began to increase dramatically. Since the Italian surrender in the summer of the previous year, the Germans had been forced to start moving those prisoners who had been held in Italian camps into Germany itself. Later on this new flood was to be followed by thousands of captured Italians, whose country had dramatically changed sides and joined the Allied war effort.

This influx swamped the camp's resources and caused massive logistical problems for guards and prisoners alike. Fortunately, from our point of view, the Italians were merely transient prisoners destined for elsewhere. There was a great deal of resentment and anger felt towards these men by their former Allies, and they were not treated particularly well. As there was no room for them in the barracks, they were obliged to sleep outside. The majority of them had received very little to eat and next to no medical attention. They were in a very poor physical and mental state and their death rate was extremely high. I had my first sight of what sick and starving men looked like, dying on their feet and where they lay. They brought disease and vermin with them, and it was a constant battle to prevent these problems from spreading and taking root in the more favoured areas of the camp.

Bed bugs and lice were a constant headache. The Germans allowed us to take our bunks outside in order for us to take them apart and strip them down into their smallest component parts in order to dig out both the bugs and their numerous eggs. Once this had been done as well as could be expected, they were coated with lime and reassembled. This battle was one that the bugs always managed to win, and it wasn't long before our beds were infested once again with the little devils. As well as this, we all became lice-ridden, and the only way to combat this discomfort was to strip off and embark on a hunt for eggs and the creatures themselves within our clothing. On a rotating basis we would pass through the delousing showers and have our clothes fumigated but again, this was another losing battle and, as the population of the camp soared, access to these services became fewer. The fact that we had pinched the coal ration (and could hardly return it) didn't help — we had effectively cut off our collective nose to spite our collective face. Our physical condition deteriorated as the year wore on, and even news of the Allied invasion of Normandy wasn't able to cheer us all that much. We were still a huge distance from our countrymen who were fighting through the hedgerows of northern France, and our liberation seemed a long way into the future. People were becoming desperate and morale was at an all time low, even amongst those who had remained strong and positive up until then. As far as I could see, there was only one realistic option that was open to me. I discussed this with Steve Powell and he was in agreement, and despite all the associated risks, we decided to pay a visit to the escape committee. After speaking to them, we were given permission to plan our departure from a camp which was becoming more and more chaotic, miserable and dangerous every day.

The plan was relatively simple. We were to change identities with soldiers who were reluctant members of a work commando. As I mentioned earlier in this chapter, there was no shortage of such people and, in due course, I ceased to be Flight Sergeant Tom Lancashire from Manchester and became Private W.L. Hutchings of 13, High Park, Knowle, in the city of Bristol. We duly met and traded our identities, briefing each other on our lives so far, schools attended, family make-up and service career. The commando was due to depart within the week so there was a great deal to take in in a relatively short space of time. As to where we would end up on this commando, that was anyone's guess. Coal mining and farm labouring were the two most common occupations for the likes of us, but there were plenty of other potential options.

Two days later our commando, consisting of ourselves and eight others, was called out and Steve and I assumed our new identities. We began by being placed into a departure hut to await our transport to our unknown destination, staying there for two nights without the luxury of bunks and doing little else other than keeping the resident rats and mice company. At 04:00 on the morning of the third day, we were roused from our deep sleep and introduced to our two guards before heading off to Mühlberg station in order to catch a local train which deposited us at a town named Torgau. Here we were divided up into three separate groups in order to be sent to different locations to work. Thankfully, Steve and I were kept together and joined by a fellow "private soldier", forming a party of three. We then boarded another train at Torgau, which took us to Bitterfeldt where we were introduced to our future colleagues, who included New Zealanders captured at Tobruk, Britons captured at Dunkirk, South Africans captured in Egypt and Canadians captured at Dieppe — a very cosmopolitan group which now numbered about thirty but only included we two clandestine members of the Royal Air Force amongst all of the "brown jobs".

We now found ourselves in the railway marshalling yards at Bitterfeldt. I recalled that we had once spent a night there in a siding en route to Mühlberg while RAF bombs fell all around us. Our task was to maintain the railway tracks which passed through the vicinity, and we were housed in a single hut surrounded by a barbed wire enclosed compound. This hut was reasonably roomy and furnished with the usual bunks which allowed us plenty of personal space. There was a tap with running water, a toilet block which was just as luxurious as the one in the camp, and a small cookhouse which was staffed and run by ourselves — mainly those who were recovering from illness and injury and had been placed on restrictive duties. Although the food was provided by the Germans, it needed to be heated up and made into the sort of soup that our captors seemed to love feeding us. There was plenty of black bread available and often we would be provided with other "delicacies" in order to supplement our diet — it was always palatable if sometimes unidentifiable. There were the occasional Red Cross parcels but, for the reasons I have already mentioned, these were becoming few and far between.

The railway consisted of a steel track bolted to sleepers which had been laid on top of a base of crushed rock. Over a period of time the rails settled and compressed the rock, thus sinking down and becoming uneven. Our main job consisted of lifting the track, replacing the ballast and levelling it out again, after having fitted new pads between the steel rails and the sleepers beneath. These pads helped to reduce the noise level which was produced whenever a high speed passenger mainline train passed over them. On the national German rail network the rails were bolted to the wooden sleepers using steel shoes. The large nuts that were used here had inevitably rusted and corroded over time, and had virtually welded themselves to the bolts, making them extremely difficult to undo by conventional means. The Germans had tried to get around this problem by producing a large, electrically driven wrench. This piece of machinery was so large and unstable that two men were needed to operate it. As my rotten luck would have it, I was one of the two men assigned to this thankless and godforsaken task. My partner was a six foot tall, 250lb Romanian labourer. I find it very difficult to explain exactly what it was like having to operate that beast of a machine. Taking just one nut off produced the sensation of being shaken to the point of death, with every joint in my body feeling as though it was coming apart at the seams. My Romanian colleague was helpless with laughter at my plight but eventually the German foreman became aware of the problems I was having and shouted at the Romanian to instruct me properly in my task before the machinery killed me. He taught me that the secret to using this mechanical monster was simply to hold it in place while the bolt was loosened, rather than trying to force it myself. This made life a great deal easier for me, but in all reality this should not have been a job for a malnourished prisoner of war with a then paltry physique.

The following day we found ourselves working on the section of track that passed through the railway station itself, and which constituted the main passenger line between Berlin and Leipzig. We had raised the portion of track that we were working on, supported by jacks which were positioned so that we had plenty of time to lower them when an express train was due to pass through. However somebody somewhere had miscalculated and soon it became apparent that a train was approaching. Full scale panic broke out as we dropped everything and worked flat out to lower the track in time to avert disaster. As the train entered the far end of the station we scattered, leaving the last remaining jacks still in place. The foreman, assisted by an extremely courageous South African POW, remained on the tracks and between them they just managed to remove the jacks with seconds to spare. It is possible that the momentum of the train would have simply pushed the jacks out of the way, but there was the equal possibility that the train could have derailed, with catastrophic results. Added to that potentially gruesome outcome was the fact that we may well have been accused and convicted of deliberate sabotage, in which case we would have all ended up facing the firing squad. This was not exactly a pleasant thought, and we felt extremely grateful towards our South African saviour. As the train shot through the station and past me at high speed barely a few feet away, I remember that my reaction to this terrifying situation was to scream at the top of my voice, as well as shouting all the obscene words I could think of in order to try and balance the transient air pressure on my eardrums. I was briefly reminded of my youth back in Manchester when, as a twelve year old, I went on a day trip to Crewe station which was about thirty miles away from Denton, and on the LMS (London, Midland and Scottish) Railway network. The sole purpose of this trip was to see the high speed train *The Mancunian* pass through the station at a great rate of knots. The main platform area at Crewe station was covered by a great glass canopy thereby forming a very large tunnel. As the train approached the station, heading towards London, the porters busied themselves with the task of hustling people and baggage back from the edges of the platforms. When the train passed through, with its whistle blaring, it pushed all the air ahead of itself, creating a suction effect as it passed out of the "tunnel". This suction was entitled "The Doppler Effect" and to have experienced it was considered by my generation to have been one of the greatest thrills on earth. Having said that, I can't truly say that I was entirely thrilled by my ordeal in Bitterfeldt, and I decided there and then that the sooner Steve and I carried out our escape the better.

We started by concentrating on working out the routine of the camp. The morning roll-call took place at 05:00 hours every day, when the guard would unlock the hut's only door, having first removed the steel bars that held the shutters in place. Everyone had to fall in outside for a head count, with the result reported to the duty sergeant. There then followed a hut inspection, before we were dismissed to have breakfast and to prepare to start work at 06:00. The evening routine was more or less the same, but in reverse, concluding with the guard closing the window shutters, placing the steel locking bar in position, then entering the hut, calling everyone to attention and carrying out another head count. He would wish everybody goodnight and then leave, securing the door behind him. We were informed that these procedures were repeated each day, seven days a week, although on Sundays we would not be required to work. The barbed wire fence that surrounded the camp was ten feet high with wire strands at six inch vertical spacings. These strands were then secured to horizontally spaced wires twelve inches apart. Each intersection of the vertical and horizontal was secured with a piece of twisted wire, and the fence was hung between poles ten feet apart. It appeared that the minimum distance to a "safe" shadowed area outside the compound was about twenty five feet and then it was another hundred feet on to the road which led away from the marshalling yard. The whole area was illuminated by a single searchlight which was left on all night.

The principle of escaping from here seemed relatively easy — all we needed was a plan. The first thing to consider was that we would have to untwist the wires that fastened the vertical and horizontal strands, and create a hole big enough to allow a man to pass through. This would have to be achieved before the day of our departure and in as unobtrusive a way as possible so as not to alert the guards to its existence. Then on the evening of our escape, someone would have to wait in the latrine until the guard had passed, watch him close the hut window and secure it with the steel bar, then remove the steel bar from the window once the guard had entered the hut, before following him inside in time for the roll-call. Once this had been completed, the plan was for the guard to leave, locking us into the hut and then securing the compound. Obviously it was essential that he did not see that the steel bar had been removed. We decided that the best night to go would be a Saturday, since the roll call did not take place until 10:00 on our solitary day of rest, which would give us an extra few hours to get clear of the compound. Added to this was the fact that many of the guards would be enjoying a Saturday night out and, therefore, be less likely to be on the alert for escaped prisoners of war.

The next Saturday Steve Powell and I were given countless presents of chocolate and biscuits from our fellow prisoners, and it was decided that once our escape was discovered, the remaining prisoners would "reluctantly" tell the Germans that we were planning to head south towards Switzerland. In fact we had decided to head due west to try and reach the Allied lines in France, but any diversion would be welcome. It had snowed heavily, which did not really fill either of us with joy or enthusiasm for the long cold trek ahead, but we decided that we were going to go whether we liked it or not. In actual fact, the escape went like clockwork. The guard had not spotted that the bar had been removed and neither had the carefully constructed hole been discovered. Getting out onto the road proved to be a simple task and soon we were on our way westwards out of Bitterfeldt. After we had walked about two miles we saw that we were being approached by a small group of POWs who were being accompanied by a guard. It was too late to take any kind of evasive action and the only option was to "brass it out". As the party marched past us, we said "Gute Nacht" to the guard and saluted him. He returned the salute in a

176

half-hearted way and otherwise ignored us, doubtless wanting to get his charges back so that he could go out for a night on the town with his friends. We had been walking for about four hours without incident before we decided that the time was right to leave the road and strike out across the snow-covered countryside in order to try and reach the railway line that we knew lay to the south. Walking through the deep snow made progress difficult, but after a while we intercepted the railway tracks and walked along them until we reached a workman's hut and went inside in order to keep out of sight and debate our next move. This hut also contained a telephone, and all of a sudden it began to ring. We guessed that perhaps somebody had seen us walking along the tracks and that the best move we could make would be to get out of there quickly and find another hiding place away from the railway. Having said that, cover was hardly in abundance and all that we came across was a nearby hedgerow. We tried to conceal ourselves within this but it was not comfortable and sleep was impossible. Added to the discomfort was the fact that it had begun to snow again and that dawn was rapidly approaching. We didn't have very much time to get ourselves more permanently out of sight. However in the distance I could make out the silhouettes of a couple of haystacks, and we both agreed that these would be ideal — apart from anything else we would be kept extremely warm. We immediately made tracks for them — with "tracks" being the operative word here. As we trudged across the deep virgin snow, it never dawned on either of us that we were effectively giving every German in the area a map with our location marked on it in red pen. We were both sleeping very soundly when I was woken up by the sound of voices in the distance, but getting closer. Cautiously we peered out but discovered that we had been surrounded by a large group of assorted country folk armed with pitchforks, spades and, in the case of one individual, a shotgun.

This was no time to play the hero. I knew when I was beaten. So with our hands up in the air, we said (in our best schoolboy German): "Guten Morgen mein Herren." The man wielding the shotgun replied with: 'Ja, Ja, alles ist kaput. Kommen Sie mit uns, bitte.' Having given ourselves up, we were then escorted to a small village nearby which consisted of a number of houses backed onto each other in the shape of a quadrangle, and housed in a small local jail which probably had not been used for a very long time. I guessed, by the smell of the place, that pigs had been its most recent tenants. After a short while a local Nazi official arrived, resplendent in his brown uniform, and we were briefly interrogated about where we had come from. We were then fed, watered, and put back in the jailhouse.

Some time later there was the unmistakeable sound of aircraft engines in the sky above the village, and a number of B-17 Flying Fortresses could be seen through the window, passing overhead. This had the unpleasant knock-on effect of all the local kids emerging and throwing stones at the jailhouse, shouting and swearing at us in very vicious sounding German.

This carried on until an old man appeared and chased them away. At about 19:00 hours we were moved into a building that formed part of the local dairy, which seemed to be a great deal more secure than the jail had been. We were given food, water, and bedded down for the night. However perhaps "bedded down" would not quite be the appropriate expression here, as we had the choice of either sleeping on the cold, wet, hard, concrete floor, or on wooden beams about eighteen inches high, a foot wide and eight feet in length. In both cases we would have the resident rats for company. Having been POWs for over a year both Steve and I were well used to rats, but these were something else. They were genuinely as big as cats, well fed, and extremely curious as to who we were. Needless to say this curiosity on their part had the effect of keeping us awake most of the night.

The dawn brought relief, and also brought the appearance of a guard from our work commando whose duty it was to escort us back to Bitterfeldt. He wasn't exactly pleased with us as he had been one of the guards on duty when we had escaped, and none of them had yet managed to figure out how we had managed to get away. Our fellow POWs had been most unhelpful, and this attitude had clearly wound the Germans up even more. Our guard looked as though he was ready to smash his rifle butt into one or both of our faces at the slightest provocation, so we decided that the best way to placate him would be to explain how we had managed to pull it off. When we arrived back at the compound everybody was at work and to our surprise we were ordered to carry out our duties in the kitchen rather than join them on the railway tracks. They obviously didn't want to let us out of their sight as the next day we were taken to Bitterfeldt to face our punishment for the offence of escaping. The Wehrmacht captain who presided over our tribunal was surprisingly sympathetic to our plight as we told him about the hardships that we faced and the poor diet that we suffered, and that all we had been trying to do was bring this to the attention of the Red Cross authorities in Switzerland. We really laid it on thick, with the result that we were only sentenced to two weeks solitary confinement on bread and water and after our release would be taken to another location to continue working. I was expecting that this new location would be a coal mine at the very least.

There were many foreign forced labourers in Germany at this late stage of the war and they were often housed in blocks built in the grounds of the factories in which they worked. These quarters had a secure internal area used to contain any workers who found themselves in trouble with the authorities, and it was into one of these areas that we were placed for the duration of our two week stay. It was clean and dry and had comfortable bunks for sleeping on. We were each given two loaves of bread on entering and told that this was all we would have to eat for the next fourteen days, but that we could have all the water we required. The guards in such places had all been invalided out of front line service, and many had missing limbs. One of my guards had lost an arm and he would regularly visit me after his sergeant had done the rounds in the evening. He spoke English and would give me the odd cigarette and we would chat about the war. He told me that if we carried out certain chores around the factory compound, then we would be entitled to extra rations which were supplied by the factory workers and usually consisted of hot soup and more bread. Unsurprisingly we both managed to take advantage of this offer and, coupled with our regular contact with our guards and the factory workers, we succeeded in making a mockery of our sentence, much to our delight.

Having served our time, we were duly collected by a more able-bodied guard and transported by passenger train to our new destination, a small medieval town called Zorbig, which lay some fifty miles south of Berlin. At this stage we still didn't know what our new working environment would be, but far from slaving away in a coal mine as I had expected, our commando (consisting of ourselves plus six South African POWs), was merely required to perform menial tasks around the town, such as chopping firewood, maintaining air raid shelters, cleaning the local school and sweeping the pavements. We were housed in a redundant dance hall that had been closed in February 1943, after Hitler's decree following the defeat at Stalingrad that there would be no more dancing in Germany until the war was won. This hall consisted of a large dance floor at street level, surrounded by a balcony above on the first floor. Rooms branched off from this balcony and we used a number of them as our sleeping quarters. The building itself was situated adjacent to a large hotel with which it shared a quadrangle shaped courtyard. Horse troughs within this yard comprised more than adequate washing facilities, and there were plenty of toilet facilities within the hall. Our rations consisted of the usual vegetables, plus plenty of bread and whatever else came our way, and these were prepared for us by an elderly German lady. It wasn't exactly cordon bleu cookery, but the food was warm, nourishing and edible, and that was what counted. Not everybody agreed with me though. On one occasion, one of the South Africans took exception to what had been placed on his plate and shouted out: "Not this bloody f . . . ing shit again?" However the elderly German lady must have acquired from somewhere a working knowledge of the English vernacular, because she replied with: "Mama versteht, Mama versteht, bloody f . . . ing shit, Mama versteht." As can be imagined, this broke the tension somewhat.

All things considered, life in Zorbig was proving to be rather pleasant, to the extent that Steve and I decided to continue being army privates until the end of the war. However the German authorities were having none of it and one morning, during roll-call, we were both told to fall out and report to the guard commander. It seemed that our little secret was out and we were informed that we would be charged with changing our identities and returned to Stalag IVB to face the music, with our counterparts making the journey in the opposite direction. However this discovery on the part of the Germans may have actually saved our lives. After the war I learned that the peaceful, delightful town of Zorbig had been the recipient of a full bomb load which a crippled B-17 had jettisoned while en route to Berlin. Our former commando had been among the casualties, and both of the privates with whom we had changed our identities had been killed outright. Such is the hand of fate.

We were initially taken to Torgau where our thumb prints were checked in order to confirm that we definitely were Flight Sergeants Powell and Lancashire, and then it was on to Stalag IVB to take the consequences of our actions. On our arrival we were both placed into solitary confinement and allowed to see a representative from the British contingent who gave us each chocolate and cigarettes before telling us that in due course we would both find ourselves appearing before the German authorities. This might take a while, but we would have to serve out whatever punishment was handed down before returning to normal barrack life. Before too long, we both found ourselves in front of yet another court martial presided over by a Wehrmacht captain, and given a second scrupulously fair trial before being awarded a further stretch in solitary confinement — three weeks on bread and water. I was getting rather used to this.

Once again, my time in solitary was made a great deal easier than it was supposed to be. Our fellow POWs had bribed the guards to smuggle items from Red Cross parcels into our cells, and we were allowed out on a daily basis to exercise. We were still not allowed access to books and were not allowed to talk to one another or anyone else, but there were no restrictions on keeping the vocal chords exercised by talking or singing to oneself. The cell block was well heated and before the end of our three week stay we were allowed a nice hot delousing shower before re-entering the main camp. It was now late November, and things within the camp had not improved. However we had been able to spend an invaluable period outside the wire and had achieved our stated aim in being able to escape, albeit only for a short period. Our health had not suffered at all — in fact I felt better than I had for a long while — we had met lots of new faces and seen lots of different places, and generally enjoyed every minute of our time away from the camp. Even though the winter had more or less arrived without any immediate prospect of victory and release, I felt as though our escape had provided me with a new lease of life to assist me with the ordeal of coping with the harsh months that 1945 was bound to bring.

We returned to the same barracks that we had been housed in before our departure, and life within it was not any different either. Red Cross supplies had dwindled down to almost nothing due to the intensive bombing campaign by the RAF and USAAF which had left the German transport network in tatters. As the Americans flew during the daylight hours, we would regularly witness their huge box formations passing over the camp, often being engaged by Luftwaffe fighters as they did so. These scraps were spectacular and, on one occasion, I can remember a B-17, which had been repeatedly hit, dropping out of the formation. It was soon surrounded by scores of fighters, eager to finish it off, and the Fortress cut a pathetic figure as it staggered about the sky, eventually smashing into the ground some two miles away and exploding in a fireball. I had seen two parachutes open, and a third survivor managed a delayed opening only a short distance above the ground. Ironically he landed only just outside the camp entrance, to shouts of encouragement and welcome from my fellow prisoners, and surely setting a new record for the shortest time spent on the run.

I also remember the day a fight took place right over the camp itself involving an American P-51 Mustang and a Focke-Wulf 190. The 190 pilot was desperately trying to out-dive his pursuer and this resulted in their both ending up almost at ground level, with the bullets from the P-51's guns spraying the camp. The two fighters disappeared out of sight and I never did find out who won that particular encounter. Air activity in the locality of the camp increased dramatically in the last six months of the war when Allied fighter-bombers roamed the area looking for targets of opportunity. Although Red Crosses were displayed upon the hut roofs these did not always guarantee us the protection we deserved and many prisoners were killed by what is now termed "friendly fire" or "collateral damage". The Canadian wireless operator in my last crew, Samuel Ramsden, was one such casualty. All seven of us survived being shot down that night, as it later turned out. The skipper, Flight Lieutenant Covington, and the rear gunner, Sergeant MacKnight, managed to succeed where Steve Powell and I had failed and made it back to England to resume the fight, both surviving the war.

The rest of us became POWs but, on 22 April 1945, barely two weeks before the end of the war, Ramsden was killed when a roaming RAF Mosquito tragically mistook his POW column for German troops on the march and strafed the barn in which they had all taken cover, causing multiple casualties.

By now we were all speculating like mad as to when the war would finally be over. The camp wasn't as overcrowded as it had been in the past, mainly because we had missed the huge influx of Italians and the thousands of Polish women who had been captured during the Warsaw Uprising in August. All had been quickly processed and shipped out to various destinations. These prisoners had been segregated from the rest of the inmates, but their very presence caused the temperature within the camp to rise rapidly, with the result that their transfers had been rushed through by the Germans in order to prevent a possible riot. The failure of Operation Market Garden to bring about a hasty end to the war also guaranteed a new batch of prisoners through the gates of Stalag IVB, and many of these were arriving at the same time as Steve Powell and I were released back into the camp. Amongst these new boys I was able to find two young lads from my home town of Denton, Private Arthur Edwards of 51, Hyde Road and Private Arthur Williams of Beach Avenue. We chatted about people and places we all knew back home but it wasn't long before, as privates, they were moved off into work commandos and I never did get around to looking them up after the war, so I don't know whether or not they made it home. They made me feel very old and responsible — after all by then I was a gnarled old veteran of twenty-four. The daily coal ration was reduced from 75 kilos per half barrack to 25 kilos and, as a result, we ended up with virtually nothing at all to heat the barracks. There was barely even enough to supply the cookhouse and it wasn't long before this ration eventually ran out. The commandant gave his permission for work details to leave the camp and search for wood and windfalls in the nearby forests but, with trigger happy Allied aircraft patrolling the area, it was safest to stay within the compound, so there weren't many volunteers for these working parties.

In mid-December the Nazis played their last card in the west and began a massive armoured offensive through the Ardennes Forest in Belgium, with the intention of carving through the Allied lines and retaking the port of Antwerp, thereby decimating the Allies' supply route. The troops that bore the brunt of this assault were raw young Americans who were fresh out of the United States, and the Germans encountered little difficulty in overrunning them and taking large numbers of prisoners. We had been kept well informed of the military situation and we knew that many, if not all, of these unfortunate men would end up staying with us in Stalag IVB. In the meantime, however, we had been preoccupied with trying to organize and arrange morale boosting shows and celebrations for Christmas. It wasn't easy, as we only had enough stockpiled Red Cross parcels for one between sixteen, but nevertheless variety shows were organized in the same vein as those we had staged the previous year. The poor Russians were in a dreadful state by this time, and unrest began to foment within their compound. This resulted in the Germans locking them in their barracks, and one night the Russians showed their contempt for our captors with a concentrated display of noise — shouting, stamping and cursing — which seemed to get louder and louder until the guards had had enough. Dire threats of retribution had no effect, and so large, fierce police dogs were brought up and pushed into the barracks, presumably to cause and spread fear and confusion. However these dogs never re-emerged, and all that could be found the next morning was their skins. Even their bones had vanished, as the starving Russians fell upon them and tore them to pieces. We speculated as to whether or not the same thing would have happened to any guard who had ventured inside.

The first trainload of prisoners from the Ardennes offensive arrived at the camp within a few days, and just in time to swell our ranks prior to Christmas. Thousands were to follow in a steady stream over the next week or so, and before too long there were no bunks for them to sleep in. They arrived with only the clothes on their backs and a more dejected bunch I have never seen. They had not long been out of training and for many of them this was their first taste of war. They had arrived in Europe convinced that Germany was on her last legs and all that lay before them was an easy progression to Berlin and victory. In a flash they had been overwhelmed and suddenly they found themselves prisoners of war in a country that was finding it difficult to feed her own people, let alone the thousands of foreigners that she was now obliged to care for. The Red Cross report on the welfare of the camp, dated 5 February 1945, spoke of the poor physical state of the Americans, and their high mortality rate, caused by:

> The debilitating condition in which men arrive at the camp due to long marching, inadequate food and water, and inadequate shelter. A typical example is that of the column which Capt. McKee accompanied; they marched a total of sixty miles in three days, the ration for the entire time being one third of a loaf of bread per man, and one bucket of molasses per 100 men. Most of the troops arriving here have spent 48 to 96 hours in a box car with no heat or straw, very little food, no water, and no facilities for defecation or micturition. (WO 224/12)

The old hands immediately began to attempt to reorganize the barracks in order to accommodate these new arrivals, and we were forced to "double-up" in order to free up bunk space. This was not so much of a hardship as it may have seemed as many of us had been doing this for a while to try and compensate for the lack of heating. Since the new prisoners had nothing at all, possessions were pooled and shared out in unsuccessful attempts to try and cheer up the newcomers. The vast majority of them just sat there with blank looks on their face, whilst others were in tears or simply muttering to themselves. One of their sergeants, a far more experienced soldier, told us that his charges had been even worse during their trip to Mühlberg in the freight wagons. Quite how we got through that first night I'll never know. I don't think that I slept at all. All I can remember was hearing the sounds of these young boys calling out for their mothers, weeping, praying and clambering aimlessly around the barracks. Fortunately I had doubled up with Steve Powell so I was spared the sheer torture of having to sleep with one of these devastated young men. The next day was Christmas Eve, the poignancy of which seemed to make it even worse for our new arrivals. The Red Cross parcels were now even more diluted but at least they were a token and sharing their contents about did at least give us all a sense of giving and a reminder of the spirit of Christmas. As had happened the previous year, the camp resounded to the sound of thousands of men singing *Silent Night* and other carols, but the atmosphere was much more tearful and subdued than it had been in 1943, and very few of the new prisoners could be brought out of their deep depression.

With Christmas over and done with, the German authorities began to speed up the processing of the new arrivals, but we would be well into January before we would see the last of them, and their prolonged stay had caused a fair amount of trouble within the camp. The most serious issue had involved the problem of racism, as plenty of black GIs had been captured in Belgium along with their white counterparts, and the

Germans treated them all as Americans regardless of the colour of their skin. This mean that they were not segregated, and the inevitable happened with race riots breaking out — usually instigated by the white soldiers. The Germans were completely oblivious to the causes of this discontent and delegations were ordered to appear before the commandant in order to explain to him what was going on. He simply could not understand the racist attitude of the white soldiers — which was touchingly naïve given the policies his country had been putting into practice for the past twelve years — and proclaimed that there would be no segregation policy within his camp. However in order to keep the peace he would allow anyone who did not wish to share barrack space with the "other side" to live outside for the remainder of his stay. With deep snow covering the ground, and sub-zero temperatures chilling the air within our lungs, this offer was not taken up. However the whites aptly demonstrated their disdain for their black countrymen by choosing to sleep together in a huddle on the brick barrack floor, thus passing up the relative luxury of the bunks, and giving the rats of Stalag IVB plenty of night time company.

The other issue that caused problems with the prisoners was the old chestnut of theft. Our new arrivals were, of course, ignorant of camp etiquette, and did not realize that stealing from their fellow prisoners was regarded as the cardinal sin by the rest of us. Each prisoner was automatically issued with a cigarette allocation, whether they smoked or not and, as tobacco was the chief currency in the camp, the non-smokers found themselves in a desirable situation. Their cigarettes could buy them almost anything, within reason, and they were a jealously guarded commodity. It didn't take long before the more sticky-fingered element of the newly arrived American contingent began to get into their stride and things started to go missing, including the precious cigarette stocks. However a POW camp is not the sort of place where it is easy to conceal things and before too long the guilty parties were exposed and called to account. The standard punishment in these circumstances was a beating, and the message obviously got through to the new arrivals because although the matter was never officially raised or spoken about, the pilfering ceased and things calmed down once again.

It wasn't long before the camp authorities began to sort out and organize the new arrivals, and those eligible were dispatched to form work commandos, providing us all with a great deal more breathing space. However one particular incident stuck in my mind in relation to this. The night before he left, a black GI stood up in our barracks and made a little speech to us in which he thanked us for our kindness towards him and his fellow black prisoners. He added that he was disgusted by the attitude shown by his white countrymen and that he would never forget how badly they had behaved. In the meantime, the cold winter weather got worse and worse, and food became scarcer and scarcer. The local aerial activity, which had provided us with so much entertainment, dwindled to almost nothing as the Luftwaffe's losses increased and the Allies gained control of the skies. Red Cross supplies dried up completely due to the, by now, relentless attacks on the German rail infrastructure and although in February some parcels reached us having been brought in by road, it was nowhere near enough to make our lives any more comfortable. With Germany on her last legs and tottering fast, all we could do was sit tight, try to keep warm and fed, and await our liberation. Our war maps kept us up to date, and the BBC news kept us informed. It seemed as though the Russians, who were already inside Poland, had opened up a massive offensive aimed at crossing the border into Germany. This objective was successfully attained within two weeks and, in late February, the western Allies began their own push into the Rhineland along the whole length of the front and soon they were consolidating on the west bank of that mighty river. We were naturally keeping a closer eye on the Red Army's progress towards Berlin, as it seemed as though Mühlberg would be lying directly in their path if they continued on their present course.

We began to see Soviet reconnaissance aircraft in the skies above the camp, and I assumed that they were spotting just ahead of their main forces. They obviously knew we were there because occasionally they would pass over the camp at low level and the pilots would acknowledge our cheers and waves by waggling their wings. In early March the Remagen bridgehead over the Rhine was taken and held by the Americans, whose vast armies poured across it and encircled the Ruhr conurbation before heading towards Berlin. Further north, the British were planning an airborne crossing of the river, and the Soviets were making steady progress towards Berlin from the south and east. Because of our position in a "corridor" which stretched from Berlin to Dresden, we were effectively caught between the two sides. This "corridor" contained the only north-south running railway line in the eastern part of Germany — a tempting target indeed for the fighter-bombers which were now roaming at will. Soon it became too dangerous for any rolling stock to move during daylight hours, so the Germans built sidings leading into the surrounding forests where trains could be concealed and protected during the day. One of these sidings ran adjacent to the camp, and one day a prowling P-51 Mustang, flying at almost ground level, spotted an ammunition train which had been hidden on this siding. Presumably the pilot radioed for rocket carrying P-47 Thunderbolts to come and take it out, because a short while afterwards these aircraft appeared and one of them scored a direct hit on the ammunition containers. The train virtually disintegrated, and debris rained down on the surrounding area which, in this case, meant the camp compound. Tragically there were a number of fatalities amongst the prisoners. I particularly remember seeing an axle, with both wheels attached, smashing into a barracks block and killing several unfortunate men within — a terrible thing to happen considering all that they had gone through to survive up until that point.

As March wore on, the American daylight bombers began to return in greater numbers and once again there were plenty of dogfights overhead for us to watch. However by the end of the month, the Luftwaffe had seemed to all but disappear and the B-17s and B-24s met with little opposition as they flew on to Berlin in support of the Soviet advance. We had no idea where the western Allies were but, by the start of April, we knew that the Red Army was very close. The commandant considered it his duty to evacuate us all away from the potential battle zone in which we were sitting and began to discuss the matter with the senior POWs. Unfortunately the situation was far from ideal, with heavy fighting to the east and west, not to mention the predatory fighter-bombers up above. There was no transport available to us except our feet, and in the end the decision was made to stay put and "brass it out". This we did until the rainy morning of 23 April when, with dawn breaking and the sounds of battle resonating all around the camp, we realized that the guards had vanished. A few hours later, a small party of Cossacks on horseback appeared at the camp entrance and informed us that we had been liberated by the Red Army. However this announcement was coupled with a dire warning that there was still plenty of fighting in the area and that if we ventured outside the wire then we would be shot on sight without any exceptions to that rule.

Life in the camp suddenly became very different following our "liberation". The Cossacks left almost as quickly as they had arrived but not before they had rounded up all of the Russian prisoners within the camp and set them marching eastwards towards their homeland. However since Stalin had decreed that any Soviet soldiers taken prisoner were little more than traitors, there were no joyful homecomings waiting for these poor men, only the gulags and the firing squads. We had not been given any extra food and we were not allowed to leave the camp in order to go foraging, so all that we could do was to stay put and await the arrival of the support troops that we had been told were on their way. The electricity supply had dried up and there was no fresh drinking water available. All we had to sustain us was the camp's supply of potatoes and beets. Things didn't look good.

In the meantime, groups of German refugees began to show up at the camp, having been driven from their homes further east by the rampaging Red Army. These were mostly the elderly, together with women and children who literally had nowhere to go and nobody to help them. The women were in particularly bad shape as many of them, regardless of age, had been repeatedly raped by their conquerors. The camp padre gathered his flock together in order to try and do what he could for these people, but there was not a great deal of enthusiasm present on anybody's part as far as helping a bunch of German civilians was concerned.

A few weeks previously, and unbeknown to us, forward units of the Russian and US armies had in fact made brief and limited contact at a place called Strehla, a few miles south of the camp. However it was only some time later that a staged link-up took place at Torgau, with propaganda film crews from both armies on hand to record the event for posterity. The encounter at Strehla was kept in the background and then airbrushed out of history. There were very good reasons for this. Strehla was a small ferry crossing point on the River Elbe, and shortly before the arrival of the American patrols, the Russians had come across a horde of German refugees attempting to cross to the western side. They had put the ferry out of action and then fallen upon these defenceless people and slaughtered hundreds without mercy, regardless of who they were. It would not have made good propaganda to have shown the link-up amid the scenes of carnage.

By 26 April support troops had arrived at the camp to organize the POWs but, by that stage, many prisoners had gone outside the wire in order to forage for whatever food the surrounding countryside had to offer. It is amazing how easy it is to ignore danger and how quickly the survival instinct takes over, if one has had no food for a few days. The main aim of the Red Army was still to prosecute the war and our comfort and welfare came a very poor second to this. The support troops did not bring any rations with them, and the situation continued to be made worse by the steady flow of refugees who sought safety with us in the camp. Before too long they were immediately being turned about face and sent away again. With no drinking water available, a rapidly deteriorating sanitation system, and a severe lack of food, the situation was heading towards catastrophe. Already huge fights were taking place in the surrounding countryside between groups of prisoners searching for food. I remember seeing a fight break out over a large pig which had been found and slaughtered, with prisoners carving huge chunks of meat from the carcass and eating them raw in their urgency — with the inevitable result that they quickly fell ill. There were many other examples of people acting like wild animals in the course of the desperate hunt for something to eat, but thankfully a few days later the Russians finally provided us with limited rations. They then impressed on us again that they hadn't yet made the area safe and that now they had supplied us with food we were forbidden from leaving the camp on pain of death. This was all well and good, but they had omitted to issue us with drinking water, so the need to leave the camp was as great at that point as it had ever been. There were still pockets of Germans fighting on in the vicinity, and the trigger-happy Russian soldiers guarding the Elbe ferry crossings had been ordered to shoot anybody who was attempting to get across the river. The smell and sight of death was everywhere.

By 30 April, a group of us had decided that we would risk the dangers and head west to try and link up with the Americans. The only direction that we could initially head in was north, since Strehla was to the south and we knew all about the fate that would await us there if we showed our faces. Eventually we reached a ferry crossing at a village called Belgem. This was also guarded by the Russians but the area was a little safer than further south and the soldiers were not quite so jumpy. The ferry itself was over on the west bank of the river, and this fact encouraged some people to continue north to try and find some intact bridges at Torgau. A few others and I decided to stay put in Belgem, at least until we had searched the town to see what we could find that would be of use to us. It was almost deserted, with the vast majority of the population having fled westwards across the river towards the American lines. Later that day I heard gunfire on the west bank of the river, and this turned out to have come from a Jeep borne American patrol. Shouting across the river to them, we explained who we were and asked them to send the ferry over to pick us up. This they did, much to the initial surprise of the Russian guards, who hadn't got a clue how to deal with the situation. Before too long, however, they realized that they too had finally linked up with their American Allies and in the joyful confusion, we were able to slip across the Elbe and into somewhat more friendly territory. The GIs welcomed us and handed out packets of cigarettes before advising us to head west and keep our eyes open for any renegade German units. They couldn't really do much else for us as, like the Red Army, they were still very much in the middle of fighting the war, and we were prancing around in no man's land getting in their way.

We immediately set off west from the river in order to put as much distance as possible between us and our Russian Allies. We soon reached a large, well maintained farm which backed onto a huge quadrangle. Dead animals lay all around this quadrangle and we all considered this to be rather strange since the Russians hadn't yet passed through the area, A quick search of the house revealed the answer to this mystery as we found the body of the farmer, who had presumably killed all his animals before ending his own life. Perhaps we had underestimated quite how much the German population feared and hated the army that was closing in on them from the east. The cellar was full of home prepared food that had been stored away, but strangely, none of us could bring ourselves to touch it. We moved off and stopped for the night in a deserted village, bunking down in the abandoned post office building. In the morning we went out foraging for food and came across a number of chickens, who proved to be extremely elusive. Eventually we managed to catch one of them, but at least our abysmal performance was compensated for somewhat by the discovery of a number of eggs.

Our little group carried on west towards Leipzig, and before too long we came upon a farmhouse which was being besieged by a number of slave labourers who had freed themselves and were bent upon taking their revenge against their former masters who were holed up within the building. The smell of death was everywhere and bands of POWs and forced labourers were roaming around, having armed themselves and were taking great delight in killing almost anything that moved, almost for the sheer hell of it. There was a great deal of pent up rage, hatred and frustration in the air. We left the besiegers to it and carried on until we reached a small town called Schildau, which was more or less intact with the majority of the population having stayed put. Other bands of POWs were also roaming around and were searching houses for loot and also in many cases, for women to rape. There was a nasty atmosphere in the town and we decided not to hang around too long. We met up with another forward American patrol, and the GIs told us which was the best road to take out of the town, but warned us that the River Mulde was ahead of us and that it wouldn't be easy to cross it since all the nearby bridges had been destroyed. We didn't really have a great deal of choice so we thanked them and pressed on, after first having taken possession of some freshly baked loaves of bread. We reached the river at a place called Wurzen where, as expected, we found that the bridge had collapsed into the river. However all was not lost as the lower spans were all pretty much in place, and it was possible, albeit with difficulty, to traverse them just above the waterline. We were hampered somewhat by the crowds of terrified elderly refugees who were having a great deal of difficulty clambering over the spans, but eventually we reached the other side and, having acquired some abandoned bicycles, picked up the Leipzig/Dresden autobahn.

Before too long we arrived in the city of Leipzig, which was little more than a heap of ruins. It had been the target of sustained RAF attention since the resumption of raids on Germany the previous summer, and the boys had done their job well, to the extent that it was almost impossible to move within the city. We soon realized that we were getting nowhere fast, so the decision was made to turn about face and bypass the place before continuing westwards. Once again we picked up the autobahn and headed north-west towards Halle, which we had been told had been garrisoned by

American troops. After cycling some distance along the motorway, I heard the sound of gunfire up ahead and we stopped, uncertain of what we had come across. The shots were coming from a overpass some distance away, where a number of German soldiers were sniping at anyone approaching them along the autobahn. We were without weapons but other armed groups who had suffered casualties took off and managed to outflank the defenders, who were duly shot. It was only then that it was discovered that the "soldiers" were little more than schoolboys who had found rifles and decided to "do their bit" for their Fatherland, with predictably fatal results to themselves and the few others that they had managed to take with them.

Now that this obstacle had been eliminated, we were able to continue unimpeded towards our destination. As night fell we sought shelter in an abandoned factory situated in a wooded area just off the autobahn. It appeared as though this factory had been involved in the production of Junkers jet engines, and by some miracle it was completely undamaged. We discovered an old fire truck and spent a good few hours trying to get it to work, but unfortunately a group of French forced labourers who were also seeking shelter had already laid claim to it by removing and hiding the ignition rotor arm and distributor cap. We gave up and climbed back on to our trusty bicycles the next morning, heading once more for Halle.

However as it turned out, luck was on our side. We encountered a number of American soldiers in 2½ ton trucks who had been dispatched along the autobahn in order to try and find stragglers and POWs like ourselves and before too long we found ourselves in Halle. The place itself was a typically medieval German town, which had suffered extensive bomb damage but was not ruined. We were billeted in an old warehouse, deloused with DDT and given clean underwear and our first proper meal for ages. This consisted of tinned American "K" rations, white bread which had the consistency and appearance of soft cotton wool, ice cream, real coffee and plenty of cigarettes — not exactly the meal that I had dreamed about during the harsh and hungry winter in the camp. We remained in Halle for a few days while awaiting transportation further west, and therefore had the opportunity to explore the town at our leisure and try to get used to the idea of being free once more. The town had, as its centrepiece, a beautiful park with a large lake within it, and a number of swans, geese and ducks lived on and around this lake. These wonderful creatures were being casually used as target practice by bored GIs who had nothing else to do except waste the ammunition with which they had been issued. To my war weary eyes, these idiotic soldiers merely resembled loudmouthed high school students. An officer and a sergeant were yelling at them to desist and behave like disciplined soldiers but these youngsters merely ignored their request, laughing and shouting obscenities at them. A sad state of affairs.

After three days, we were taken by truck to an airfield at Merseberg and put on a C-47 Dakota transport aircraft bound for Brussels. Once in Belgium we were again deloused with DDT, allowed to have a hot shower, and given more clean underwear. We were then required to register and therefore confirm our status as surviving prisoners of war before being officially put on standby for repatriation to England.

So finally, on 18 May 1945, ten days after the end of the war, I found myself on board another C-47 as it took off from Brussels and headed over the Channel towards England. By coincidence, we landed at RAF Upper Heyford, the very same airfield that I had left in 1941 at the start of my training as a flight engineer. It was almost as though things had turned full circle on me, and after nearly two long years of evasion, captivity and escape, I finally stepped back onto English soil for the first time since 11 August 1943.

The irony was not lost on me that when I had volunteered to become a flight engineer four years previously, it had only been in a temporary capacity for a period of no more than six months. This was the length of time that it was estimated would be required in order to train new recruits for the role, allowing we pre-war regulars to revert to our ground crew duties. Looking back, it is quite clear that I should have known better, and taken heed of the old motto — "Never Volunteer." Still, despite all of the trials and tribulations I had been through in the intervening four years, I had somehow managed to survive, more by luck than judgement. With hindsight I can't help thinking that the lack of planning shown by the failure to train sufficient numbers of recruits as flight engineers, resulted in the loss of many highly and expensively trained airmen. We were promised that we would be able to resume our roles once these new flight engineers had been made operational, but this state of affairs never materialized and, in my opinion, in the long term this amounted to nothing more than a total waste of the backbone of the Royal Air Force.

CHAPTER
SIX

Peacetime and into Civvy Street

So, I had arrived back home in dear Old Blighty at exactly the same airfield which I had left back in 1941 to embark on my flying career. My fellow ex-prisoners and I were immediately given railway warrants to various Personnel Receiving Centres (PRC) dotted all over the country where we would be given medical examinations, re-inducted into the Royal Air Force, issued with new kit and generally smartened up. After all, the war wasn't quite over yet as the Japanese were still fighting on in the Pacific and plans were afoot to send a large Bomber Command force to assist the Americans with their strategic bombing campaign. Steve Powell and I were sent to No. 106 PRC at RAF Cosford, near Wolverhampton, where it was confirmed that I was fit for a quick return to active service. I was given a period of home leave and told that I would receive my orders during this period. I had been reclaimed by the Royal Air Force once again.

I found that just moving around at leisure in a free society was an extremely strange experience and, following my incarceration, I found the abundance of females most unsettling. Just finding the right things to say and the right way to say them was extremely difficult, and the first few days back in England were something of a trial. The trip home to Denton was to be the ultimate test of my sanity, but I was lucky in that my "partner in crime", with whom I had shared most of my experiences over the past two years, would be accompanying me for most of the way. Steve Powell was a Liverpudlian and he would be changing trains at Crewe in order to catch his connection home, and as we sat on the LMS train as it headed north out of Euston station, the butterflies in my stomach refused to be still. We talked and talked about our feelings and we both agreed that it seemed unreal to be able to travel freely without the company of a gun-toting German guard. By the time we got to Crewe and said our farewells, we had agreed that Steve would take our "imaginary guard" with him towards Liverpool and try and get rid of him on the way. This may seem strange but after two years of incarceration there were still plenty of ghosts knocking about and this was our way of exorcising them.

So, for the first time in years, I was totally on my own. We had been told to send telegrams to our families to inform them that we would be arriving home sometime in the late afternoon. My train duly arrived at London Road station, Manchester, and I stepped onto the platform which was thronging with servicemen in almost every uniform you could imagine and their weeping relatives who were enthusiastically welcoming them home. Unfortunately there was nobody there to welcome me, so I slung my kitbag over my shoulder and headed out into the street to try and find a number 19 tram to take me home to Denton. Unfortunately it was the evening rush hour and the queue at the tram stop was enormous. Nobody seemed all that keen to allow an airman with his full kit to get on ahead of them and it was only with the help of a burly female conductor that I managed to get on at all. Even then I had to stand until halfway when some of the seats became vacant and I was at last able to slump down gratefully. I began to take an interest in my surroundings as the scenery became more familiar. We passed through Ardwick, West Gorton, Belle Vue and Reddish, all of which appeared to have escaped the worst of the bombing and seemed similar to how they had been in pre-war days. As the tram entered Gorton, the only noticeable change I could make out was that the golf clubhouse now consisted of a pile of rubble. It had been the recipient of a stick of jettisoned bombs from a struggling German bomber back in 1940 but, as far as I was aware, these were the only bombs that Denton had received during the course of the war — I don't remember hearing about whether there were any casualties from this incident.

When the tram reached Seymour Street, I disembarked and stood for a moment looking down the street towards my home. Not a soul was in sight as I slowly walked the two blocks to number 53, pausing from time to time to take it all in. Suddenly I found myself standing outside the front door and, after taking a deep breath, I knocked, pushed the door open, and went inside, shouting "Is anyone home?" I was confronted by my tearful mother who welcomed me back with a hug, before leading me into the kitchen and putting the kettle on, in traditional English fashion. Nobody else was at home — Dad was at work, my brothers Albert and Douglas were away in the Army and Navy respectively, and my sister Joyce was with the WAAF. My other sister, Elsie, had married in 1940 and was living nearby with her husband and their new baby. Having said that, my arrival didn't seem to have that much of an effect on them and I had to visit their house rather than the other way round as it appeared as though they were much too busy. I did pop round to see my new nephew, but Elsie was still in the "protective mother" phase and I was only allowed to admire, and not to hold.

Later that evening, once the flick house had closed, Dad returned and welcomed me home with a firm handshake and "It's nice to see you back, son". In the meantime the neighbours had periodically begun to drift by to pay their respects, I began to feel that at last I was back at home sweet home. I spent the following days visiting people and places. I went back to my old school, Audenshaw Grammar, where I had a long chat with my old headmaster, who actually listened to me for a change and said that I should write a book. Mother insisted that I should go and see our Methodist minister, Reverend Keely, who listened to my story and then declared that God had indeed watched over me. It had been arranged in my absence that I would act as best man to the groom at the forthcoming wedding of Brenda Rothwell, as the Rothwells were a big church family. I was expected to say a few words at the reception, but I honestly can't remember what I came out with. I do remember that my speech wasn't all that well received, with a distinct lack of applause. I later heard that Brenda had had her marriage annulled once she had realized what would be expected of her as a wife. Mrs Rothwell blamed me for some reason and went around telling everybody that I had put a "hex" on the union. What kind of a place had I come home to? I started to get extremely bored and irritated by people and things around me. One day, I was sitting alone in the parlour when Dad came in and sat down. He told me that although I appeared to be under the impression that everyone and everything had changed, this was not the case and that I was the one who had changed.

Thankfully, my movement orders arrived in the post. Firstly, I was to report to MI9 in London in order to be debriefed about my time as an evader in France and Belgium and then, on 4 October, I was to travel to my new posting at RAF Bishop's Court in Northern Ireland. By now the atomic bombs had been dropped and Japan had surrendered, but I was still a regular serviceman and would not be demobbed until I had completed my agreed term of service. RAF Bishop's Court by the coast underneath the mighty Mountains of Mourne, was a now-redundant wartime air navigation and air gunnery school. It was reached by taking the train from Euston up to Stranraer on the south-west coast of Scotland, then a short ferry trip across the Irish Sea to Larne on the Irish coast. Once there, I had to take a ride on the Belfast and County Down railway to the nearest station at Ardglass. This railway was narrow gauge and everything about it was Lilliputian, including the stations, carriages and engines. It was 90 per cent single track with by-passes at the various stations so that the north to south trains could wait until the south to north trains had gone past. The whole arrangement was extremely casual — if one of the drivers saw a pal of his who was a little late in getting to the station with his churns of milk, he would just sit tight and wait, regardless of passengers and timetables. Having said that, the trip around the coast was extremely beautiful, and well worth the little Irish idiosyncrasies that accompanied it.

The accommodation at Bishop's Court was basic, consisting of Nissan huts which were almost located right on the seashore. This meant that seagulls were in abundance, and would noisily remind us of their presence early each morning, from their perches on top of the huts. Autumn was now turning to winter, and the weather was getting bitter, with cold winds whipping in off the Irish Sea and interminable rain. I was never without my mackintosh for the entire time that I was at Bishop's Court. The only centre of civilization that was within walking distance of the camp was Newcastle, a small fishing village. The main hub of the village was a pub which seemed to have been plucked straight out of the Middle Ages. The floor was earthen, with spittoons, and one long bar ran the whole length of the room. On this bar top were secured, by chains, several pewter tankards. The only brew that was served there was Guinness stout, which was pumped from huge vats which stood against the back wall of the pub. You could also get what was officially termed "whiskey", but was in fact a clear, colourless liquid with the kick of a mule. Such was the nightlife on offer for those of us stationed at Bishop's Court.

There were plenty of other ex-aircrew there and, of course, all had senior NCO rank. This made it rather difficult for the existing senior NCOs, used to yelling at and disciplining lowly airmen, to maintain discipline amongst those who were almost equal to them in rank, and who had seen plenty of action over enemy territory. I was the only ex-Brat fitter there, so my "reward" was to be placed in charge of the more unruly men who were awaiting demob and who were becoming rather restless. There was no flying at that time, and the station's Avro Ansons were all up for airworthiness inspection. The main test of these aircraft's serviceability was to inspect the main spars of the wings by piecing them with an ice-pick to see whether any water oozed out. If it did, then the wings were classed as Category E, and put up for scrap. After a good few years outside in the cold County Down drizzle, this was the fate that befell many of them, and the discarded wings would be stacked behind one of the hangars. Here they constituted a perfect breeding ground for rats, which caused us a number of headaches — the main one being how to get rid of them. A local vet got to hear of our problem and recommended the services of a local "ratter", who turned up with the tools of his trade: a number of Yorkshire terriers and a couple of ferrets. The ferrets would squeeze into the tight spaces and narrow gaps, and flush out the rats. The terriers would be waiting for them and one bite per rat was all that was needed before it was on to the next one. It didn't take long for the rat population of Bishop's Court to dwindle down to almost zero and at last the sensible decision was taken to burn the rusty wings, something that should have been done a considerable time earlier.

This was about the most exciting thing that happened to me during my time in Northern Ireland. I hadn't been overjoyed about being posted there in the first place, and after a while I began to complain that as an ex-POW, I was entitled to a posting much nearer home, as per the regulations. In due course I was told that I would be posted back to England, to No. 16 Maintenance Unit at Handforth, near Wilmslow in Cheshire. It was just before Christmas 1945 and, as I was to find out, the journey home wasn't exactly going to be easy or comfortable. Once again, the Larne/Stranraer car ferry beckoned and as this was to be the first post-war Christmas, there would be a huge number of servicemen heading home for leave. The boat was absolutely packed and, typically, the December weather was dreadful to the extent that the captain had considered cancelling the crossing before eventually deciding to risk it. The ferry itself was hardly the most luxurious vessel on the high seas and seemed to me just to be a rusty old hulk. Once we got out onto the open sea, the ferry did almost everything bar looping the loop. We were all confined below decks, where everyone (including the crew) suffered dreadfully from seasickness. The smell of stale vomit was terrible and water was breaking over the bows and the sides of the ship before finding its way down below to where we all shivered in the cold. As an inexperienced sailor, I can honestly say that I have never been so frightened in my life, not even when I was on ops over Germany. I began to think about what the Royal Navy and Merchant Navy must have gone through in the North Atlantic, in weather worse than this, for days on end, and I mentally took my hat off to them. Two and a half hours after leaving Larne, we finally reached the calmer waters of Loch Ryan and everyone began the process of cleaning up before we docked at Stranraer and climbed gratefully on board the waiting London-bound train. We had all gone through three hours of hell but at least I had the consolation of knowing that I had brought with me a lovely fat turkey for our Christmas dinner, the first that my family had seen for ten years or more. A very happy Christmas was had by all in the Lancashire household that year.

Life at Handforth took on pretty much the same pattern as it had at Bishop's Court, complete with the similar problem of bored and restless aircrew personnel awaiting demobilization. Attempts were being made to keep them occupied, but regular servicemen like me who held aircrew rank but were also prewar fitters were given positions of responsibility. I was placed in charge of a site which prepared surplus propellers and other parts for eventual disposal. Everything was assumed to be scrap metal and was placed up for public auction. Some site commanders, usually ex-aircrew officers, recognized a good thing when they saw it and would "tip off" bidders when certain items came up for sale. My immediate superior was a flight lieutenant who was the son of a local farmer. He advised his father to purchase a number of large wooden boxes, made from 6 inch wide tongue and groove, for 10/- a box. He had ensured that each box was packed full of tongue and groove boards equivalent to fifty extra empty boxes. Other scams included lead being labelled and sold as iron and Packard Merlin aero engines which were sold as mixed scrap metal, together with a "complimentary" tool kit which was worth far more than the engine itself. The engines were supposed to have been smashed up with sledgehammers prior to being sold, but the clever use of bribery meant that these orders were easy to circumnavigate. The amount of money that the government must have lost in the sale and disposal of surplus war materials must have run into millions of pounds, but I never heard of anyone being prosecuted for being involved in such scams — I had always thought officers were supposed to be men of honour.

One of the main advantages of working at Handforth was that I was able to live at home and commute to work daily by using local trains and buses. However this comfortable existence came to a sudden close when, without warning, I was posted to No. 39 Maintenance Unit at Colerne, near Bath. This was where Lancasters, Horsa gliders and assorted miscellaneous aircraft such as Miles Magisters ended up immediately prior to being scrapped. As at Handforth, there were many other cons and scams in operation, with the largest and most important concerning petrol. All the aircraft which were flown in for disposal contained residual fuel in their tanks. These were siphoned out, placed into 5 gallon drums and found their way onto the black market. Petrol, of course, was rationed and remained so until 1950, so a great deal of money was made from this "forgotten fuel". By this time I had acquired a new motorcycle — a 500cc Calthorpe — with a sidecar attached, and I would use this sidecar in which to transport these fuel drums and salvaged lead acid batteries from the scrapped Horsa gliders. These also became useful black market commodities and I remember that at one stage so many of these heavy batteries were stacked on the storage hanger floor that their weight caused a complete collapse of the concrete.

I had arrived at Colerne on 24 June 1946. On 20 October that year I was informed that I should never have left Handforth, and was immediately sent back to Cheshire. It turned out that this was to be my last ever posting within the Royal Air Force as I remained there until my final discharge. During my second stint at Handforth I reverted back to being a Fitter 2 and was reduced to the peacetime rank of sergeant. I was puzzled by this and compared my service record to those around me, drawing the conclusion that I should at least be holding the rank of flight sergeant. One of my colleagues had an identical service history to mine but a greatly inferior record, and I reckoned that my past brushes with authority at Wyton and Waterbeach were finally catching up with me.

Although I had let it be known that I would be leaving the service in September 1949 when my time ran out, on 26 October 1948 I was sent on a Planned Servicing Course at No. 2 School of Technical Training at RAF Cosford. Before leaving I went to see my CO and stated my objections to this, including my grievances over my substantive rank. He was very sympathetic and said that I was a victim of circumstances, but also that I had trodden on too many toes in the past. He finished by saying that he could do nothing about it, so I bit the bullet, finished the course and passed it with credit. I also swallowed my pride and took the cut in pay caused by dropping from warrant officer rank, but I was more determined than ever to leave the service and try my luck as a civilian. My CO advised me against this course of action, reminding me of the security of RAF life and the unpredictability of life on "civvy street", especially as I had never worked there before. This was undeniably true, but surely it was a challenge worthy of an ex-Brat, and a 33rd entry ex-Brat at that.

So much for my service life up until that point. However my private and family circumstances had changed rather dramatically during my first stint at Handforth, as I had met a girl and got married. During the war I had followed the example of my former skipper, Flight Lieutenant Parkins, and decided to wait until the end of my operational career before considering taking the plunge. Of course spending the last two years of the war in a prisoner of war camp solved that problem for me. In any case, not long after I had been posted to Handforth, I was invited to a birthday party and was immediately swept off my feet by the birthday girl herself. Things moved quickly from there, with the result that, at 14:30 on Tuesday 21 March 1946, at the Church of St Lawrence in Denton, I married Miss Dorothy Cordingley. The congregation sang:

Thine for ever. God of Love, Hear us from they Throne above, Thine for ever may we be, Here and in Eternity

We left the church to the sound of Mendelssohn's *Wedding March*. My old bomb aimer Steve Powell was my best man, and off we went to Torquay for our honeymoon where I managed to "hit the bullseye", with the result that nine months later our eldest son Andrew was born.

I'll cover my married life later in this chapter, but for now I'll return to my time at Handforth as I waited to be discharged. On one occasion I managed to get myself put on a charge by the station warrant officer for failing to turn up for orderly sergeant duties. This was because the orders were always posted on the noticeboard in the Sergeants' Mess, but as I lived away from the station I very rarely went into the Mess as I had little reason to do so and I hadn't seen the orders. The warrant officer was well known for his dislike of aircrew and I soon found myself up before my CO.

Thankfully, my CO was an ex-aircrew man himself and he quickly dismissed the charge, before informing the warrant officer that in future it would be his duty to notify the orderly officers in person. Doubtless that went down well.

During my last few months at Handforth I was involved in a road accident when my motorbike was in collision with a refuse truck on the way in to work. I managed to nurse my machine through the gates but the medical officer took one look at me and sent me down to Cosford to be x-rayed and to have the chips of loose bone in my right elbow manipulated back into place. Of course this meant that I needed time to recover, which ate nicely into my remaining few months in the service. On 24 August 1949, I was posted to No. 101 PDC at Warton, where the paperwork required for my discharge was put together, and where the formalities were completed. The final release officer signed me out, having read what had been written on the page of my release book where recommendations are made to potential future employers and then, for some reason, tearing up the book and replacing it with a brand new one. I was a bit annoyed that it was never even noted that I had been a "Trenchard Brat", but on 23 September 1949, having swapped my uniform for a complimentary civilian suit and hat, I walked out of Warton, a thirty year old husband, father, inexperienced civilian and free man, with the rest of my life to live.

Now I have to turn the clock back again in order to cover the way that my domestic and marital arrangements developed since the first few months following my return to Britain in 1945. For the previous few years I had looked forward to being a married man and I had always wanted to have at least four children — spending two years as a prisoner of war gave me plenty of time to reflect on such matters — and once I had met my bride-to-be I was glad to discover that she had absolutely no objections to my dreams of a large family. Dorothy Alice Cordingley was the daughter of Cyril and Ethel Cordingley of 43, Kendon Grove, Denton. Her father was a delivery driver for Robinson's Jam and her mother was the local insurance agent, so all of her good and bad points were well enough known by everybody locally. During the war both Dorothy and her father had been in the auxiliary fire service, but their time spent in the service had not been particularly arduous: their unit had been on standby during the Manchester blitz in the autumn of 1940 but had not been called upon, and they told me that most of their time had been taken up with playing cards. The courtship was fast and furious — so much so that one evening Dorothy's parents came home unexpectedly early and found us in something of a compromising position on her bed. Our explanation that we were just trying to get to know each other better cut no ice with them.

I discussed my forthcoming marriage in some detail with my parents, who were also well aware of Mrs Cordingley, but were not altogether that impressed by my future mother-in-law. They knew nothing about Dorothy's father except to say that Dad did recall seeing them both in the dock at the local magistrates' court but couldn't remember why they had been there or what the charges had been. However I had made my mind up and was not to be put off by anyone. Dad said that he hoped that I realized that when you married a girl you also married her entire family, lock stock and barrel, but this pertinent warning went in one ear and out the other. I was determined and nothing was going to stop me. At the time I was stationed at Handforth and living at home, as was my sister Joyce, who had been demobbed from the WAAF. During the war, as did so many young English girls, she had met an American and had recently become engaged to him. His name was William Walden, and he came from Atlanta in the state of Georgia. Joyce planned to emigrate to the USA to live with him and although they did not really know each other very well and the general feeling was that she too was inviting trouble upon herself, Dad did take the time to have a long chat with his future son-in-law. Of course she was head over heels in love, as was I, and neither of us was in the mood to listen to any form of parental advice. My elder brother Albert had married while I was a prisoner of war, but this had been to save his girlfriend's honour and this situation went down like a lead balloon with my mother, who was extremely hostile to his wife Minnie from then on. Of course this was mainly because she was concerned about what the Manchester Road Methodist mothers' circle would think of her and her family. It completely escaped her memory that during the Great War, she had found herself in a similar position to Minnie when she found herself expecting

Albert out of wedlock. This fact, together with Mother's attitude, eventually resulted in a bitter feud between Albert and herself which was never resolved and even when she died in 1974, Albert refused to go to the funeral. The only one of the Lancashire children who was not now living at or very near to home was my younger brother Douglas, who was still with the Royal Navy as a submariner, although believed to be making his way home from the Far East.

Neither Joyce nor I were paying any rent during this period, but one day Dad took me to one side and informed me that money had become rather scarce and that he would have to ask Joyce and myself to start contributing to the housekeeping. He explained that before the war he had put everything he had got into his New Central Cinema, which had reopened just in time for the start of hostilities in 1939. For the first six months, things were good and takings were healthy, but costs began to rise once government regulations were introduced which stipulated that a fire warden had to be present on the premises at all times. His projectionist was then called up and he had to take over the job himself. Mother was pressed into service in the ticket booth, and before too long Dad began to sleep at the cinema in order to act out the role of Fire Warden during the night. As the Luftwaffe began to target Manchester in late 1940, the building was hit by a number of incendiary bombs but, thankfully, the area was largely left well alone and no damage was done. Then to cap the whole thing off, takings started to fall away as the war began to bite home and people had less money to spare. Added to this was the fact that the local people were finding it difficult to keep warm during the winter weather, so as many of these were Dad's friends and customers, he would open the doors of the cinema to let them in for nothing once the evening performances had started: not so that they could watch the films but so that they could keep warm for a couple of hours. As a result he could not afford to support a couple of freeloaders, and we were quite rightly shamed into starting to pay our way.

When the war started, I began to send a proportion of my pay home to Mother in order for her to put into a Post Office savings account that I had opened. This was so that I could build up a little nest egg for when the war ended, which was when I planned to get married. After I returned home from Germany I discovered that most of the money in the savings account had gone and I was initially extremely angry, jumping to the conclusion that Mother had frittered it away on herself. In actual fact, my parents had been extremely hard up during the last few years of the war and my savings had kept their heads above water. I was deeply ashamed of myself to have thought that my parents would have needlessly spent my savings on themselves but, in my defence, I was so far removed from reality during my time in Germany that I would never have known just how bad things had become at home.

After Dorothy and I had got married, we lived for a while with her parents at 43 Kenton Grove. From my point of view, the house was relatively luxurious. It had a separate bathroom with hot and cold running water, and two small gardens at the front and back. It was one of the semi-detached houses that were built in the 1930s which cost £300 and could be secured with a down payment of £25. My in-laws, who did not have that sort of money in those days, had borrowed the money for the deposit from Dorothy's maternal grandmother, on the proviso that she would come and live with them. However the home that they created for her was most unpleasant, and the old lady had soon had enough and moved out. She died just after the war's end, and with her died any obligations that the Cordingleys had towards her, with the result that the house subsequently became theirs. Their joint income was not great, and not long after I moved in with them the decision was taken to sell the house and set up in business themselves. With the money raised from the house sale, a down payment was made upon a house and shop in Llysfyn, a small village in north Wales. This was a wonderful opportunity for them in a beautiful setting, but the property had been much neglected during the war and required plenty of refurbishment and modernization. My skills were also required when it came to servicing the old Jowet delivery van which had been included in the sale. All orders from the shop were delivered free of charge, and if the van was not running it would result in irate customers and lost business. The van had a two cylinder air-cooled engine, a chain drive, and solid rubber tyres. It had been the type used by the various tea companies in the immediate post-Great War period and, although the engine was of sound working order, the other parts were quite rotted and decayed. I spent all my spare weekends and all my leave away from work grappling with this piece of machinery just to try and keep it roadworthy. My move to north Wales had made it impossible for me to commute from Handforth, but my workshop training at Halton stood me in good stead for making working parts during the week with the material that was widely available and I used to smuggle these out of the camp in my motorcycle sidecar when I left on Friday afternoons, and fit them over the weekends.

Unfortunately the atmosphere at home was not good and deteriorated quickly despite all that I was doing for them. My father-in-law was quite a lazy man, and didn't feel inclined to pull his weight as he seemed to consider that "work" was an infectious disease. This led to all sorts of rows and recriminations and it became obvious that before too long Dorothy and I would have to find somewhere else to live. On 14 December 1946, at Nant-y-Glyn Nursing Home, Llysfaen Road, Colwyn Bay, Dorothy gave birth to our eldest son, Andrew. The arrival of a baby who cried all day and all night did little to soothe the troubled atmosphere at home. Dorothy had had very little experience with babies, but my mother-in-law was a self proclaimed expert and my father-in-law contributed to the whole situation by criticizing everything and everybody. As far as he was concerned, and in his own words, we were: "Stupid idiots who should have had more sense than to start a family", and he pointed this out to us on a regular basis.

During this period my mother had been using all her contacts to try and secure us a new prefabricated house but unfortunately demand was far in excess of supply. She did manage to get me onto the waiting list, which was a feat in itself. In the meantime, my wife announced to everybody that she was expecting once more. This news marked the end of our time in north Wales as we were virtually kicked out of the house. Fortunately my sister Elsie offered to take us all into her home, and on 10 December 1947 we arrived back in Denton, with Dorothy eight and half months pregnant. Two weeks later, on Christmas Eve, she gave birth to our second son at Gee Cross Maternity Home. We named him Stephen and I remember spending the whole of Christmas Day in the maternity home with my rapidly expanding family. In mid-January 1948 things started to look up for us as my name came up trumps on the housing list and we were offered a house and immediate occupancy. I immediately hired a lorry and driver in order to transfer all of our belongings from north Wales to our new home in Denton. When the driver and I arrived at the shop, we loaded the lorry up without any help from the in-laws, although presumably in their relief to be rid of us they did stretch to a drink, a sandwich, and a "goodbye", and they did ask after their daughter and grandsons. We then returned to Denton and settled into the new house, with the help of Elsie and my mother. This was the house that I returned to after being demobbed on

23 September 1949, the date of my thirtieth birthday. It was the first type of house supplied under the Labour government's subsidy programme, and consisted of a semi-detached 3 bedroom two storey dwelling. It was built at minimum cost but it did provide us with a good sturdy roof over our heads, albeit with minimum extras, and I was very glad to get it even if Dorothy did consider it a step down from what she was used to.

My first priority was to find work. My entire life savings of £500 had been lent to my in-laws to help get them started with their business, and the Lancashire cupboard was pretty bare. In preparation for leaving the Royal Air Force I had taken advantage of an existing educational programme called EVT (Educational Vocation Training). If you successfully completed the training, then the cost and initial outlay was refunded to you. I took a course called Machine Drawing and Design, which was more or less a rehash of what I had learned at Halton, and completed it quickly and without any problems, so as a result I was given a certificate which confirmed that I was now a graduate of the Institute of Engineering Design. My initial forays into the labour market were unsuccessful and I began to run out of contacts. Things were looking decidedly uncomfortable when all of a sudden, a neighbour told me that he had seen an advertisement for draughtsmen with an aeronautical background and experience in detail drawing. The company concerned was English Electric, and the vacancies were at their drawing office in Warton in Lancashire. I immediately sent off a CV and obviously it impressed them enough to call me forward for an interview and a test. The interview part went very well, and it was clear that my time as a Halton apprentice did impress them, not least because the interviewing panel seemed to know what one was. The test required me to draw a detailed part that they showed me. Mr Crowe, the chief draughtsman, said that he could see that I had had little drawing experience since I had managed to get the projection the wrong way round. However he agreed to give me a three month trial as a junior trainee draughtsman to see how I coped with the work and at the end of this period my progress and position would be reviewed and, if it was satisfactory, rectified.

My Halton training soon showed itself and I progressed rapidly. To assist me with my new profession, I enrolled in the night school at Preston Tech, in order to gain National Certificates in engineering. By the time the three month probationary period was up, I was coping with intermediate drawing without the slightest problem and was allowed to look at minor problems that were occurring on the factory floor. Over the next year I found a place in Preston for the family and me to live in, as I was finding it a struggle commuting from Denton each weekend, and my schooling was taking up all my spare time. Unfortunately Dorothy was not happy living in Preston and there were some unpleasant things said about how I had dragged her down to my level. In the meantime her parents had sold their business at a tidy profit, and had moved into a pleasant middle class area nearby, where they had bought a large semi-detached house.

This did mean that I was repaid my loan of £500, naturally without any offer or mention of interest. My position at English Electric was now stable as the company had received the contract to design and build the Canberra bomber, which was now in the delivery stage. As well as that, another important contract was won, that being to design and build a fighter which would eventually take to the skies as the enormously successful Lightning. Although my responsibilities had increased, my pay had not caught up and I began to feel undervalued. I repeatedly voiced my frustrations to Mr Crowe but his reassessments never seemed to arrive and were constantly being put back. Something had to give.

By now it was approaching Christmas 1950, and one day my attention was drawn to an advert in the newspaper which offered posts in Canada for draughtsmen. I was extremely interested in this opportunity and applied immediately. On 31 December I was called for an interview and thankfully was able to impress the interviewer to such an extent that I was offered a post there and then with the Avro company at Malton, Ontario. I was told that I would have to pay my own way over there, but that I was guaranteed a job on my arrival. This was a boom time for Avro in Canada, as the company had taken over the wartime Victory Aircraft Company facility and had recently won a contract from the Royal Canadian Air Force to design and build a new jet fighter aircraft. As well as that, Avro was busy producing a new jet engine, and the prototype of the world's first civilian jet airliner was nearing completion. I was told that it was expected to make its maiden flight in the next few days. It all seemed like a dream, and when I discussed it with Dorothy I was surprised to discover that she was very much in favour of going. It appeared that some years earlier, her aunt and uncle had emigrated there and her family had been due to follow but the outbreak of war had scuppered their plans. There was more good news, as my in-laws were running low on funds and had taken a live-in position looking after two elderly ladies, so there was plenty of room for Dorothy and the boys in north Wales. I would establish myself at work and find us all a place to live and then when the time was right, they would come out to Canada and join me. In view of the problems and objections that we had been forced to put up with in the past, it was difficult to take in the fact that everything was going right for a change. I returned to work after the Christmas holidays and, with all the paperwork being sorted out, I tried to arrange a passage to Canada. For four months I badgered the shipping lines until finally, on 23 April 1951, I received notice from Thomas Cook and Sons that a berth was available on the SS *Franconia*, which was bound for Quebec. The ship was due to leave Liverpool on 27 April and so I immediately accepted the offer and paid for the trip in full, before handing in my somewhat truncated notice to Mr Crowe at English Electric. This had the effect of him offering me an immediate pay rise and responding to the complaints I had made over the last year or so, but it was too little and much too late. My mind had been made up.

In the meantime my passport and the necessary paperwork had been obtained and correctly stamped, and I had packed my case. I was ready to go, and early on the morning of 27 April I said goodbye to my wife and children, picked up my case and walked to Preston railway station, where I caught the Liverpool train. I had no trouble finding the Cunard wharf and I was soon aboard the SS *Franconia* and safely ensconced in my steerage berth. We pulled away from the dock and into the Mersey estuary amid the usual fanfares, and finally I was on my way. I had £5 in my pocket and the guarantee of a job when I arrived at Malton. My new life was about to begin.

With it being April, the weather in the North Atlantic was anything but calm, and like many others I soon began to suffer from terrible seasickness. The *Franconia* had been a troopship during the war but had now been completely refurbished and improved, and was actually quite luxurious. The food was wonderful, but unfortunately my sickness meant that I wasn't able to enjoy it as much as I would have liked. After five uncomfortable days the ship entered the Gulf of St Lawrence and the waters calmed down significantly. For the first time since leaving Liverpool, people started to show their faces and the dining rooms noticeably filled up. Before too long, we docked at Quebec and, after making my way through Customs and Immigration, I boarded a sleeper train bound for Toronto. On waking up in the morning, I discovered that we had arrived and had been shunted into a siding to await the arrival of a more sociable hour. It had been arranged that my wife's aunt and uncle would meet me at Toronto station. These were the relatives who had emigrated just before the war, and I was to stay with them until I had settled in and acclimatized. This I did and I must say that I was made to feel extremely welcome. I had finally arrived, and I had a whole new experience to look forward to at Malton. I could hardly wait.

CHAPTER
SEVEN

My New Life

After a few days spent acclimatizing in Toronto, I decided that the time had come to take the plunge, and I made my way to the Avro plant at Malton, where I was received with open arms. I was put through a stringent medical examination, which I passed without any problems, before being immediately accepted and inducted into the company. I was then introduced to a project engineer named Bob Lindley who assigned me to a structures design group so I could begin my duties as a draughtsman. I settled in and found that I had no difficulty with the workload, although I did find it strange that there were no entry orientation lectures for new employees such as myself — I was merely given a booklet which contained information about working at Avro, and government leaflets that contained advice and assistance for brand new immigrants. I found that the attitude towards the job was completely different to that which I had experienced in a British design office. Every individual was encouraged to put forward his ideas on exactly how a design project should be tackled. The management listened to you, and full consideration was given to your ideas, regardless of what they were.

More importantly, if your suggestions were implemented, you were given full credit for them. In the English Electric Company, the plaudits would invariably be snapped up by some project manager or chief draughtsman, but here it was much easier to obtain promotions on merit. I soon advanced and wasted no time in picking up my college education from where I had left off. I was certainly enjoying my time in Canada, and I was progressively given more and more responsibility as time went on. This rise in seniority was reflected in regular salary increases, and before long I was given the position of senior design draughtsman and tasked with ironing out the production glitches on the new CF100 jet fighter. I was starting to come to the notice of the senior engineering management team and things were looking good for me.

There was also plenty of overtime on offer, so I was able to start saving for the deposit for a new house, and at the same time send the surplus money home to my wife. The Canadian government had introduced a scheme whereby those who worked in the defence industry could apply for a mortgage at a very low rate, as long as a 10 per cent deposit had been paid. Within twelve months I had managed to raise the required sum and I had begun to save for my family's passage across the Atlantic. In the meantime I had laid down plans to have a new house built in the nearby town of Streetsville and, as the building work progressed, I gave my wife the go ahead to book tickets for herself and the boys, advising her to arrive as near to the end of August

1952 as possible, so as to coincide with the estimated completion date of the house.

However, under pressure from her parents, she took it upon herself to book the family's passage on the SS *Ascania*, which sailed from Liverpool on 15 May 1952, bound for Montreal. This meant that I would have to find accommodation for us all over a three month period and, as funds were extremely tight, I had no option other than to take out a bank loan. This was anathema to me as I have never liked the prospect of debt, but I did not know of anybody who could or would loan me the required sum. Reluctantly, I took out the loan for $1,000 — an enormous amount of money, especially when you consider that my new house was costing ten times that, and that my government-backed mortgage would take me thirty years to repay. My security consisted of my job and my bank balance would regularly be down to nothing at the end of the month, overtime notwithstanding. This was not a very healthy time for me on the financial front but, when my family arrived at the end of May, I was able to get them into the same boarding house in which I was living.

There were to be other expenses too. I had managed to cope without a car since my arrival but clearly this would not be possible now and I managed to acquire an old Standard Vanguard in time to collect everybody from King Street railway station in Toronto. The voyage had been rather rough and uncomfortable, but the boys were in good spirits and very excited to have finally arrived. Their mother appeared to be somewhat less so, and could not seem to stop complaining about almost anything and everything that had happened to them since leaving England. The very sight of my wife made my heart beat like the clappers and after not seeing her for over a year all I wanted to do was touch and hug her. However it was obvious that she did not feel the same way towards me, and when I asked her what was wrong, she replied: "Do you believe that all I had to do was to think about sex?" Naturally this was hurtful and the atmosphere between us became rather tense, but I threw all my energy into my work and reasoned that she must have been under considerable pressure from her parents over the last year. I hoped that things would improve now that we were an ocean away from my in-laws.

Thankfully, we moved into our new house in mid-September, as planned. We didn't have a great deal to put into it at this stage, the only furniture being our beds and an old dining set that we had managed to pick up at a local auction sale. I made some bits and pieces from the left-over lumber, and our new neighbours chipped in with items that they had no further use for. Compared with what we had been used to at home in England, our new house was a palace. It stood in the middle of a wooded acre of land and it contained three bedrooms, a separate dining room, a kitchen/living room and a full basement, all with central heating. We quickly settled the boys into the local school and, with things going well for me at work, the future looked rosy. There was to be a huge cloud on the horizon though, and its arrival was heralded by the delivery of a letter from my wife's brother, Arthur. He was writing to tell us that he, his wife, and their two children had booked their passage on one of the "Manchester Liners", and would be arriving in time to spend Christmas with us. I was astonished. How could this be? He didn't have a job, and his family didn't have anywhere to live? I couldn't understand what was going on, but before too long Dorothy let the cat out of the bag.

Before the war, it seemed that Dorothy's parents had decided to emigrate to Canada but the outbreak of hostilities meant that these plans had to be put on ice. After I had declared my intention to move to Canada they saw this as a great opportunity for themselves, so they told my wife to encourage my ambitions but not to mention their little scheme until we had committed ourselves to the idea. So not only was my brother-in-law's family planning on coming, but also (to my absolute horror) my mother and father-in-law. As of yet they had not booked their passage, but they would not be long in appearing. With that in mind, as well as the fact that we would doubtless be required to provide board and lodging for them all, Dorothy agreed to take a job in a local grocery store in an attempt to bring in some extra money.

Arthur and his family arrived on schedule and we enjoyed a rather crowded Christmas together, but I managed to get through it all in one piece. He had brought with him the expected but unwelcome news that my in-laws would be sailing on the SS *Spinner* in the first week of March and would be arriving before the month was out. So that gave us only three months to find Arthur a job, accommodation for his family, and whatever else it would take to fully house my mother and father-in law. As he had no means of getting around on his own, was completely unfamiliar with his new surroundings, and did not seem to possess any initiative, it was left to me to try and sort him out. I made enquiries at Avro, telling them that Arthur had been an RAF mechanic and assuring them that he would be competent enough to work on the flight line. They granted him an interview, and subsequently offered him a post, subject to a three month probationary period. The job itself wasn't all that pleasant, as it involved working outside in all weathers, and it was not unknown for people to suffer frostbite during the depths of winter. Of course he was not aware of this fact, and I wasn't about to tell him because a job was a job, and it provided us with a chance to get him out of the house. Dorothy did her bit as well, finding them an apartment, and we loaned them bits and pieces of furniture to start them off. Of course with the in-laws about to arrive we had to shell out to replace the furniture that we had lent them. The grim day was upon us — 20 March 1953.

The weather that greeted Dorothy's parents upon their arrival was typically Canadian; bitterly cold, windy and with deep snow piling up around the house. Naturally this caused both of them to moan and whinge incessantly. I did point out that it would have been easy to have waited a couple of months and sailed in the summer, but my opinions fell on deaf ears. In fact it probably wouldn't have made much of a difference anyway and they were both still complaining three months later. My father-in-law had made no attempt to try and find work, and when I broached the subject with him he said that he had supported Dorothy and the boys for twelve months after I had moved to Canada, and that I owed him. Of course the fact that I had sent home monthly financial contributions and parcels of supplies during that year had completely escaped him. I was beginning to feel extremely bitter and resentful and my mood was not improved by the fact that he declared that the Canadian summers were too hot to work in. There were plenty of jobs to do, such as creating a garden, but he never lifted a finger to help. My whole life seemed to revolve around my in-laws and their needs. Even Dorothy, who was normally a staunch defender of her parents' behaviour and actions, began to get fed up with the situation and joined me in urging them to try and find work. As luck would have it, an advertisement had been placed in the local newspaper asking for a husband and wife to keep house for a retired "gentleman farmer". After much persuasion, to my relief they applied for and were subsequently offered the post, even buying themselves a car to help them get around by themselves. It seemed as though things were looking up at last.

However the strained relationship between Dorothy and myself had not improved following the arrival of her family, but now I hoped that we could try and rebuild it into something more meaningful. My job had been going well and there was plenty of overtime on offer, which enabled me to spend plenty of time away from the family home. My wife remained cold and aloof towards me, but my feelings had not changed. I was still crazy about her and the thought of breaking up our marriage never entered my mind. As far as I was concerned it was a matter of "till death us do part", and it was as simple as that. Dorothy remained in daily contact with her parents but she never told me anything of what was being discussed and kept trying to reassure me that everything was fine. However I knew that the main topic of conversation was the possibility of finding another job. The fact that we had our own beautiful new house made my mother-in-law seethe with envy, and ongoing medical expenses began to eat into the meagre savings that they had accumulated, which hardly helped the overall situation. They began to find fault with me once more, accusing me of neglecting my wife and children by spending long hours at work, and of always considering myself ahead of them. Then my mother-in-law came up with the notion that I owed them $1,000 to cover what they had spent on Dorothy and the children during the year that I had been away trying to sort out our new life. This running debt even included the cost of their passage across the Atlantic, which I had paid for in its entirety. I even produced the bank statements to prove this, but my in-laws were having none if it. I talked it over with Dorothy and she said that we should pay them the money, as it would go some way to helping them out and easing the tensions. I saw what she meant, but I couldn't help thinking that agreeing to these outrageous demands would only result in their trying to pull this scam again in the future. Eventually I decided that I would pay, but only on condition that they left us alone and ceased to have any contact with us in the future. To my surprise Dorothy readily agreed to this, and I drove up to the farm and told them of our decision.

A few weeks later, we all travelled up to the Canadian National Exhibition for a day out, and seemingly by chance, we ran into my in-laws. Dorothy and the kids openly hugged them, and I stood there dumbfounded. It appeared that she had contacted her parents the day after our agreement had been made. That revelation spoke volumes, and I found myself being forced to back down. I threw myself into my work in order to try and retain my sanity, and began numerous DIY projects at home. I was always busy with something or other, and I was accused of never having the time to do anything else. That wasn't strictly fair as we did go out to plenty of dinner dances, to functions organized by a local association of ex-Brats, and we had plenty of family picnics and outings. I even told Dorothy that she could plan and arrange any holidays that she wanted, but I will admit that I did keep myself to myself during those months — probably rather more so than was wise to, under the circumstances.

In early 1954, when things finally seemed to be settling down, out of the blue Dorothy told me that she wanted another child. She never really said why, but I guessed that it was either because all of her friends seemed to be expecting, and that she felt a little left out, or that she wanted to have a little girl. I was a little taken aback, especially considering the negativity that she had displayed after the birth of our two boys, but things went as planned, she quickly fell pregnant and our new arrival was scheduled to appear on 6 December. I felt as though the presence of an ally would be a good idea, so I asked my mother to come over for a visit which would coincide with Dorothy's due date. The pregnancy went without a hitch except for the fact that Dorothy became more and more agitated as December approached. Our youngest son was born on the way to the hospital and we named him Peter. Although there had been no complications, when she came home from the hospital after a couple of days, Dorothy was in a foul mood, and all of us, including both grandmothers, had to bear the brunt of her aggravation as she ranted and raved. As far as I was concerned, that was it — we were definitely not having any more children. My mother went home to England and tried to cheer me up by telling me not to worry, and saying that she would soon "get over it". I wasn't so sure. Things were hardly improved by the fact that my mother-in-law seemed to consider that the new arrival gave her carte blanche to visit whenever she wanted, and it appeared as though we were now right back to square one.

However by the summer of 1955 things had calmed down and we were back on a more even keel. Work was going well and I was extremely pleased with the progress that I had made within the company. The world's first jet airliner (the Avro Jetliner), designed and built by Avro, had successfully flown a couple of years earlier and multiple orders had been taken from potential customers. But with the Korean War in full swing and showing no signs of ending, the Canadian government had decided to pull the plug on the entire project and concentrate instead on designing and building military aircraft. We all considered that this change of emphasis was rather strange as Canada was hardly a major contributor to the war effort, and it was obvious that there was a hidden agenda at play here. No real satisfactory reason for the demise of the airliner was ever given, and the matter was simply played down.

A new proposal for an advanced interceptor aircraft had been submitted for evaluation by the Royal Canadian Air Force. In anticipation of Avro being awarded the contract to build the new aircraft, a project office had been created and I had been promised a role within it. This was the chance that I had been waiting for, and I felt that at last I would have a real chance to show what I could (or could not) do. I was subjected to vetting and security clearance checks, but my RAF background ensured that this was not a problem, and I found myself part of a twenty-five strong engineering team, all housed in a secure office. I had been assigned to work on the wing structure, although at this stage the project consisted of little more than a blank sheet of paper. The chief engineer, Jim Floyd, had a picture in his head of exactly what he wanted, but he had no idea whether or not it would be possible to turn this idea into reality, or if the available technology existed which would be needed to meet his requirements.

The aircraft itself was to have an arrowhead-shaped wing, with two engines hung underneath one another on either side of its centre line. All the fuel was to be carried within the wing structure and the armament was to be housed in a compartment between the engines. The cockpit would be situated directly in front of this compartment, together with the as-yet undesigned navigational equipment. The landing gear would be built into the underside of the wing structure, and a vertical fin/rudder would be mounted on top of the wing. This was a classic delta configuration and it was necessary in order to allow for a 3 per cent wing structure — the maximum thickness would not be able to exceed 3 per cent of its chord. This thickness to chord ratio was considered by the aircraft design world of the early 1950s to be impossible to achieve. This made it even more of a challenge for us. The above criteria was to be used as a guideline and after a few weeks of tinkering around with this and getting nowhere, Bob Lindley, who was the project engineer, called us all to a meeting. The essence of what he told us was this; we should throw away all of our books, test reports and findings, because when you were trying to achieve the impossible there was no point in relying on orthodoxy. He told us to start again with clean blank pieces of paper on our drawing boards and to use our own ideas and our own innovations. This advice was both inspired and inspiring and all of a sudden we started to make rapid progress on the project. It was a great feeling to realize that we were challenging established notions and working towards achieving the impossible.

In due course Avro received the confirmation from the Canadian government that the contract had indeed been won. The new interceptor was to be known as the CF105 Arrow. It would meet all the design, production and delivery criteria that we had promised, and would be completely compatible with the latest electronic navigational and armament systems that were being developed in the United States. Further developments were made in order to equip it with the brand new Avro Orenda engines, which were made by our sister company. It truly was a winner in all respects and it was set to put the Canadian aviation industry right up there with the best in the world. Everybody was thrilled and proud to have played a part in the development of this beautiful aeroplane and the future was looking bright. I had also taken on other responsibilities at work, and these allowed me to visit the RCAF CF100 squadrons which were based in Europe as part of the Canadian commitment to NATO. They had been having problems with the wet weather conditions and I was sent there to iron them out. I was treated like a VIP, and for an ex-Brat like myself it was a very strange feeling to find myself dining at the group captain's table.

However following the 1957 general election, a lawyer named John George Diefenbaker was voted into power and took over the office of Prime Minister. He was from the rural wheat producing region of the country and he seemed to believe that Canada's future prosperity depended more on agricultural exports than military technology. The United States was more than happy to supply Canada with all the hardware that she required in order to ensure her national defence, and the Arrow project began to lose support and funding at the highest levels of government. At 11:00 on 20 February 1959, a day that has come to be known in Canada as "Black Friday", I was in the middle of a normal working day when the public address system suddenly and unexpectedly crackled into life. We were told that:

> All contracts relating to the CF105 Arrow have been cancelled immediately. There is no other work available, making it necessary for all personnel to gather up their personal belongings and go home. Your termination papers and final pay cheque will be sent to you as soon as possible. See the news media for details.

With these few words, 14,000 people, including yours truly, had had their lives altered. I was one of the luckier ones, as I had been there a relatively long time and my financial situation was reasonably good. Many others were in debt up to their eyebrows and had relied upon the success of the project to keep the creditors away, and I knew of at least one person who committed suicide as a result of the cancellation.

The shadow cast over the nation as a result of this catastrophe has never really gone away and in Canada the controversies of Diefenbaker's decision are still being debated to this day. There is no doubt that the

Arrow was an absolutely inspired concept and that it could have been one of the greats. In October 1957, the magazine *Aviation Week* gave its opinion on the CF105:

> The Avro CF105 Arrow has given Canada a serious contender for the top military aircraft of the next several years. The large, decidedly advanced delta-wing fighter was rolled out of the Malton plant a few days ago . . . The Arrow's power, weight and general design leave us with little doubt of its performance potential.

There was little we could do about it now. All I will say is that I felt extremely flattered to have been a part of the project office that established the configuration of the Arrow. Under the leadership and tutelage of men like Jim Floyd, Bob Lindley, Guest Hake and Jim Chamberlain, I learned more in months than I could ever have done in decades elsewhere. However now my first priority was to try and find some new employment so that I could secure the financial future for my family. With all this talent now up for grabs, aviation companies in Britain and the United States launched huge recruitment drives. For the time being, my services were still required by Avro as I had been recalled from the Arrow project to continue the ongoing design, procurement and testing of the CF100. However, I knew that this wouldn't last forever but it at least gave me the opportunity to shop around for the best position available to me, and also to try and sell our house. This wasn't going to be easy, as the newly depressed locality was swamped with houses for sale and the best that one could hope for was to find someone to take over the mortgage payments for a $1 transfer fee. My first serious job offer came from the North American Aircraft Corporation, based in Columbus, Ohio. In the meantime I had sat through many interviews with representatives from British aviation companies but I was put off by the general approach that they seemed to adopt. I formed the impression that they were trying to recruit staff on the cheap, by offering the sort of reduced salaries that only the most desperate would be tempted by. I was reminded of the unsatisfactory working conditions that I had experienced ten years earlier at English Electric and this helped to convince me that the best opportunities lay south of the St Lawrence. Not only were the salaries far higher in America, but the companies paid all your moving and relocation expenses. With that in mind, I accepted the offer from North American, and prepared to move to Ohio. We sold our house, unfortunately and unavoidably at a very low price, but on the day before I was due to leave, I received a cable which informed me that the job was no longer available because an important contract had been cancelled. However all was not lost, as in the meantime Avro had taken on a design contract with Lockheed Aviation, which was based at Burbank, California. I was immediately sent down there, so I put all the furniture in storage, found a temporary home for my family and set off in my car to complete the 3,000 mile journey.

Now on such a long trip, one can experience some very interesting moments, especially if one is alone. On reaching the state of New Mexico, bored with the endless highways, I decided to try an advertised scenic route through Walnut Canyon. Near the start of the route, there was a conveniently placed lay-by which afforded spectacular views of the canyon twisting away into the distance, and also of a narrow road winding down over 1,000 feet. The cars on that road looked like Matchbox models, as they twisted and turned on the tight switchbacks. It was a wonderful sight to see the canyon disappearing over the horizon, and then the daunting realization hit me that the same road I that had been gazing at in wonderment was the road I was about to take. I descended through dense forest, seemingly driving for miles along the switchback roads, but in fact only travelling short distances at a time, as the crow flew. At the bottom I emerged onto a desert plain with nothing in front of me except mountains in the distance. I stopped at an isolated petrol station and restaurant, and noted that the sign outside proclaimed that there would be no more amenities for the next 100 miles. I asked the attendant where the mountain pass was, and he replied that there wasn't one as the road actually went over the mountains, passing through an abandoned mining town called Jerome, which had been built into the steep sides of the incline. The attendant also added that the area was infested with rattlesnakes and that if it became necessary to stop for a "comfort break", it was important to keep a good look out for them as the previous week somebody had failed to do this and been bitten on the backside. I thanked him and set off again through the steep switchbacks which ran through Jerome, all of which caused me to thank the Lord that my brakes were working. The town itself looked relatively modern and presentable and it seemed to me that the only thing it lacked was people. Not long after I had passed through it, I found myself driving along rough mountain roads without barriers, around hairpin bends and often with sheer drops of hundreds of feet on one side. Fortunately there was no other traffic at all, from either direction, and I guessed this was because the locals weren't stupid enough to try and navigate this treacherous road in the diminishing daylight.

I was extremely surprised by how quickly night fell in this part of the world, and the onset of total darkness did little to calm my nerves. All I could see were the stars in the night sky and my headlights stabbing into the darkness in front of me as I went around hairpin bends. I suddenly felt very lonely and unbelievably frightened. I was more terrified on that winding mountain road than I had ever been in the skies over Germany and, in fact, even now I find it difficult to put my true feelings into words. The nightmare lasted for another twenty minutes (which seemed like hours) before the worst was over and I managed to hit the main Phoenix highway. I found a motel and booked in before falling asleep in an exhausted state as the adrenaline levels within my body began to subside and return to normal. The next morning I drove north in order to pick up the famous Route 66 which took me over the Arizona state border and into California at the town of Needles. This town was located in the area of the Mojave Desert, where it was so hot (with temperatures of over 100 degrees) that many people who drove through it did so at night. Even then, it wasn't wise to attempt the journey without suspending water bags from the radiator, just in case.

The drive through the desert was a strange experience for me. With all that vastness stretching away in front of me I found that it was easy to unconsciously press the accelerator pedal down until it eventually touched the floor. The road was so smooth and there were so few obvious points of reference, that I did not realize how quickly I was travelling until I glanced at the speedometer. This was obviously a common phenomenon, and the many crosses at the side of the highway bore witness to numerous fatal accidents, many of which were doubtless the result of excess speed. However I managed to survive the trip and I arrived at the town of San Bernardino without any further problems.

That afternoon I reported to Lockheed's Burbank design office and I was asked to start work the following day. On the first weekend that I was there, I found and rented a furnished house in North Hollywood and phoned Dorothy with the news that she and the boys should take the next available flight out to Los Angeles. She was ready and they arrived on the following Tuesday. On the Wednesday the boys were all enrolled in the nearest school and they started immediately. On the first free Saturday we all went to Disneyland for the day and had a great time at the newly opened theme park. The next free weekend we all went to the beach at Santa Monica and then on to visit the movie sets at Corrington-Ville, where films such as *Robin Hood, Fort Apache* and *Gunsmoke* had been made. They staged mock gunfights every day on the *Dodge City* set, but unfortunately the stars didn't show up. On our third Saturday excursion we spent some time in Beverly Hills gazing at the homes of the stars, before heading to downtown Los Angeles to see Grumman's Chinese Theater, the handprints on the "Walk of Fame", and the zoo in Griffith Park. We finished our day with a walk through Forest Lawn where I admired the perfect replicas of Michelangelo's David and The Tree of Life, and then on to the Mausoleum where many deceased members of the Hollywood aristocracy lay in their final resting places.

Two days later, I went to work as usual to be greeted with the now-familiar news that the contracts that we were working on had been either terminated or pulled back into the main plant for completion. We were all given two weeks' notice at fortnightly intervals over the next six week period. I was one of the first to be made redundant, and was handed two weeks termination pay as well as expenses to cover our move back to Canada. Our brief but enjoyable stay in California had come to an end and, once again, it was "all change". In the light of this, I was forced to make a trip to the United States Internal Revenue Service office. I had been pre-warned about the notorious income tax reviewers who worked there and, as I awaited my turn in the queue, I began to speculate as to which of these monsters I would be called in front of. I decided that the worst of the bunch looked something like the Wicked Witch from *The Wizard of Oz* and, as luck would have it, she was the one who called me forward. I could have sworn that she had a smirk on her face and an evil gleam in her eye as she looked at me. I tried to ignore her but I found myself firmly hooked on the end of her wiggling index finger and had no choice than to seat myself in front of her. Much to my surprise she was extremely softly spoken and was fully aware of the cutbacks at Lockheed. She immediately picked up on my northern English accent and we made friendly small talk about England for at least twenty minutes before finally getting down to business. I wanted to know exactly how much I owed the taxman and I had estimated that the total sum was probably somewhere around the $4,000 mark. She looked at my paperwork and then told me that she would have to discuss the matter with her supervisor. I was left sweating in the office for a good few minutes before she returned, telling me that due to extenuating circumstances I would have nothing to pay. She then issued me with an exit permit which declared that I was free to return to Canada and that I owed nothing to Uncle Sam. It just goes to show that you shouldn't listen to rumours, and you should definitely not judge a book by its cover.

Since I had relatives living in San Diego, we decided to go and visit them before making the long journey back north. These relatives were Skinners from my mother's side of the family. My grandfather Skinner's brother had emigrated to America at the end of the previous century, together with a friend of his named Williams, who had been sixteen at the time. They were spike drivers, and had been attracted by the prospect of working on the myriad of new railways that were being planned and built there. One of these new railways had its terminus at the Mexican border which ran just south of San Diego, but the railway company that they were working for was made bankrupt, owing thousands of dollars to its workforce, and the decision was taken to pay them off with parcels of land that had been owned by the company. With the rapid expansion of San Diego (which had only been a colonial Spanish mission village up until then), these parcels of land suddenly became prime real estate. The descendants of Great-Uncle Skinner now controlled the lease on most of downtown San Diego, and the money was pouring in. His friend, Mr Williams, was still alive, although very elderly, and he was absolutely delighted to receive us. After so many years he was at last able to chat and reminisce with people who actually knew his beloved West Gorton, and it was wonderful to see just how happy our visit had made him. On the day that we were due to depart for our long return trip to Canada, we decided to get up in plenty of time and pay a short visit to the world-famous San Diego Zoo before heading off. To our delight, Mr Williams unexpectedly turned up bright and early, dressed in his Sunday best, in order to accompany us to the zoo. We spent the next couple of hours touring the complex in an open-topped double-decker bus and having a wonderful time seeing all of the animals. I have never seen a happier looking person than Mr Williams that morning, and when the time came for us to leave, he had tears of joy in his eyes.

The trip home was made by car, and we spent a large part of the journey travelling eastwards along Route 66. I had learned my lesson and wasn't tempted to make any "scenic" detours on this occasion, especially as my wife and children were with me. We had settled the lease on the house, withdrawn the boys from their schools, returned the rented television set and packed up the car with all our worldly goods. The moment had come to leave for the Canadian border at Niagara Falls, some 3,000 miles away.

On the first night we stayed in the small town of Barstow, which was at the western end of Route 66. The next morning we set off again in the cool pre-dawn in order to traverse the Mojave Desert before the temperatures got too hot. We managed this without any problems, stopping every two hours to change the boys around in the car and stretch our legs, and carried on through Arizona into the thinly populated state of New Mexico. On the second night we had something of a problem finding anywhere to stay, but eventually we came across a very run-down looking motel/garage/ store complex. I filled up the car, and we bought supplies from the store before turning in for the night. Unfortunately the place was riddled with rats and mice, all of whom made a beeline for the grocery bags containing the food that we had just bought. We couldn't keep them away and finally, in desperation I gathered up everything I could and locked it away in the car. I am quite sure that our room mates spent the rest of the night trying to discover where we had hidden our supplies because none of us was able to get much sleep. We would have liked to have got away at the crack of dawn once again but I discovered that the car was coated in thick ice and it was impossible to open the door, so we had to wait for the sun to rise and defrost it for us. We passed the time sitting around the stove in the store, drinking the owner's coffee and listening to him telling us tales of rattlesnakes, armadillos and rats as big as cats. Although the night time temperatures in that mountainous part of New Mexico were very low, they were normal for early December, and the days were clear, warm and bright which made for ideal driving conditions. We crossed the state line and entered Texas, driving through the flat, windswept, treeless plains that dominated the area which was known to all as the panhandle. Here the highway veered north-west and entered Oklahoma. The weather was still good, but conditions began to change rapidly once we began to cross the Ozark Mountains. Cloudy skies appeared overhead and, as the light got worse, it began to snow heavily. Soon I was driving through thick snow and I decided that we should stop and find a motel as soon as possible. Unfortunately, lots of other drivers had the same idea and it was very much a case of "first come, first served". We had to carry on for another two hours through the freezing and treacherous conditions with my petrol gauge hovering above "empty", and my terrified family sitting in the back. Eventually, at the fourth time of asking, we managed to find an available room, with the five of us sleeping when and where we could, extremely grateful to have found anywhere at all.

The next morning, after a long delay as we waited for the snow-ploughs to finish clearing the roads as best they could, we set off again, heading northwards out of the Ozarks. Unfortunately it started to snow heavily once again, and this had the obvious effect of slowing us down and restricting our progress. We had been aiming to stop for the night at a town in Indiana called South Bend, which was only a day's drive away from Canada. However when we reached there late in the evening, we were again unable to find a vacant motel room anywhere in the town, not because of the weather this time, but because our arrival coincided with the start of a large convention which was being hosted there. We had to carry on until we eventually found a room in a town called West Elkhart. By this late stage, all the restaurants were closed or closing, and we hadn't eaten since breakfast. Hearing of our plight, the motel owner appealed to his restaurant staff, asking them to stay on a little bit longer and prepare something for us. Thankfully, they were happy to do so and we all enjoyed some delicious hot soup before turning in for the night.

It was still snowing heavily, and yet again our morning departure was delayed. This meant that we didn't reach the Canadian frontier until 23:00 and I spent an anxious few hours pondering whether we would be allowed into the country, as I wasn't quite sure just what our immigration status actually was. I had left Canada, as an employee of Avro, in order to work under contract with Lockheed Aircraft in California. To this end I had been given a temporary work permit which had now expired, along with the contract. We also had our validated American Green Cards which entitled us to permanent residence in the United States, and which had been issued to us (but never subsequently cancelled) by North American Aviation. In addition to all of this, I was driving a car that I had purchased under a diplomatic licence from the Ford Motor Company — under a loophole in the law that immigrants could take advantage of. Ford had delivered the car to the point of entry, and in order to do so, had to obtain Canadian licence plates. So technically I was driving a Canadian registered car back into Canadian territory, which was all very correct.

This then was the true story that I told the Customs and Immigration officers at the Canadian border at 23:00 in a howling blizzard with a wife and three kids trailing along behind me. Christmas was a week away and I had no idea where we would be spending it as we had no home to go to. These weren't exactly ideal preparations for the festive season, putting it mildly, and I am quite sure that the officers on duty had no idea what they were letting themselves in for when they turned up to work the night shift that evening. After listening to my story, they referred the matter to their supervisors who, in turn, liaised with their opposite numbers on the American side of the border. After two hours deliberations they concluded that I would not be breaking any laws by crossing back into Canada. We were Canadian citizens, the car had been licensed in Canada, and our Green Cards had not been invalidated by the State Department. We were told that we were free to proceed. I then informed the customs officers that I had a car boot full of items which I had purchased in California and which I wished to declare to them. Their reply to me is not printable, but the gist was "Just get the hell out of here". It was now 01:00 and fortunately we found a place to bed down for the night, completely exhausted from our efforts.

The following day we arrived back in Streetsville and I reestablished contact with Avro and began to hunt for somewhere to live. The boys were put back into their old school and we passed word to our relatives and friends that we had returned. We found a place at 33 Britannia Road just in time for Christmas. However as 1959 turned into 1960, I discovered that in my absence, matters at Avro had gone from bad to worse. The government had ordered the complete destruction of everything that had been connected with the Arrow project: drawings, records, test reports, models, jigs, tools, and even the six completed prototypes. No financial offers would be accepted from the United Kingdom or anywhere else, and the extensive library was never to leave Avro. The Arrow was to be erased from existence, and nobody knew the real reasons why. With that in mind, I again started to send out CVs, but I steered clear of British companies as I had decided that America offered our best chance for a stable future. My first application resulted in a request from

Capital Airlines, based in Washington DC, to present myself there for an interview. The vacancy was in their engineering group and I seemed to give them the impression that I would fit easily into the slot. I was subsequently offered a job there in March 1960. My start date was to be 25 March but on my arrival in Washington I was told that Capital Airlines had filed for bankruptcy that very same day, although the airline was expecting to be taken over by United Airlines so the job offer was still valid, if a little uncertain. I was given an additional thirty days to reconsider, but as I was south of the border I took the opportunity to visit a number of companies that I had already contacted to see if they would grant me any speculative interviews. One such company was the Vertol Corporation, which was based near Philadelphia. I had actually received a rejection letter from them a couple of months earlier, but they were happy to talk to me on this occasion. The interview went well and, on my return to Canada the next day, I found a cable from Vertol offering me a position, with a good salary, excellent benefits, all moving expenses paid and an immediate start date. I accepted straight away.

The work would be a little different from what I had previously been used to, but the principles were much the same. Vertol was an offshoot of the Sikorsky Helicopter Corporation, and there was a total workforce of around 1,000 people. In fact the company was in the process of being taken over by the mighty Boeing Company of Seattle, but there was no uncertainty as there had been at Capital Airlines and

260

everyone's job was guaranteed. The two main projects that were being worked on were the twin-rotored Chinook helicopter which had been ordered by the US Army, and the huge Sea King which was under development for the Navy. So on 2 May 1960, having left my family in Canada for the time being, I started work for Vertol Corporation, at a post in a development design group with responsibility for resolving problems originating in the field as the newly designed helicopters entered service. These problems included handling cargo, retrieving crashed aircraft, delivering cargo to ships in bad weather, operating in muddy terrain and many others. From my point of view, the main benefits of this job were the close contact and liaison that I was expected to maintain with the US military and government agencies, who naturally kept a very close eye on the development of these projects. I found the intricacies of writing proposals, submitting them, negotiating contracts, and the execution of these contracts very interesting and fulfilling. It was also fascinating to see how these achievements were ultimately used by the military, and the satisfaction of standing on a podium presenting solutions to the top brass of the US Navy was both nerve wracking and stimulating. By now the Vietnam War was in full swing and with money being plentiful Boeing was doing brisk business with the military. Who would have guessed that the sixteen year old boy standing on the platform of Marylebone station that January morning in 1936 would one day be standing in an auditorium in the Naval Department building in Washington DC, addressing an audience of such exalted standing? Or lecturing the top engineering staff in the US Air Force Research and Development laboratories at Wright Field in Ohio? I was both staggered and proud of how far I had come in the preceding thirty years, and I put most of that down to the exceptional training that I had been lucky enough to receive at Halton.

After I accepted the job with Vertol, Dorothy and I decided that I would get myself settled down there, and she and the boys would remain in Canada until such time as we were ready to move lock, stock and barrel. My first priority was to try and find somewhere for us all to live, and it wasn't long before I came across a nice big house in the town of Westchester, Pennsylvania. It was in the process of being completed, and as it was not far from being ready, I put a deposit on it and arranged a mortgage. My family moved down without a hitch and although Steven in particular resented being taken away from his Canadian friends, we all settled in quite nicely. Over the next few years, the time that I spent at home was reasonably limited owing to the vagaries of the job, but I was earning good money and this seemed to compensate in part. I was able to buy my wife her own car, and we hosted legions of relatives who regularly came down to stay, notably my in-laws who travelled down from Canada at what seemed like every opportunity. I was able to bring my mother over from England for a brief visit. She was on her own now, and had been for a number of years as Dad had died before I left England, following a fall from the roof of his cinema in West Gorton where he was attempting to fix a leak. Jet aircraft were not yet in regular service so it took Mother fourteen hours to cross the Atlantic in a noisy old DC7, but she found it a thrilling experience, if not just a little tiring. The almost constant presence of my wife's family did nothing to ease the relationship between myself and Dorothy, which was starting to become somewhat strained, and did not provide an ideal environment for bringing up three boisterous sons.

As time went by, my eldest son Andrew began to get into trouble — firstly at school and then later with the law. According to my in-laws, I was to blame for this, and they informed my wife that if he was to spend time apart from me then he would return to the straight and narrow. I resented being made the scapegoat but I was more concerned with Andrew's best interests, so I bit my tongue and when it was decided that he should move back to Canada and live with his grandparents for a while, I reluctantly accepted. Of course this move was a complete disaster. Andrew behaved (and was treated by his friends) as a returning hero, and subsequently tried to live up to this image, chasing every girl who was available. Before too long, my in-laws were badgering us to take him back again. In the meantime I had been having talks with lawyers, psychiatrists, the school authorities and officials from the juvenile court in order to obtain guidance as to what to do in order to try and prevent him ending up in court.

So Andrew returned home but my worst fears were soon realized and he once again found himself in serious trouble with the police. A warrant was issued for his arrest, and we all ended up in the local juvenile court to hear the verdict. Andrew was as cocky as ever and had gathered all his mates together so they could celebrate his release. However the court did not see it this way, and he was ordered to be detained indefinitely in Kislyn Juvenile Facility. I did not think that this measure would help in the long run, but it did at least give us the time and breathing space to try and work out how to help Andrew to put his behavioural problems behind him. I am not trying to make excuses or to load all of the blame for this state of affairs onto one particular person, but I did (and still do) feel extremely resentful towards my in-laws who meddled incessantly with my marriage and my family and I am sure that the knock-on effect caused by this interference did ultimately contribute towards what eventually happened to Andrew.

Dorothy and I visited Andrew every week at the detention centre. He did not undergo a miraculous transformation, and neither did the resident psychiatrists notice any obvious change, but we gradually talked things over with him each week and between us we decided that a spell in the Army would be a good idea. He was quite receptive to the idea once he realized that joining the Army would give him the opportunity to partake in training courses in all sorts of subjects that he had an interest in. He also felt as though it would be helpful to him to get away from the home environment for a while, and that the Army would help him to straighten himself out. After his release he came home, full of good intentions, but trouble seemed to come looking for him and once again it wasn't long before somebody filed a complaint against him. The probation officer called and told me that it was a serious matter and would possibly end up in the criminal court. Andrew had already met and talked with the local Army recruiters, and I sat him down and told him that he had a simple choice: he could either join the Army or he could end up in court and face another jail sentence. Fortunately, he chose the Army and joined up immediately, with the result that the charges were dropped and the prospect of another spell in prison disappeared. Almost immediately things started to improve, although I am sure that he would have tried it on once or twice with the drill sergeants at his "boot camp" until he realized he couldn't win. The Vietnam War was in full swing at this time and, of course, there was the prospect that he might find himself being posted there but, by a stroke of good fortune, he was sent to Germany. While there he studied hard to obtain his high school diploma and then began training in the field of electronics and telephone communications. After he had finished his stint in the Army he returned home and talked over his future career aspirations with friends who had contacts in the Bell communications company and began to work for them until his eventual retirement many years later.

Life in the neighbourhood was otherwise pleasant for us all as the 1960s turned into the 1970s. From the beginning of our time in Westchester we got on very well with everyone and held regular parties to which all of our friends and neighbours would be invited. In fact our annual New Year's "bash" became the talk of the town (or so I was led to believe). Unfortunately we didn't travel as much as I would have liked and we never seemed to get a great deal of time on our own because the in-laws regularly descended upon us. I used to look forward to their returning to Canada so that peace and quiet would descend upon the house once again. They would have liked to move to the USA permanently but, in order to obtain the necessary residential status, they would have needed sponsor and I certainly wasn't foolish enough to put myself forward as one.

The Vietnam War was drawing to its conclusion and all the touchy political machinations that accompanied the American withdrawal resulted in cancelled contracts and limited funding for development projects. These signified a major recession in the defence industry and Boeing was hit by numerous layoffs and redundancies. The senior management team in Seattle began to examine the possibilities of getting involved in more and more civilian engineering projects. They sent out a directive to Vertol with an order to form a group to look at the feasibility of designing and building vehicles for the urban transportation market. The government gave considerable financial and material subsidies to such projects, so this might have been one of the reasons for Boeing's interest. I was attracted by the prospect of trying something new, so I immediately volunteered my services and was accepted into the steering group. It was a huge switch from being involved in the design of the huge 747 to looking at ways to build new trams (or "trolley cars" as they were known in the United States), and our project was regarded by many people as little more than a huge joke. This atmosphere of mockery meant that people were deterred from joining the project and we had to work hard to attract the people that we needed. Of course the knock-on effect of this was that we had individuals seconded to us from other teams and these people were often sub-standard and had effectively been dumped on us by their former supervisors who had been looking for ways to get rid of them.

However we weren't deterred by these early setbacks and began to learn the language and terminology of the urban transportation industry and to study the details of the existing systems, both in America and the rest of the world. We began to make progress and not only got our toes in the door, but also began to win small contracts which were largely obtained on the back of Boeing's good reputation. These grew in scale as time progressed and we found ourselves in the position of being invited to bid for any future design/build contracts that came up. Of course this rattled the established companies who saw us as upstarts trying to step on their toes. As far as they were concerned, Boeing should stick to building aeroplanes and leave surface transportation systems to those who knew what they were doing.

So it came to pass that one day the cities of Boston and San Francisco both issued an invitation to bid for the contract to replace their ageing fleets of trolley cars. We asked permission from the senior management team in Seattle and they told us to go ahead and put in an offer. The requirements were that the new cars should be built to conform with the Federal Department of Transport specifications, as only this would guarantee a Federal subsidy. We had no problems with the design and build phase, and the project would be simple to manage, but there were concerns over the costs that would be involved. Seattle agreed with the proposals and was prepared to subsidise the bid, with the result that Boeing was awarded the two contracts, much to everybody's surprise.

Since over 90 per cent of the material used in the creation of the cars would be subcontracted, the initial task was to source and make contact with those companies who could and would make component parts for the cars. In order to give some idea of the magnitude of this task, I bought a business card file which eventually held over 200 cards, all relating to this part of the project, and this was only a small portion of the total number of approaches that were made by the team. My main responsibility was to configure the vehicle to ensure that all of the sub-systems were accommodated within the confines of the portfolio, and that it conformed to the Federal SLRV (Standard Light Rail Vehicle) specification. This included overseeing the layout design of the basic structure in sufficient detail to be used as a baseline for the award of a sub-contract to design and build the bodies of the trolley cars. Since my experience up until this point had involved fastening together bits of aluminium alloy by using rivets and bolts to create aeroplanes, I was a little out of my depth. Trolley cars were traditionally constructed from steel and welded together by techniques that were completely alien to me and it was decided that I should enrol in the next available welding course at the local vocational college and take on a full apprenticeship. I was also to combine this with the apprenticeship course in air-conditioning, since the installation of such systems within the cars would also be within my remit. As these were both evening classes, they did not eat into the time I spent on the project and I was able to carry on as before, learning in my spare time as I did so.

In due course, a sub-contract for the car bodies was awarded to a Japanese firm: the Tokyo Car Manufacturing Company, and I would have to travel to Japan in order to liaise with them and oversee the development of the cars, ensuring that they conformed with the specifications. The factory was a pre-war plant, built by and for Japanese workers and so the problems caused by the Lilliputian nature of the production lines, together with the different work ethic and the inevitable language barrier, all had to be overcome. There was also a lingering suspicion of the Americans and the British which some of the older workers had been unable to shake off, although I did notice that they did seem to trust me a little more than they did my American colleagues. This mirrored the attitude of the German guards in the POW camp at Mühlberg, who used to allow unguarded British prisoners to leave the camp in order to unload Red Cross parcels at the railway, but would not dream of allowing Americans to do so.

There were some quaint daily rituals at the factory, which I rather appreciated and enjoyed. On arrival, a little old lady would mysteriously appear from nowhere in order to serve you a cup of green tea, accompanied by a formal bow and a pleasant greeting. I later used this ritual to my advantage, as on one of my first trips back home to America, I bought a small silver necklace and on my return to Yokohama, I presented it to this lady as a token of my appreciation. News of this gesture seemed to spread like wildfire through the factory, and from that moment on the spell was broken and we were treated as guests rather than intruders. I was given complete freedom to wander the factory floor as and where I liked, and my escort was now dispensed with. The toilet arrangements also provided me with something of a surprise, being similar to Western conveniences in the "stand up" department, but nothing more than a hole in the ground was provided for the alternative function, at least in factories built prior to the last war. One day I was standing at the urinal relieving myself when all of a sudden I felt one of my feet being lifted off the ground. I looked down and to my amazement I saw the cleaning lady holding on to my ankle and mopping furiously where my foot had been. It seemed that she just wanted to clean under my foot without causing a fuss. I also noticed that older restaurants in Yokohama solved the problem of having to provide male and female conveniences for their customers by placing two doors into the same public toilets, one labelled "Male" and the other "Female". Of course I only discovered this arrangement by trial and error.

In the office, back at the factory, I learned that after concluding a presentation or a meeting, one had to be very careful to ensure that everybody present had fully taken in what you had been saying. This was because the Japanese would always answer "Yes" if you asked them whether they had understood, but some of them meant "Yes, I do understand" whilst others meant "Yes, I do not understand". This linguistic quirk caused predictable chaos and, in the end, I found that the best way to ensure that all was well was to ask the senior Japanese engineer present to repeat the conclusions that had been reached in the final part of the meeting. Only then could we be certain that they had understood what had been said. Another initial roadblock was caused by the fact that we used inches and feet in our drawings and plans, whereas the Japanese used the metric system. Eventually it was decided to use both formats on the plans, but not before a great deal of confusion on the part of our hosts.

Working with the Japanese on a daily basis meant that as time went by, we grew to know them as human beings and the stereotypical image of the Japanese, that many of us had been exposed to during the war years, began to fade away into the background. During our free time we were shown around and taken on numerous excursions by our Japanese colleagues. I visited such places as the old capital of Kyoto, Mount

Fuji, many Buddhist shrines, and we ate at traditional Japanese restaurants where we all sat cross legged on the floor and were served and entertained by Geisha girls in their spectacular costumes.

On one occasion I was taken out to a Chinese restaurant in the Chinatown district of Yokohama. The principal dish was carp, and this fish could be seen swimming around in a huge tank as we entered the restaurant. When the time came, it was lifted out of the tank and dropped straight into a pan of very hot fat. In its death agonies the carp curled its body round into a large arc, and it was in this position that it was served to us as the *pièce de rèsistance*. Our host then cut it up and it was served to his guests. The fish's head, complete with wide staring eyes, was reserved for me as I was the guest of honour. The thought of having to look the carp in the eye while eating it was a little too much for me and I was forced to decline. Since my host was Japanese, there was no loss of face or loss of honour, but had he been Chinese, my refusal would have constituted a grave insult and I would have felt obliged to grin and bear it. My cowardice was laughed off by my dining companions, and that was the end of the matter.

There were many trials and tribulations associated with my time in Japan, but it was a wonderful experience and I came to make many new friends. I began to understand the complexities of the Japanese people, but I sensed that many Americans still held them in great contempt. In particular, a group of American consultants, who had been hired by our municipal customers to oversee the production and monitor the quality control aspects, displayed blatant prejudice in doing their job. I often heard them openly expressing their views and opinions about the Japanese, always in full earshot of our hosts. I subsequently made representations to Vertol about their embarrassing and insulting behaviour, which at least had the effect of shutting them up, but the damage had been done and my job had been made a great deal more awkward than necessary. This was not the first time that I had been face to face with racist behaviour from white Americans, and I am afraid to say that it is still thriving in many sections of American society.

Overall, I made six trips between Philadelphia and Yokohama over that prolonged period of time, but as compensation for the long flights I was allowed to break the journey with an overnight stop in Hawaii where, on one occasion, I was able to visit Pearl Harbor. On another occasion I was asked to return via England, where I visited the Westinghouse Brake Company in Chippenham which was producing the door systems, in order to iron out a problem. This was a special assignment for me, as this visit home gave me my first and only experience of flying round the world. The day eventually arrived which would see the first trolley car bodies being shipped across to Philadelphia from Japan. I stood on the dockside at the port of Yokohama and watched as they were winched onto the *Export Bay* which was bound for the east coast of the United States, via the Panama Canal. It had been agreed that my presence in Japan was no longer required after the arrival of the first car body shells and that future liaison with the factory would be the responsibility of others. I was to return to Philadelphia and work on the project from there. My continuing assignment with the SLRV programme was to create other configurations of the new and very successful Light Rail Vehicle in anticipation of future bids and contracts from other municipalities.

Before too long, Vertol's home town of Philadelphia issued a call for bids to replace their own ageing PCC cars and, incredibly, Seattle decided to send over their own team, which had no experience in such matters, to try and win the contract themselves. In all there were ten companies involved in the bidding and it was no great surprise when Boeing not only failed to win, but ended up being rated in last place. When you consider that the demand for commercial aircraft was now overwhelming, with Boeing developing the new 757 and 767 airliners, and that the bid would at least keep the company in the frame for any new surface transportation contracts, it is not difficult to conclude that the team was sent over with the express intention of losing the Philadelphia bid. Unfortunately for me, this clever strategy on the part of the management meant that I would soon be out of a job once again.

I was transferred to the helicopter division and started work on the configuration group. This was a unit that I had worked on before and my first assignment was to configure a 107 helicopter which would be used by the logging industry. I gave a presentation of my proposals for this machine to the managers involved who, I had previously regarded as friends and colleagues, and you could have cut the atmosphere with a knife. I had never before felt such hostility directed towards me in all the time I had been with Boeing. It seems that they regarded me as having left them in the lurch when I volunteered for the SLRV project and they viewed my return as a calculated attempt to tread on their toes. This was not an ideal situation to be in and I was made to feel most unwelcome.

In the meantime, there had been a momentous upheaval in my personal life. In 1974, almost out of the blue, my wife informed me that she was seeking a divorce and that our marriage was over. The boys had all grown up and were making their own ways in the world, and my in-laws naturally threw all their support behind my wife's decision, with her mother mumbling "Good riddance", and her father stating that we should never have got married in the first place. This turn of events was a great shock to me. Although when I had married Dorothy in 1946 I knew that married life would never be the fairytale that I had dreamed of as I lay alone in my bunk at Mühlberg, imagining a devoted wife and at least four happy children, I had been brought up to believe that marriage was a contract that was binding for life, regardless of what came to pass. A lawyer was called in and tallied up all of our assets, dividing them in two. Dorothy didn't want the house as she had never really liked it, and moved out, buying an old place in the locality that required a great deal of work doing to it. However she never really left me, always coming round to see how I was getting on and, of course, I encouraged her as I still had hopes of a reconciliation. Eventually and to my deep joy, this happened, and I sold up and moved in with her.

I spent a great deal of time and money in renovating the new house, but after a few years it became clear that things were still not "lovey-dovey" between us. With my position at Vertol being somewhat unhappy, in 1978 I decided to apply for a transfer to the Seattle factory. The new 767 airliner project was now in full swing and with the imminent start of the design phase of the 757 project, it seemed that they were short of engineers to work on it. I had four years to go until my scheduled retirement and this post would hopefully carry me through and make a fitting conclusion to my career. I put my proposal to Dorothy and she was extremely enthusiastic, seeing it as an opportunity for us to start over again, in a new location, with the opportunity of finding and making new friends. Foolishly, I fell for it and, having been offered the position, I began to make the arrangements for our move to the west coast.

I drove to Renton, the town near Seattle where Boeing was based, which was a journey of nearly 3,000 miles and involved crossing the Rocky Mountains. This was a new experience for me but as it was May, the winter snows had thawed and it was a relatively easy trip. Having arrived at Renton and clocked in at the factory, I then set about finding a suitable house to buy. Our idea had been that I should invest in a home in a good location, and that we would take plenty of time to

276

hunt around for a suitable piece of land on which to buy our dream retirement home. I subsequently found and purchased a house which I thought would be a good investment, and then flew back to Philadelphia, leaving my car in Seattle. On my arrival at the airport, I was annoyed to find that nobody was there to meet me. I phoned Dorothy and was told that she was busy and that I should travel home by public transportation. This took me five frustrating hours, as a result of infrequent connections, and I arrived at the house in Westchester to find that she wasn't at home, and didn't return for another two hours. It was hardly the lovey-dovey reconciliation that I had been hoping for after a few weeks away. I managed to sell the house and tidied up all of our affairs, before we began the long journey westwards in Dorothy's car. I had been annoyed by Dorothy's uncaring attitude since my return but I was determined to make a go of it and we arrived in Renton without having experienced too many problems — the engine running short of water in the Columbia Gorge being the only setback. Once there, we eventually managed to locate a piece of land large enough to suit our needs. It was six and a half acres in total, and before too long our house had been designed and built. The land was a little too large for both of us to maintain properly, but it was certainly a good investment for the future.

During the search for the plot of land, we saw a roadside sign advertising "Western Dancing". We thought that this would be a good way of spending plenty of time together and learning something new.

The real-estate agent, who had handled our purchase, introduced us to the art of square dancing and we met plenty of others who had similar interests. We both became avid dancers and progressed on to round dancing, a form of American ballroom dancing that is fairly similar to square dancing. Dorothy had danced as a teenager, but my only experience had been when the Methodist mothers used to get their offspring together after Sunday School, in order to try and teach us how to waltz. Of course being at that tender age I considered having to put my arm around a girl's waist to be disgusting, and never really gave it my full attention. My (former) in-laws would visit from time to time, but thankfully the greater distance, coupled with their advancing years, meant that we didn't see all that much of them.

The 757 programme was going well, and other than dancing and making local excursions, I didn't really have time for much else. The house was in a wonderful location and both of us enjoyed gardening, so there was plenty to do at home. Dorothy got herself a job in order to make new contacts and meet new friends but, in spite of her new social life, she didn't seem satisfied and began to spend more and more time with the real-estate lady who had introduced us to dancing. In 1982 I retired from Boeing with a full pension, and me suddenly being at home twenty-four hours a day proved to be too much for Dorothy, who walked out on me once more and went to live with her friend. This was the final straw for me and, despite my commitment to marriage and to our relationship, I decided that it was over. However Dorothy did not seem to be able to let go: showing up at dances to see who I was dancing with, regularly calling me up to see how I was getting on, and generally refusing to allow me to move on. With my patience at an end, I offered her $100,000 from my pension fund to encourage her to move back to the east coast. The offer was too good for her to refuse and she took it. On the day that she left, she turned up to say goodbye and, as she got into her car, she put her head out of the window and left me with the following words: "Well, you know there was no point in staying because I don't love you. In fact I have never loved you." With that parting gesture she drove away, and after thirty-six years, she had finally gone out of my life for good.

So here I was, sixty-two years old, alone and with my pension fund some $100,000 lighter. If my retirement was to be comfortable, that money would have to be replaced. I still had good contacts with Boeing, so I made enquiries to see whether I would be able to fit back in and I successfully applied for a job in the customer service department, which was being expanded to include the new 757 aeroplane which was moving into production, as well as the 707, 727 and 737 aircraft which were already in service. I started in the post production group of the department in order to carry out the necessary engineering work relating to any repairs or modifications that were brought to our notice by the clients. I was now a contract engineer hired on a temporary basis and there was lots of work available. Aircraft only make money for their owners

279

when they are airworthy, and any that are grounded (classed as AOG — Aircraft On Ground) are considered to be a drain on resources. Any assistance and expertise on our part was to be executed as soon as possible. This meant that lots and lots of overtime was on offer and, as contract engineers, we were paid good rates of pay. I was able to live on my full Boeing pension, coupled with my Social Security pension, so all my wages went directly into my bank account. Within two years, I had managed to replace all of the money that I had given to my ex-wife and, in 1984, I was able to retire for the second and final time.

In the meantime, I had continued with my dancing and used my contacts there to maintain a healthy and active social life. As I was now an eligible male I was surprised but not unhappy to find myself in great demand by the many single females in my age bracket. Dance partners were numerous and many were actively looking for a "live one" just like me. I had been a one-woman man all my life and, quite frankly, this situation scared me to death — I had never quite realized the lengths that a determined woman would go to in order to snare a man. I was no coward but being sixty-six years old, I was not in the least romantically inclined and, in fact, my experience with marriage had made me vow not to go down that road again. Despite this, I settled on one permanent dance partner because of her excellent ability. She was a widow who I had first met while dancing with my ex-wife and we would often dance in the same "squares". Funnily enough she was also called Dorothy and her husband, whom she had lost to cancer some years previously, was also called Tom — how is that for coincidence? It became inevitable after a while that she would try and make a play for me. By that stage my attitude towards romance had softened and I was more than receptive towards her advances. In fact I can't have been much of a challenge — I never had been much of a ladies' man and I had forgotten many of the tricks of the trade that I may have possessed at one time. So after a while we moved in together and, much to my surprise, our arrangement seemed to work extremely well and we were actually a very happy and compatible couple. On the other hand, my attitude towards marriage did not falter, but thankfully she understood and readily accepted the situation. We considered ourselves married but not "churched", as the saying goes. Most of our friends were happy for us, with the odd exception amongst the more religious of them who considered us to be "living in sin". We settled down and there began a very happy and fulfilled period of my life. After all of the trials and tribulations of the previous years, I finally felt as though the gods were beginning to smile upon me at last.

CHAPTER EIGHT

There and Back Again

There now followed an extremely satisfying period of stability in my life. Dorothy (Dottie) took a trip across to England to visit my sister, Joyce and, as she had never even ventured out of the north-west of America, it was a great thrill for her to fly across the Atlantic and then travel around Britain by train. On her return we visited Canada to meet up with other ex-patriate Brats from the 33rd Entry and then went to Oregon to stay with my youngest son Peter, who at that time was working for an electronics firm, Textronic Inc. At about this time the Berlin Wall fell and Germany was reunited, and my thoughts turned to planning a series of visits to Europe in order to try and retrace my wartime journeys.

First of all, I took a trip back to England to attend a reunion of 33rd Entry ex-Brats. Some years previously my sister had seen an advertisement in a magazine which had been placed there by an appropriately named ex-Brat named Wilbur Wright, who was in the process of creating a 33rd Club. I put my details forward, and was later contacted by former Leading Apprentice Eden "Chaka" Webster, a former room mate who I had not seen since we passed out in December 1938. He invited me to his home in Ashbourne, Derbyshire, and I went to the next reunion in Oxford and there met up with him. There were many still around, a few of whom I knew, but I didn't go to any other reunions for quite a while as I preferred to think of people as they were in their prime, as opposed to in their so-called "Golden Years". Many of them were in a pretty bad shape. There were those who had never managed to achieve anything or had never been able to go anywhere or do anything, and there were also those who had been in the right place at the right time and who had ended up in positions that they hadn't really earned or deserved. They seemed to spend the whole time constantly talking about themselves, usually bragging of mythical exploits in "never-never land". One poor soul had been put down and accused of lacking in moral fibre during the war. He had had to live with this awful stigma for his entire life. I knew him well and when I visited Chaka we tried to set up a meeting with him as he also lived in Ashbourne, but he refused as he was too ashamed to see us. The expression "lack of moral fibre" should be taken out of the English language and its usage banned. There are cases where men who had risked their lives time and time again over Germany, having been decorated for their efforts, finally broke under the interminable pressure and were stripped of their medals and their rank. They would be demoted to the lowest rank in the Service and would deliberately be handed the lowliest, most humiliating tasks such as cleaning the latrines. All because they had supposedly "lacked moral fibre". What the hell is "moral fibre" anyway? Chaka and I kept in touch even though we didn't go to reunions. He and his wife travelled to Canada and the United States in 1990 and managed to find time to stay with us in Renton. It was great to natter about old times, but a little sad to reminisce about those we had known who didn't make it through the war. Another Brat named Jim Constantine was living in Seattle, so we took the time to dig out his address and visit. They also went to visit Bill Young in Calgary, and George Reddy in British Columbia, and Chaka's wife, Joyce, was able to look up a former nurse she had known in Montreal and not seen since 1945. All in all, a very successful trip for both Chaka and Joyce, and it was great to see them.

Not long afterwards, I received a surprise phone call from England, where the caller asked if a Tom Lancashire lived there? I confirmed that he did and was asked if I remembered somebody called Jim Ely. I certainly did and replied that I had known somebody by that name at Waterbeach in 1942, and that as I recalled, he had been about 5 feet 10 inches, with blond hair and a blond moustache. I mentioned that I had attended his wedding to Dorothy, a WAAF who worked in the Sergeants' Mess and whom Jim had placed fairly and squarely in the ranks of the "pudding club". I also remembered that Flight Sergeant Mackie had been the best man, and that Dorothy's sister and father attended the ceremony, but not her mother. Jim (for it was he) was absolutely staggered that anyone could have remembered such detail. What had happened was that a young English student who was researching the deeds of 15 Squadron had made contact with me. I had given him Mac Mackie's name and he had subsequently met up with him. He had told Mac my name and phone number and Mac had passed this on to Jim, with whom he was still in touch. I also learned that Dick Strachan, the navigator in my first crew, had been in touch with Mac as part of his forty year quest to try and track down his old flight engineer. I telephoned him immediately and promised to visit him at his home in Ayrshire the next time I was in England.

We all met up the following year, in the pretty Lincolnshire market town of Stamford. Unfortunately Dick wasn't able to make it, due to the fact that he had been diagnosed with cancer and had been forced to remain at home. A great time was had by all, and it was followed up the next day by a visit to the still functioning RAF Wyton, the home of 15 Squadron between 1941 and 1943. Jim Ely had been in touch with the Station CO and arranged the whole day. We were provided with a flight lieutenant to escort us around the base, taken wherever we wished, and to end it all, treated to a meal in the Officers' Mess. The icing on the cake was being shown a collection of wartime photographs, which had been mounted on one of the walls of the lounge bar, and finding ourselves in our former glory. A wonderful ending to a wonderful day.

The next day I flew up to Glasgow and visited Dick at his home in Carnoustie. After all, if he had spent forty years trying to find me the least I could do was to spend a day with him. I was shocked to see how frail he looked, and privately I doubted that he would survive for much longer, but we had a very emotional meeting and it was well worth the effort. I learned that Dick had never returned to Stirlings after the end of his tour, but had finished the war as a Pathfinder Mosquito navigator.

The following year, Dottie and I travelled to Scotland to visit Dick, who had seemingly recovered from his illness. We enjoyed a picturesque train journey through the Lake District before reaching Carnoustie, and this time we were able to stay there for two days, being shown the local sights and enjoying a wonderful Scottish meal served in a local hotel complete with waiters wearing kilts. We talked ourselves to a standstill and Dick paid me a very touching compliment when he said that he had never met anyone as cool as I had been when under intense enemy fire. Little had he known the utter panic that I had felt at such times. Unfortunately, within a few months of our return to the United States I received a letter from Dick's wife, Celeste, saying that Dick had suffered a relapse and passed on. I was so glad that we had been able to meet up before he had died and I still keep in touch with Celeste to this day.

In 1992, having once again retired from Boeing, and having amassed sufficient funds, I decided that the time was right to plan our first trip through Europe to try and find out what had happened to my old POW camp at Mühlberg. I planned to visit Belgium as well, in order to meet up with Blanchette, the daughter of the farmer with whom we had stayed on that fateful night in 1943. Over the years we had exchanged Christmas cards, so I knew that she was alive and well, and still living in the same house. To begin with, I wrote to the mayor of Mühlberg, bought a detailed road map, and informed Blanchette of our plans, as well as asking for instructions as to how to find the house. I didn't have to wait long for replies. The mayor explained that he would love to receive us and that now that the Communists had gone, things were a great deal better there. The camp itself no longer existed, but a local group was being formed in order to set up and maintain a museum concerned with keeping its memory alive. Blanchette was very excited at the prospect, and sent directions to the farmhouse, as requested. We decided that the best thing would be to fly into Brussels and hire a car there, before driving down to the Ardennes and then on into Germany. Of course we were both seventy-three years old, with very limited French and German skills, so it was going to be a bit of a challenge but, as an ex-Brat, with all the associated confidence that I had had instilled in me, I was more than willing to meet it. Unfortunately, I subsequently fell ill and the decision was made to postpone the trip until the following year as I was not in a fit state to travel and undertake what would almost certainly be quite an arduous journey.

A year passed, and now that our plans were almost complete, we visited a local travel agency and sat down to finalize and pay for our trip. We had decided to be away for one month, which would include visits to

Belgium and Germany, with the obligatory stop off in England to visit my family, as well as Chaka and Joyce in Ashbourne. The travel agent routed us from Seattle to Washington DC, where we would connect with a trans-Atlantic flight to Brussels. These were two long flights either side of a short twenty minute stop at Washington, and we finally arrived in Belgium early one morning, tired, confused and disorientated. We eventually managed to locate our hire car and headed out of the airport complex, only to find that my careful route planning had been a waste of time due to the fact that all the approaches to the airport were in the process of being redeveloped and all the diversionary instructions were in French. By some miracle we managed to free ourselves from this trap and I realized that we were now heading east. In fact we were looking for the E411 motorway which ran south towards the Ardennes, and so I turned round and tracked westwards until we found it. At last we were on course.

Desperately in need of some refreshment after our long journey, we pulled into the next service area that we came across, and found the restaurant. Having enjoyed a quick meal and a couple of cups of coffee, I headed to the cashier's point near to the exit in order to pay. I handed her a 2,000 franc note, not really having got to grips with modern day Belgian currency, and she said something in French which I took to be "Have you got anything smaller?" Unfortunately I only realized afterwards that this was what she must have meant, and at the time I just stood there with a blank look on my face and told her that I didn't understand. This exchange caused something of a delay and those in the queue behind us started to get a little bit agitated and angry until finally the manager appeared to sort things out and smooth them over. So much for our arrival in Belgium. Once back in the car we got the maps out, familiarizing ourselves with our location and trying to make head or tail of Blanchette's directions. Eventually we came across a village called Froid Fontaine which was almost silent and deserted, save for the noise of a hammer being used in one of the nearby houses. As I had done fifty years earlier in a similar situation, I took a deep breath, walked up to the front door of that house and knocked. Eventually a man opened the door, and a rather extraordinary conversation ensued. He could not speak English and my French was extremely limited, but by using gestures I managed to let him know that I was looking for Blanchette Pochet's house. He didn't know her personally but went across to a neighbouring house where the occupants did, and finally I discovered that she lived approximately two kilometres away, down the hill that was on the other side of the village. We followed the directions and, sure enough, arrived outside a house that I immediately recognized. We stopped, parked and were greeted by a large Labrador dog who barked loudly at us. Alerted to our presence by the noise, Blanchette appeared. The young lady of 1943 had been replaced by the grandmother of 1993, but she was still the same Blanchette and she joyfully welcomed us to her home.

The next forty-eight hours were a bit of a blur. We were inundated with visitors from all over the area, from the local aristocracy right down to the man who dispensed the petrol at the local garage. I think they rather viewed me as some kind of ghost who had appeared from the past, as suddenly as I had appeared in their midst that August morning fifty years earlier. The adulation showered upon me was totally unexpected and difficult for me to take in. What I thought would be a few days of personal reminiscence was starting to turn into something else altogether, and I found it more than a little unsettling. I decided that it was time for us to take our leave, so after a visit to the old White Army hideout in the nearby woods where I had stayed for a while back in 1943, we said our goodbyes and headed towards the German border, after promising to call back in on our way to England. I hoped that this would give everybody a little time to cool down and return to normal.

Our journey took us through Luxembourg and into the Moselle valley, following in reverse almost exactly the same route taken by the German panzers in May 1940. We were now on the German autobahn system and we made rapid progress, following almost exactly the advance of General Patton's forces along these same autobahns in the spring of 1945. It was not difficult to sit back and imagine yourself driving a Sherman tank into the heart of Germany, with "Old Blood and Guts" himself spurring you on. The speeds reached on the autobahns were extremely high, but the quality of the other drivers was excellent and all you had to do was get into the habit of giving everybody else a wide berth. We didn't encounter any problems until we crossed over into the former East Germany, where the roads and bridges had clearly been neglected by the communist government and were only now being repaired and rebuilt. The subsequent traffic jams backed up as far as the eye could see and it was a good three hours before we found ourselves on the open road again, putting us well behind schedule. As we hadn't booked anywhere to stay it was clear that we would quite late in hunting for a bed for the night. With that in mind we left the autobahn at the next major town, which was called Gera. It was the rush hour and the roads were extremely congested. We pulled into a service station to fill up, get the maps out and try and work out a way into the city centre. While paying for my fuel, I got talking to a fellow customer who said that the easiest way to find the centre was to follow the tramways and they would guide us there. He did add a warning that they were not all being used, and that we should disregard those that were dull and rusty as they would lead us in the opposite direction to where we wanted to go. I thanked him, got back into the car and pulled out of the forecourt into the flow of traffic. To my absolute horror, I found myself staring straight at the oncoming vehicles as I was heading the wrong way and there was nowhere to turn around. I managed to make use of a small gap in the traffic, and crawled over to the hard shoulder, to the tuneless fanfare of what seemed like hundreds of car horns. The situation didn't look good. There wasn't enough room to turn around, and it looked as though we were going to be in for a very long wait. Thankfully, an articulated lorry driver had witnessed my plight and he very kindly blocked off the oncoming traffic long enough for me to complete the necessary manoeuvring and point us in the correct direction. As I had been told, the tramways did guide us into the city centre, but we had absolutely no luck in trying to locate a hotel. We had reached the stage where I had decided to stop the car, get out and ask the nearest English-speaking local. As I stepped onto the pavement, I looked up and saw a six foot high sign that read "HOTEL". That particular stroke of luck was followed by another, as the hotel was excellent, having been graded with five stars. It had recently been refurbished and the room we were given was wonderful. We enjoyed a superb dinner (if a little pricey), and had enough time to look around the city centre and enjoy a beer or two before retiring for the night.

The next morning we paid up and resumed our journey eastwards. Having had a quick glance at the map, we decided that we would be able to save a little time if we left the autobahn and continued to Mühlberg on the minor roads. Unfortunately we ran into some severe thunderstorms. These were so bad that it became dark and that, together with the heavy rain, caused us to get lost. Somehow, we managed to end up in the middle of a farmyard with a suspicious-looking farmer's wife peering at us through closed curtains. We managed to extract ourselves from that situation and carried on in the same direction in the hope that we would eventually meet a main road. This theory proved to be correct and thankfully we connected with one of the major highways heading north from Dresden. We left the road at the junction for the town of Reisa, which was to be our next destination.

Before leaving America, we had been warned that the former East Germany was still very unstable, and that we shouldn't trust anybody, least of all the local police. Since Reisa was the place where we were to cross the River Elbe and head north towards Mühlberg, we had taken the time to study our maps of the area carefully, as well as reading all of the information that we had at our disposal. Therefore we knew that all we had to do was to travel along the road running from west to east, through the middle of the town, until we reached the river bridge. After crossing, we would need to take the first turning on the left and that would give us a clear run to Mühlberg. Unfortunately our detailed planning and preparation had been a complete waste of time as roadworks had forced the closure of the main road and large signs were posted, describing the two available detours. Naturally these were written in German and my schoolboy grasp of the language was not up to the task of reading them. We gambled and took one of the detours, and half an hour later found ourselves back in exactly the same place, having completed rather a large circle. We now tried the alternative detour, and after a while the road split into a fork. I took the left hand road only to discover, to my horror, that it was a one-way street. Things were going from bad to worse, and to compound matters, I became aware of a green car directly behind us — a police car. I pulled over to the side of the road and hoped that the police officer would follow. Thankfully he did and there began a conversation carried out in broken English and very broken German. I managed somehow to get the message across as to where we wanted to go but his efforts to try and describe the route that we needed to take, resulted in frustration and eventually he threw his arms up in the air and signalled for us to follow him. He gave us an escort through the town until we reached the turn-off that we required, pulled over to the side of the road and told us to stay on the road until we reached Mühlberg. We thanked him profusely and Dottie asked him if she could take his photograph. He politely declined, as he had a prisoner in the back of his car who he was transporting to jail, and that because of this he had broken the rules by helping us. He left us with an impression of the old East German police which was completely at odds with what we had previously been told about them.

We set off as directed, through an unbelievably quaint landscape which had probably remained the same for hundreds of years. Each village that we came across had its own castle or *Schloss*, and the roads were made of cobblestones which must play havoc with the suspensions of the local cars. Eventually we arrived at the town of Mühlberg, the former site of M-Stammlager IVb POW camp, which had been my home for almost two years between 1943 and 1945. The town itself could not have changed much since its foundation and heyday in the thirteenth century, with its narrow cobblestone streets, and its total lack of chain shops, banks, hotels and gaudy restaurants. The women all seemed to be wearing dresses and the highlights of the week were the market days where almost everything could be bought or sold. There were a few cars and a small local bus service, but in all other respects it was like being in a very pleasant time-warp. We found the town hall, or *Rathaus*, and parked nearby. Having entered, I found myself at the back of a very long queue of women who were all trying to reach a small counter where there was a pretty young lady serving them. Eventually, I made it to the front and discovered that the lady didn't speak English. After trying my limited German on her (with the help of the other ladies in the queue) I showed her the letter that I had received the previous year from the mayor. The effect on her was electric — she almost fainted and then ran into an adjacent office shouting "Rose-Mary, Rose-Mary Bauer, der Engländer kommt, der Engländer kommt." Rose-Mary Bauer had been the young lady who had answered my speculative letter, and she immediately came out of the office and was so excited at my arrival I was certain that she would wet herself. It was a few minutes before she calmed down and I was taken to meet the mayor in his office. Sadly he couldn't speak any English and seemed to be too nervous to carry on the conversation so Rose-Mary excused us and took us to meet the custodians of the new museum that was being created in order to try and put Mühlberg back on the map. They were also extremely excited to meet an ex-POW who had actually been in Stalag IVb, and when I had contacted them the previous year, they had arranged for us to stay with a local family. Of course we had not been able to show up because of my illness, but

I was assured that even at such short notice, they would be extremely happy to take us in.

When it had become obvious that my state of health would not allow us to visit, by way of compensation I had sent the museum a copy of an overall painting of the camp as it had appeared in 1945. It had been created by a Dutch prisoner during his incarceration, and I had obtained my copy in 1946. I was pleased to see that it now formed the centrepiece of the museum's Stalag IVb display, and I felt glad that I had been able to show them what the camp had looked like during the war years.

Since we did not know our way around the town, Rose-Mary led the way for us on her bicycle. I am sure many people were wondering exactly why a car containing two people was devotedly following a slow moving bicycle. Eventually we arrived at Kuhnereestraße and knocked on the door of number 45, the home of Anita and Bernd Grulich, a pleasant middle-aged couple. Theirs was a modest end-terrace house, but they had a spotless basement apartment and were delighted to have us stay with them. They told us that they would supply us with all our meals but apologized that they had no separate bathroom. Bernd's mother lived with them and, as she was my age, she had very clear memories of the camp and its many prisoners. We all got on very well and, as luck would have it, Bernd had arranged to take a week's leave from work. He invited us to stay for the whole of that week and told us that they would take us wherever we wanted to go. We gratefully accepted and began to plan a list of local attractions that we wanted to see.

First on our list was the site of the POW camp itself. Naturally not a great deal remained, as it had been bulldozed sometime after the conclusion of the war. However the local museum committee had been hard at work in the last few years with the original roadways being cleared and marked out, and the original building features being identified. At the entrance a portal had been erected and an enlarged, framed copy of the painting that I had sent them constituted the centrepiece, together with a number of artefacts covering life in the camp. After we had all left the camp in May 1945, the Russians had used it as a processing centre for German prisoners, prior to sending them eastwards. Naturally, this had resulted in the need for an enormous German military cemetery which was fast becoming something of a shrine. This shrine had become the focal point of an annual pilgrimage which was putting the main role of the place as a POW camp firmly in the shade. In the nearby village of Neuburgsdorf was the former cemetery for Allied prisoners, but I was a little disappointed that the only nation that had chosen to erect any form of commemoration was France. You really had to search hard to find any markers for British dead.

We then took a trip to retrace my steps when I broke camp and headed west in May 1945. We crossed the Elbe by ferry at the village of Belgem and carried on westwards, but I failed to recognize anywhere from my previous journey. Then we reached a small town called

Schildau, where suddenly something triggered in my brain and I asked Bernd to stop the car. There, partly covered, but still as I remembered it, was the word *Backerei* carved into the wall of a building that we were passing. It was from this bakery that I had taken a few loaves of bread as we had passed through the town. It's funny how the brain can remember tiny details like that and yet forgets the larger ones. From here my mind began to unravel back forty-eight years and it was an easy task to locate where I had spent the night. It was a school hall that had been converted into a small hospital ward by a local female doctor and her daughter who acted as a nurse. After settling us down for the night, they had requested an escort home through the town as the place was crawling with POWs thirsting for revenge and the two women were understandably fearful of being raped or worse. Two of our number volunteered to see them home but they never returned to their beds and were never seen again, so one can only speculate as to what happened to them and their charges. From the school we walked into the town centre, which was just as I had remembered it except for a Coca-Cola sign which signified the subsequent predictable arrival of American global culture.

We now located Torgau, which was the town that Steve Powell and I had passed through in late 1944 following our failed escape bid. As I have previously mentioned, it was also the town where the staged link-up was filmed between the Soviet and US forces in May 1945. From Torgau we travelled south along the west bank of the river in order meet up again with the

Belgem ferry that we had caught earlier that day, and that I had used back in 1945 to get across the Elbe.

Although Berlin had not been part of my wartime story — I had not even taken part in a raid on the German capital — I was still quite keen to see it as I had always wanted to walk through the famous Brandenburg Gate. Bernd was not all that enthusiastic about the prospect but he did agree to drive us to the edge of the city so that we could park the car and make our way to the centre using public transport. I had failed to realize that my hosts were country folk who had only ever been to the big city a couple of times in their lives, and that the thought of driving in Berlin traffic was upsetting to them. As it was, we had no trouble getting ourselves to the outskirts of West Berlin and parking in a pre-arranged spot that one of Bernd's Berlin-based relatives had secured for him. Anita and Bernd had hoped that their relative would be able to escort us into the city centre, but all he did was supply us with directions as to how to get there by ourselves, and took us to the nearest U-Bahn station. Getting onto the U-Bahn was very similar to using the London Underground. As we descended into the station our hosts just stood there with their mouths open. I worked out what line we would need to take and bought tokens for all of us. We managed to find the correct platform and got on the next train which headed east into the city. Anita and Bernd didn't say a word until Bernd asked a fellow passenger how he would know when to get off. He was shown a route map which had been fixed to the opposite wall and which showed all of the stations; these would light up depending on where we were. I don't think they believed what was happening to them and they both looked genuinely scared to death. When we reached our destination Dorothy and I stood up and Bernd and Anita followed us like sheep until we reached the open air. The station was at the site of the empty shell of the Kaiser Wilhelm Church, which had been left as a constant reminder of the pounding the city took from the Royal Air Force during the war. The site was a hub for tour buses, and so we selected an itinerary that best suited us and caught the next bus, which was an open-topped double-decker. This would have been absolutely ideal had it not started to rain, but we all had our waterproofs on so the inclement weather didn't bother us too much. The bus took us to the old Cold War hot-spot of Checkpoint Charlie, the Brandenburg Gate and the Reichstag building, and ended up by passing down Unter Den Linden and through the Brandenburg Gate, allowing me fifteen minutes worth of photo opportunities. I also sat back in my seat and was able to imagine what it might have looked like back in 1945, with the Russian tanks rolling down the Unter Den Linden and taking pot shots at the Gate itself, which still bore the scars caused by the shells that the Red Army pumped into it.

By now it was mid-afternoon, and time to think about heading back to the suburbs to collect the car. Bernd and Anita could not face the ordeal of the U-Bahn again, so we had to cover the six miles on foot, in the pouring rain. At one point we came across a station and I managed to persuade them to descend to the first level. However once artificial light took over, they both panicked and had to go back outside. I realized how frightened they both were so I did not push the issue any further. In fact, our walk back was very pleasant, despite the weather. We crossed the parkland that surrounded the Potsdam Palace and I recalled that it was there where Attlee, Truman and Stalin had met and planned how to carve up Europe, setting in motion the events of the Cold War. After an hour and a half, we reached the car and since the rush hour had not yet started, Bernd was happy to drive through the city centre from west to east to give us a last look at the place before we headed back to Mühlberg. We passed the Tiergarten (Berlin Zoo), drove up the Unter Den Linden boulevard and out through the Brandenburg Gate. I had enjoyed a most fulfilling day, I had seen what I had wanted to see, and I was happy to say cheerio to the German capital.

Our experience with the U-Bahn reminded me of my first trip to London as a twelve year old, in 1931. It was a day trip organized by my grammar school, and one of the thrills of the day was a trip on the London Underground. At King's Cross station, three separate lines crossed at different depths, and I can remember very well the feelings of claustrophobia that I experienced as I descended the escalator. It seemed that we were heading straight for the bowels of the earth on a vast one-way system which, if it failed, was sure to entomb us down there forever. I was greatly relieved to emerge once more into the daylight. Adding to my unease were the noises of the trains, the rushing of what seemed like far too many people, the speed of everything and the vivid bright lights. In hindsight, it was easy to imagine how Bernd and Anita must have felt about the U-Bahn.

The next trip on our agenda was to the town of Lubbenau in the Spreewald, near to the Polish frontier. This was the region where the River Spree branched out into countless lakes, streams and canals, all of which meandered through beautiful woodlands and meadows. It was a beautifully sunny day, and we took a two-hour river trip on what was little more than a large punt, holding up to fifty people and lying very low in the water. We found this unexpectedly fascinating — I had the impression that I was gliding on the surface of the water and that if anybody had so much as sneezed, we would have sunk.

Bernd and Anita were spoiling us and had even transformed their back garden into a miniature beer garden for our benefit. One day, we found Bernd painting something onto a large, flat rock that we had recovered from the river bed. He told us that he was inscribing my name and home address on it, as well as my POW number, and was going to place it underneath the portal at the entrance to the camp so that anybody who wished to could contact me.

The excursions continued. We visited the local *Schloss* which was still inhabited, and explored the grounds, which included a dried-up moat. Each small town had a *Schloss*, and these were built during the Middle Ages when Germany had been little more than a collection of fragmented communities, constantly threatened by their neighbours as well as marauding bands of outlaws. We also visited the run-down former railway station where I used to unload Red Cross parcels and enjoy the odd glass of beer in the café. It was decrepit but still instantly recognizable, and the word "Mühlberg" could still be seen, carved into the brickwork. While I stood there, looking around and winding back the years, a man approached me with his wife in tow. They were older than Dorothy and me, and were wondering who these strangely-dressed people were — Dorothy was wearing jeans and I must have looked like a typical American tourist. I explained who we were and what we were doing there, and the man told me that both he and his wife had worked in the railway station during the war, and they were absolutely amazed to talk to somebody who had not only been there at the same time, but had also travelled 5,000 miles just to meet them. When I shook his hand to say goodbye, I didn't think that he would ever let it go.

All the towns on the River Elbe had a ferry service, a throwback to their mediaeval past. The one at Mühlberg was located some distance outside the town owing to the fact that the river had changed its course at some time in the more recent past. It was powered by a very small gas engine which would chug along at its own pace without any problems, except during the spring floods when it would be unable to cope and would frequently stop working. Naturally it was during this period that we had cause to use it, and our suspicions were aroused by the fact that we were the only people who seemed to be on the ferry that day. We were later informed about the ferry's potential for disaster and were told in no uncertain terms how lucky we were to have "got away with it". Our time at Mühlberg was coming to an end; we had stayed there for ten days, eight days more than the two we had allocated. This meant that we would have to make good progress all the way to England and would limit the amount of time we could spend with Blanchette. We enjoyed a farewell party that our new friends had laid on for us, and began to think about the long westward journey across Germany. Our hosts had been wonderful and we could not have asked for more as they had effectively adopted us. We promised to return at some stage in the future, and off we went.

After leaving Mühlberg we headed north to Torgau and crossed the river there, before turning west and reaching the small town of Bitterfeldt, where I had worked on the railways in 1944 while impersonating a young Bristolian soldier. I was surprised to see that the same buildings in which I had lived were still standing, but the barbed wire compound had vanished. I didn't go into the station because there wasn't anywhere nearby to park, but my mind wandered back and I remembered that it was here that we had been able to see ordinary Germans coming and going, and we had taken particular note of the girls that we had seen. On one occasion I recall seeing a group of prisoners being escorted to their fate by a number of soldiers. The men all had their heads shaved and looked extremely dejected, but within the group were two very beautiful young women, with glamourous hairstyles and

304

expensive looking clothing. We had guessed that they were all Poles, captured after the Warsaw Uprising, and that the two girls were destined for the bed of some high-ranking Nazi officer. I never did find out if we were correct or not.

I managed to pull myself back into the present day and we carried on to the small town of Zorbig. This was where Steve Powell and I had been sent to following our abortive escape attempt. We parked the car and walked into the town centre. It had changed little in the intervening forty-eight years, and I immediately located the school, outside of which I had swept the snow from the pavements. The railway station had been modernized, but was still recognizable, and the roads had been smartened up and re-cobbled, but otherwise everything looked the same. However I had problems finding the place where we had been quartered, so we decided to visit the local park and try and find somebody who was old enough to be able to help. I succeeding in finding an elderly couple who looked as though they would fit the bill, and I introduced myself to them, using my very best German. I managed to make them understand that I was looking for the location of a dance hall which had been used to house prisoners of war in 1944. The man didn't know anything, but the lady recalled that after the defeat at Stalingrad it had been forbidden to dance anywhere in Germany, and that there had been a large dance hall on the other side of the town which had been part of a hotel complex. She added that she didn't know if it was still there, but supplied us with directions and wished us luck in our quest. Lo and behold, as directed, we found the hotel with a familiar large square building attached to it. I immediately recognized the large courtyard which had contained the horse troughs where we had performed our ablutions.

After I had taken all this in, we set off south-west and passed into the former West Germany, heading for Koblenz. We crossed the Rhine and entered the beautiful Moselle Valley, where we were lucky enough to find a fine bed and breakfast establishment which afforded us superb views over the river.

The next morning we continued southwards along the river, reaching Trier and passing into Luxembourg. Before too long we were at the Belgian border and searching for the village of Messancy, which was the location of the famous wartime Victory Museum. We had booked a room for that night in the adjacent Victory Hotel which actually straddled the main E411 highway, and found it without a hitch, having driven through some of the most stunningly beautiful countryside that I had ever seen. The next morning it was time to visit the museum itself, which was well worth the effort. On display were countless items of German, British, American and Italian equipment and hardware, and we could easily have spent all day there were it not for the fact that we had to visit Blanchette once more. Now that we were more familiar with the environment we had no problem locating the farmhouse, and were warmly greeted once more. Blanchette's brother Norbert now took over the hospitality duties, and he and his wife helped me to retrace my steps once more. They showed me where I had landed by parachute that August morning, and where I had made my first contact with the Belgian farmer. I was also shown where our Lancaster had crashed, and given a guided tour of Blanchette's house, where we had stayed on the fateful night when her father had been taken away by the Germans. The loft area was exactly the same as I remembered it, and the secret dormer in the roof was still there after all those years.

Unfortunately, because we had spent longer than expected in Germany, our time in Belgium was cut short. A couple of days later we headed off to Brussels airport and time constraints forced us to reach the capital in the middle of the rush hour. I have never before or since been in such traffic, nor been exposed to such dreadful and inconsiderate driving, but at least we had fared better than we did when we had arrived. We had allowed ourselves plenty of time, so the thirty minutes that we spent driving around in circles and looking for the depot where we had to return the hire car did not actually make us late. We caught our short flight to Manchester without any problems, and spent the next couple of days visiting my relatives, before heading to Ashbourne to stay with Chaka Webster and his wife.

To my delight he had managed to contact an old Halton buddy of ours, ex-Sergeant Apprentice "Bullet" Reid, who I had not seen since we passed out in 1938. The highlight was a trip out into the Derbyshire Dales where we all enjoyed a wonderful pub lunch, something I had never experienced before. After yet more goodbyes, the next morning found us aboard a train to Euston station, and from there to Heathrow and the flight home. I had planned on taking a taxi across town so that Dorothy could see the sights of London, but she insisted that we take the Underground. I was reluctant to do so because it was the rush hour, and we were loaded down with luggage, but in the end Dorothy won the battle of wills and so off we went into the bowels of the earth. Well, all I can say is that she certainly got the experience she wanted. I had remembered that the end of the carriage is always the best place to stand when you have plenty of luggage with you, but even so the pushing, shoving and close bodily contact was something to behold. Thankfully the overcrowding lessened as we passed through the city centre, and we had no further mishaps, with an uneventful and relaxing flight taking us back to the United States.

After we had been back home for a while, I received a letter from the high school at Mühlberg. It appeared that the English class had been on a field trip to the camp, and had come across and read the stone which Bernd had placed at the entrance. They had asked their teacher to try and find out who this mysterious ex-prisoner was, and the result was the letter that I had been sent. I was told that I had been "adopted" by the school, and I was asked to set up a regular correspondence with them in order to tell the story, in instalments, of how I had come to be a POW there, what conditions had been like, and how I had made my way home after my liberation. This was to become their final project before their graduation, and would end up as a document which would be given to the town's museum. I was more than happy to tell my tale, and there began an association with that particular class group which was to last for another five or so years.

Two years later, Dorothy and I decided to repeat the trip, with the intention of spending more time in Belgium and ferreting out that which we had failed to do in 1993. We decided that the best time to go would be September, so as to coincide with a number of their military commemorations, not least the fifty-first anniversary of the liberation of the vast majority of the country. As before, we flew into Brussels and hired a car, but this time we had arranged to arrive at a much quieter time of day, and I was relieved to see that the improvements to the approach roads had been completed. Unfortunately we arrived in pouring rain and could not locate the hotel where we were to spend our first night back in Europe. To add to our frustration, we could actually see the place but had no idea how to reach it. Eventually I pulled in to a petrol station and saw a local taxi driver filling up at the pumps. I went across to him and paid him to show us the way, which he subsequently did. The next morning we managed to reach Blanchette's without getting lost and met up with her brother Norbert, who once more took on the responsibility of being our tour guide.

First of all we located the field, adjacent to the village of Furneaux, where I had hit the ground. We then moved into the village itself and tried to track down the people with whom I had made my initial contact. The farmhouse had been demolished in the intervening period, and the family had moved elsewhere. The second farmhouse to which I had been taken later that day, was still standing but the occupants were renting the property from the original owners, who had retired and were now living in a nursing home in the town of Leuven, to the east of Brussels. It wasn't a difficult place to reach and we found them easily. They were delighted to receive us and I was able to thank them belatedly for their help, and drink their health. It had been at their house that I had been picked up by a monk from the nearby Abbeye de Saint-Benoît and taken through the woods to the restaurant where I had been reunited with Steve Powell. The name of this monk was Don Cyprien Neybergh, and he had later been captured by the Germans, spending the rest of the war in Dachau concentration camp. He was one of the lucky survivors, and when he got home, one of his first acts was to return my personal effects, which he had retained for safe keeping, to the British Air Attaché in Brussels. By doing this, he thereby established a contact with me and we enjoyed a friendship which endured for many years until his death from natural causes.

My next wish was to try and trace my parachute, which I had buried in the field that I had landed in. I learned that at the war's end, it had been dug up and pieces of it were distributed to the local schoolchildren as a souvenir of the Allied victory. I did remember that after landing I had ripped off the maker's label, which read "Erwin" and kept that with me until I had mistakenly left it in the loft at Blanchette's house while I had been hiding there. Naturally Blanchette had found it, and I was delighted to discover that she had kept it all those years. The next day, Dorothy and I were taken to the memorial at Bastogne, erected in honour of the brave American 101st Airborne Division, who had stood fast against the German onslaught in those last days of 1944, when Hitler had gambled everything with a massive assault to try to throw the Allies back and retake the port of Antwerp. This memorial included a museum complex which had an automated display, repeated every two hours, showing the course of the Battle of the Bulge, and reminded us all of the heroism of the American forces who, in truly dreadful weather conditions, by sheer guts and determination, brought the offensive to a grinding halt and then pushed on into Germany itself. I never could understand why, having broken the back of the German forces in the west, General Patton was never given the green light to carry on to Berlin itself, but as I was behind barbed wire at the time, I wasn't really privy to all the details.

During the time that we spent in Belgium, we were wined, dined and attended various veterans' reunions. The wonderful attention that was paid to us was marvellous to the point of acute embarrassment — never in my life had I felt so fêted or so important. After a final farewell dinner, we ended our visit by stopping off in Manchester to look in on my family, and then making the short hop over the Pennines to Ashbourne, where once again we were welcomed by Chaka and his wife for a two day stay before it was time to head home for a rest.

Our third and final trip was undertaken three years later, in September 1998. In the intervening period we had moved away from Seattle and taken up residence in Ohio, and I felt that three years was a more than adequate time for the experiences and emotions of the two previous expeditions to sink in. We would again be heading to Mühlberg as I had promised to visit the school, where the pupils I had been corresponding with were approaching their graduation. I looked forward to seeing just how much the town had changed in the years since reunification, and I was also keen to see my old friends from five years earlier. This time, we decided to cut out Brussels airport altogether and fly into Luxembourg City. This would avoid the chaos of the Belgian capital's road network and was actually much closer to Blanchette's village. The flights went like clockwork, as did the driving, and it didn't take long to arrive. Our first commemoration was the following day, and that was the ceremony to mark the executions of the "Armée Blanche" resistance members whom Steve Powell and I had lived with for a time in the woods that surrounded the village, and who had been betrayed by the "Captain", a German agent who had infiltrated the escape line. Much to my surprise, I was asked to take a leading role in the ceremony, which took place in the local Catholic church. The colours were placed upon the altar and blessed, and there then followed a parade which was concluded with me laying a wreath on the cenotaph. I must admit to finding the veneration a little embarrassing but I suppose I should have got a little used to it by then. The commemoration then moved to the site of the hideout in the woods, with tractors and farm carts being used to transport the congregation. Once the formalities had been concluded, Blanchette supplied us all with a late lunch. I remember talking to a very well-to-do local count and countess, both of whom spoke excellent English and who spent a long time extolling the virtues of Allied servicemen, particularly those from America who had come such a long distance to help to free Belgium from Nazi occupation.

At this function I was also able to speak to a number of ex-Resistance fighters and, at my request, it was decided that a group of us would attempt to follow the route I took along the famous "Comete" escape line from Brussels to the place where our group had been betrayed and captured. This took us over the border to the French town of Charleville where my time in captivity had begun on 4 September 1943. We parked at the town's railway station and I walked into the building before stepping back out through the main doors as I had done that fateful day. Letting my memory guide me, I walked through the town centre, which was a great deal busier and more congested than I remembered. At a certain point, our group had been told to cross the main road and enter a building directly opposite. I reached that spot and realized that it would be impossible to cross here now owing to the huge volume of traffic and the impossibility of reaching the other side. I had to carry on down the street for a short while and use a pedestrian crossing, then double back on myself. As I did so, almost without thinking, I looked up and found myself directly outside the correct building, which had hardly changed at all. This had been the place where our little group of Americans, Dutchmen and Britons had been set up; ambushed and captured by the enemy.

Following our capture, we had been housed for two nights in the attic rooms of a local chateau which was being used by the town's garrison. However I didn't have a clue where this was, as we had been transported there in trucks which had been sealed, and we had no idea of the name of the place. All I could recall was that the chateau had been surrounded by high stone walls, and that within these walls there had been a screen of mature oak trees, the tops of which we could see from our attic windows. Using a process of elimination, my guides had brought us to the only building in the locality that could have fitted the criteria. It was now the central part of a large medical complex, but there were no oak trees to be seen. I entered the main reception hall and was immediately struck by a sense that I had been there before, although there was nothing there that I could recognize. There were no magnificent entrances or reception areas with plush red carpets, no gold-embellished walls covered with oil paintings, and no grand stairways. The upper floors provided me with no further clues as they had been converted to doctors' waiting rooms, and the top floors had been sealed off. Enquiries with the staff revealed that there was nobody now working there who knew the history of the place, but somebody mentioned the name of a nurse who had retired last year, and wondered if she would be able to help as she had been there for a very long time. A couple of phone calls later and the lady herself arrived at the chateau and came in to speak to us. She told us that the building had been taken over by the State at the end of the war and converted into a hospital. She had seen it evolve over the years and told us that the oak trees had all been cut down, and that the wonderful red carpets that had covered the floors and the staircases had been ripped out. That, coupled with my strange sense of *déjà-vu*, was enough for me, and the discovery of numerous oak tree stumps out in the grounds merely confirmed that we were indeed in the correct place. After looking around and taking it all in, we headed back to Belgium using the same roads, as I was told, that Field Marshal Montgomery used to advance into the country in the aftermath of the Normandy breakout.

We left Blanchette's for a short return visit to see our friends in Mühlberg, and I wasn't surprised to see that the town had been rapidly modernized in the intervening five years. The women seemed to have swapped their dresses for jeans, a shopping centre had been built and banks were springing up. There were clearly more cars and trucks around, as well as evidence of the pollution that these had brought, and private enterprise was obviously flourishing. Shops, bars and restaurants were being opened all over the town and I was informed that the fledgling spirit of capitalism meant that many of these new businesses were failing almost as soon as they were being created. The camp itself had been paid a great deal of attention, and was now very clearly defined, with all the building foundations having been discovered, identified and marked. "My" students at the local high school had even located the foundations of my old barracks block, and as they were about to graduate, they put on a party in my honour. I was presented with a bouquet of flowers and thanked profusely for my cooperation and help with their project. In anticipation of this day I had collected fifty American baseball caps to distribute as gifts, and I could not have been more profusely thanked by them had I dished out gold Rolex watches. After yet more farewell parties from our friends in the town, we said our goodbyes and headed back to Belgium.

We didn't come up against any problems on the return journey and after a couple more days of sightseeing I was asked if we would be able to attend a small, routine commemorative dinner. Of course we agreed, and I was given the distinct impression that this meal would be nothing special. Of course I should have known how things were done here, and the "routine" dinner turned out to be the full scale annual banquet which was hosted by the local veterans' association. It was not until we entered, and were led to our places at the head table, that we realized that we were going to be the main attraction. After the meal, all the speeches were made in my honour, and I was toasted so many times that I was starting to feel very groggy. Then, as old soldiers do, we drank and sang, then drank and sang some more, before an opera singer stood up and announced that she was going to dedicate a song to Dorothy and myself. She sang beautifully, bringing tears to our eyes with her rendition of *Amazing Grace*. At the conclusion of proceedings everyone stood and sang *God Save The Queen* before lining up to shake my hand: a most memorable and emotional experience.

After we had returned home from this third trip, which was to be our last, we sat down and attempted to put everything into perspective. Why had I felt the need to go back? How did I find the people and how did they compare with those of my memories? What of the places themselves? Had they been as I had expected, and if not, why was that? I tried hard to find the answers to these and other questions that were buzzing around my head, but it wasn't easy. I had found my visits to be happy, yet emotional and thought-provoking. They had the effect of rounding off and bringing full circle the most intense, dangerous and emotive periods that any generation would experience. I had lost many friends, many colleagues, and many of those who had helped me and shared my wartime adventures in Europe were no more. I hoped that my pilgrimages would also act as a small tribute to those people, and I like to think that they did.

Epilogue

After my penultimate trip to Europe in 1995, I started to think more and more about putting my roots down. My three sons lived thousands of miles apart and had taken very different paths through life. Andrew lived in Ohio, Steven lived in North Carolina, and Peter lived in Oregon. Dorothy and I decided to take a motoring trip around the country and visit them all, to see if we could be accommodated within their lifestyles and environments. This trip would also have the benefit of allowing us to see vast parts of the United States that we would not normally visit.

We took a leisurely six days to arrive at the town of Strongsville in Ohio, where Andrew and his wife had retired to the previous year, following his twenty-nine years with IT&T. He had met up with a high school friend with whom he had never lost touch and who had just taken on a new car dealership in Strongsville. This dealership had been set up to supply Land Rovers and Volvos, and Andrew's friend asked him if he would like to help him establish the new business. Being a car buff, Andy jumped at the idea. We were made very welcome and were given a wonderful tour of the area by my son and daughter-in-law before we carried on towards North Carolina, where Steven lived with his wife and daughter. However, given Strongsville's relative proximity to the Canadian border, we travelled via Niagara Falls as Dottie had never seen them before. Unfortunately we were in the thick of the tourist season and could hardly make any headway at all past the Falls, let alone find a place to park. We took the decision to continue on over the border and found the place where I lived when I had worked for Avro in the 1950s. After a nostalgic meandering, we turned south and re-entered the United States, reaching Charlotte, North Carolina, a few days later.

Steven's wife, Kathy, was not there when we arrived as she had other business to attend to, and she would not actually be home until late so we were unable to see her until breakfast the next morning, before she headed off to work again. Considering I hadn't seen Steven since 1978, the reception was icy-cold and Dottie and I felt quite insulted. We all went out to supper at a Red Lobster franchise restaurant, and when we got back we decided that we would get up early for breakfast so as to be able to see Kathy, and then we would leave. We hadn't even had time to unpack, but the next morning we said our goodbyes and headed west for Oregon, on the Pacific seaboard. It was a long drive across the whole width of the States, and we followed the route of the pioneers of old, including that of the ill-fated

"Donner Party". This unfortunate group found themselves stranded in heavy snow storms in the mountain passes which led into California, and had to resort to cannibalism — their story is told in the book *Hail Hunger*. Eventually we hit the Pacific and headed north through what must be some of the most beautiful scenery in the world, keeping to the coast road and then cutting diagonally across country, and through the famous Redwood forests of northern California, before reaching Oregon.

On arriving in Portland we settled into a hotel for the night and I phoned Peter to tell him that we had arrived and would be dropping in on him the next morning for a few days. When we had been planning our trip we had furnished him with our itinerary, but we were one day later arriving than we had planned to be, and my call was diverted to his cellphone. Peter answered, and told me that he was out in town with the boys, and that he had arranged to go away for the weekend with a group of friends. Extremely disappointed, I told him to go ahead, and that we would carry on to Seattle and home. The next morning we took the time to find his house before setting off for the relatively short trip north, and so ended our grand tour. As for what we would do next, it hadn't really been a difficult choice to make, and before too long we had moved across to Strongsville and bought a house near to Andrew. We quickly settled in and Dottie and I have all the recreational facilities that our aged bodies can handle, as well as being under the watchful and loving eye of Andrew and his wife.

Is this then the end of the story of the life of this Trenchard Brat? I think not. I am only eighty-seven years old now, and I am still square-dancing on a regular basis. We belong to another ballroom dancing club, and Dorothy and I are also considering renewing our passports so my globetrotting days may not yet be over. I am able to take in my stride the death notices that arrive in my e-mail inbox informing me of the passing of yet more of my fellow 33rd Entry Brats and wartime comrades. However I know I'm on the list somewhere, and when the bell rings for me I'll be able to go willingly, knowing that if nothing else, I did my best. After all, that's what I promised my Dad all those years ago at Wilmslow station, wasn't it?

Also available in ISIS Large Print:

Growing up in Sussex

Gerry Wells

"Rescued by Father, probably startled from his newspaper, I was handed dripping and yelling over the fence to be sorted out by Mother who wouldn't have been amused. A second baptism perhaps, just to make sure."

This compelling memoir starts with a boy's journey through the early years of the 1930s — days of the rag and bone man, street lamplighters and in the background, Hitler. Then life gets real, at school where cane and cricket bat rule and even more real with army call-up and training.

In 1944/45 comes the crunch of combat in Operation Overlord. And after all that, with his ears still ringing a bit, comes the blessed call of demob and a taste of new delights, finding a woman daft enough to marry him before settling near his work on a farm to start his life as a man.

ISBN 978-0-7531-9540-6 (hb)
ISBN 978-0-7531-9541-3 (pb)

Ghosts of Targets Past

Philip Gray

"I couldn't help thinking that the Royal Air Force had a real problem on its hands. How did they figure on making a front-line, gung-ho pilot out of the sort of material I provided — a shy, reticent, non-belligerent country boy?"

Born in Scotland, Philip Gray is now a journalist living in Canada, but in WW2 he found himself captain of the crew of a "mighty Lanc", operating with 186 Squadron as the RAF took war right into the heart of Germany. Both Gray and his crew felt they were in charge of the undisputed king of the skies, but dangers lurked around every corner and on every mission. In an engaging yet frank style, Gray reveals the true relationships between himself and his team, and between the team members themselves. He also searches his own soul as he struggles to survive in love and war.

ISBN 978-0-7531-9542-0 (hb)
ISBN 978-0-7531-9543-7 (pb)

In the Face of the Enemy

Ernest Powdrill MC

"Suddenly a hail of machine-gun bullets were fired in our direction, with one or two ripping into the canvas roof of my tractor a couple of feet from my head. I was standing up at the time with both hands gripping the top of the windscreen."

In the Face of the Enemy is a no-holds-barred account of the author's experiences in an artillery regiment with the British Expeditionary Force in 1939 and 1940 and, four years later, in North West Europe closing in on Nazi Germany.

Ernest Powdrill joined the Territorials in 1935 and transferred to the Regular Army in 1938. By the time his regiment went out to France in September 1939 he was a full sergeant in command of a 25-pounder Mark 1 gun.

ISBN 978-0-7531-9534-5 (hb)
ISBN 978-0-7531-9535-2 (pb)

Night Action

Peter Dickens

"When I poked my head out of the window, his head was out further along the carriage. He smiled at me and twiddled a revolver around his finger."

In all the annals of the war at sea, comparatively little has been written about the role of the torpedo boat, and yet these small boats were at the heart of some of the most dangerous actions of the War. Travelling at high speed and amid storms and gunfire, and usually under the cover of darkness, these vulnerable craft sought out enemy convoys and escorts and wrought havoc among the German supply lines.

Night Action is Peter Dickens' account of his experiences as the young commander of the 21st MTB Flotilla during 1942-43. Lively and thrilling, while there is humour to be found, the horror of war is never far away.

ISBN 978-0-7531-8382-3 (hb)
ISBN 978-0-7531-8383-0 (pb)